Rising Tension in Eastern Europe
and the Former Soviet Union

Studies in Disarmament and Conflicts:

Rising Tension in Eastern Europe and the Former Soviet Union

Edited by

DAVID CARLTON
PAUL INGRAM

and

GIANCARLO TENAGLIA

Dartmouth

Aldershot • Brookfield USA • Singapore • Sydney

Published by
Dartmouth Publishing Company Limited
Gower House
Croft Road
Aldershot
Hants GU11 3HR
England

Dartmouth Publishing Company
Old Post Road
Brookfield
Vermont 05036
USA

British Library Cataloguing in Publication Data
Rising tension in Eastern Europe and the former Soviet
    Union. – (Studies in disarmament and conflicts)
    1. Europe, Eastern – Foreign relations   2. Former Soviet
    republics – Foreign relations   3. Europe, Eastern – Politics
    and government – 1989–   4. Former Soviet republics – Politics
    and government
    I. Series   II. Carlton, David, 1938–   III. Ingram, Paul
    IV. Tenaglia, Giancarlo
    947'.086

Library of Congress Cataloging-in-Publication Data
Rising tension in Eastern Europe and the former Soviet Union / edited
    by David Carlton, Paul Ingram, and Giancarlo Tenaglia.
        p.   cm.
        "Presented to the following courses of the International School on
    Disarmament and Research on Conflicts (ISODARCO): the Seventh Winter
    Course held at Folgaria (Trento), Italy, between 23 and 30 January
    1994, and the Eighth Winter Course held in Bressanone (Bolzano),
    Italy, between 21 and 38 January 1995"—CIP pref.
        ISBN 1-85521-666-3
        1. National security Former Soviet republics Congresses.
    2. National security Europe, Eastern—Congresses.   3. Former Soviet
    republics—Foreign relations—Congresses.   4. Europe, Eastern–
    –Foreign relations—1989–   —Congresses.   5. Former Soviet republics–
    –Ethnic relations—Congresses. 6. Europe, Eastern—Ethnic
    relations—Congresses. I. Carlton, David, 1938–   .   II. Ingram,
    Paul.   III. Tenaglia, Giancarlo.   IV. International School on
    Disarmament and Research on Conflicts. Winter Course (7th : 1994 :
    Folgaria, Italy)   V. International School on Disarmament and
    Research on Conflicts. Winter Course (8th : 1995 : Bressanone,
    Italy)
    DK293.R57   1996
    327.1'7'094091717—dc20   95–47704
                                                                                                        CIP

ISBN 1 85521 666 3

Typeset by Manton Typesetters, 5–7 Eastfield Road, Louth, Lincolnshire LN11 7AJ, UK.

Printed and bound in Great Britain by Ipswich Book Co. Ltd., Ipswich, Suffolk

Contents

List of Abbreviations

ACV   Armoured Combat Vehicle
CEI   Central European Initiative
CFE   Conventional Forces in Europe
CIS   Commonwealth of Independent States
CSCE   Conference on Security and Co-operation in Europe (now called the Organization for Security and Co-operation in Europe)
DAHR   Democratic Alliance of Hungarians in Romania
EBRD   European Bank for Reconstruction and Development
ETA   Euskadi Ta Askatasuna
EU   European Union
FSU   Former Soviet Union
FYROM Former Yugoslav Republic of Macedonia
GDP   Gross Domestic Product
GDR   German Democratic Republic
GNP   Gross National Product
HEU   Highly Enriched Uranium
IAEA   International Atomic Energy Agency
ICBM   Inter-continental Ballistic Missile
IMF   International Monetary Fund
IPS   International Plutonium Storage
JCG   Joint Consultative Group
LEU   Low-enriched Uranium
MBFR   Mutual and Balanced Force Reductions
MD   Military District
NATO   North Atlantic Treaty Organization
NIC   Newly Independent Country
NNWS   Non-nuclear weapon State
NPT   Non-proliferation Treaty
NWS   Nuclear-weapon State
OOV   Objects of Verification
OSCE   Organization for Security and Co-operation in Europe
SRAM   Short-range Attack Missile
START   Strategic Arms Reduction Talks
TLE   Treaty-limited Equipment

UN	United Nations
UNCTAD	United Nations Conference on Trade and Development
UNECE	Economic Development Commission for Europe in the United Nations
WEU	Western European Union
WTO	Warsaw Treaty Organization

Notes on the Contributors

Georgi Arbatov (*Russian*) is the Director of the Institute for the USA and Canada, as well as a member of the Russian Academy of Sciences. He is author of *The System: An Insider's Life in Soviet Politics*.

Derek Braddon (*British*) is Research Director at the Research Unit in Economics, University of the West of England, Bristol.

David Carlton (*British*) (*co-editor*) is Lecturer in International Studies at the University of Warwick. He is author of *Anthony Eden: A Biography* and of *Britain and the Suez Crisis*. He is co-editor of thirteen previous volumes in this series.

Douglas L. Clarke (*US*) is a freelance analyst of military and arms control affairs. He was previously a captain in the US Navy and served on the staff of Radio Free Europe, Munich.

Victor Gilinsky (*US*) is a former Commissioner of the US Nuclear Regulatory Commission.

Paul Ingram (*British*) (*co-editor*) is a Researcher at the Oxford Research Group and is conducting postgraduate research at the Department of Politics and International Studies, University of Warwick.

Alexander Ivanov (*Russian*) is Head of the Science Co-ordination Division in the Directorate of Foreign Policy Planning in the Russian Ministry of Foreign Affairs, Moscow.

Stephen P. Koff (*US*) is Professor of International Relations at Syracuse University, New York.

George Mourtos (*Greek*) is Consultant on Strategic Issues, Strategic Studies Section, Greek Ministry of Defence, Athens.

Alexander Nikitin (*Russian*) is Director of the Centre for Political and International Studies, Moscow. He previously served with the Soviet Permanent Mission to the United Nations in New York.

Ioan Mircea Pascu (*Romanian*) is Secretary of State in the Romanian Ministry of Defence, Bucharest.

Yuri Pinchukov (*Russian*) is Head of the Department of Non-proliferation in the Institute of World Economy and International Relations, Moscow.

György Réti (*Hungarian*) is First Secretary of the Hungarian Embassy in Rome. He has also served as a diplomat in China, Vietnam and Albania.

Gerard Snel (*Dutch*) is a postgraduate student in the Department of Political Science and Public Administration at the Free University of Amsterdam.

Giancarlo Tenaglia (*Italian*) (*co-editor*) is Senior Researcher at the Italian Agency for Energy, New Technology and Environment (ENEA).

Alexei Vasilyev (*Russian*) is Director of the Institute for African Studies, Moscow.

Ciro E. Zoppo (*US*) is Professor of International Relations at the University of California, Los Angeles.

Preface

The chapters in this volume were presented to the following courses of the International School on Disarmament and Research on Conflicts (ISODARCO): the Seventh Winter Course held at Folgaria (Trento), Italy, between 23 and 30 January 1994, and the Eighth Winter Course held in Bressanone (Bolzano), Italy, between 21 and 28 January 1995.

The organization of the courses was made possible by the financial contributions of many organizations and the generous collaboration of several individuals. To the following goes our deepest gratitude.

For all of these ISODARCO courses:

The John D. and Catherine T. MacArthur Foundation;
Dr David Carlton and Dr Eng. Giancarlo Tenaglia, Directors of the Courses;
The Physics Department of the University of Rome 'Tor Vergata';
Professor Sandro Stringari, Director of the Physics Department of the University of Trento;
Dr Carlo Alessandrini, President of the Provincial Council of Trento;
The 'Forum Trentino per la Pace' (Trento Forum for Peace);
The Union of Scientists for Disarmament, Trento Branch; and
Dr Isabella Colace of the ISODARCO office in Rome.

For the Seventh Winter ISODARCO Course our thanks are due to the autonomous Trentino–Alto Adige Region for its overall assistance and financial support. For hospitality we are indebted to the Hotel Vittoria and to the local meeting agency 'Folgaria Convegni'.

For the Eighth Winter Course our thanks are due to Dr Tarcisio Grandi, President of the Trentino–Alto Adige Regional Board; the Bressanone Town Hall; and to the Convention Bureau Alto Adige. For hospitality we are indebted to the Hotel Grüner Baum and to the local Tourist Board.

All opinions expressed in the chapters of this book are of a purely personal nature and do not necessarily represent the official view of either the organizers of the School or of the organizations with which the writers may be affiliated.

It will be obvious to readers that in this volume no *detailed* study of any aspect of the crisis in the former Yugoslavia has been attempted. This omission can be simply explained: developments there are so fast-moving as to ensure that anything published in book format will be hopelessly out-dated by the time it reaches its readership.

Professor Carlo Schaerf
President of ISODARCO and Director of the School

1 The Outlook for Russia

Georgi Arbatov

Being a Russian one sometimes feels concern that Russia as a country, with its recent history full of turbulent and at times dramatic changes and events, has made the outside world somewhat tired and, to some degree, dulled in its reaction to events there. But at the same time it is widely understood how important not only for Russia but for the whole of the world is the direction in which the country is developing.

To obtain some perspective it is perhaps useful to begin with some reflections on the main periods of the *perestroika* process. The first period, not only romantic but also highly constructive, lasted from March 1985 and until the end of 1989. This was when Mikhail Gorbachev was at his best, surrounded by a highly motivated, mostly unselfish and gifted group of people and when millions were ready to support changes. In these years *perestroika*, despite some shortcomings and mistakes, began to bring the first tangible results. *Glasnost* radically changed the intellectual, spiritual and even political atmosphere in society. Drastic changes in foreign policy soon brought to an end the Cold War – a state of political affairs which, after four decades of existence, had started to look almost everlasting. Above all, the mood in the country was predominantly optimistic and upbeat.

The second period is more difficult to define; perhaps one could call it a period of growing uncertainties and vacillations, accompanied by a partial but very dangerous retreat. It lasted from 1990 until the unsuccessful *coup d'état* of August 1991. It seemed to many that this was a period when hesitations and even fears on the part of the leadership, and above all of Gorbachev himself, about the political and social forces unleashed by their policy and the direction in which they could push the development of the country.

Without going into details of the events, the overall results could be summed up as follows. First, there was a rejection of all the plans for economic reform prepared by the autumn of 1990. All were far from perfect but they were obviously better than the programme proposed a year later by Yegor Gaidar.

Secondly, we saw a radical retreat from democratic development. Gorbachev's programme of rule by a more or less 'iron hand', consisting of eight points, was accepted by parliament in November 1990. Under the pressure of those who demanded such rule, one of the most decent men in the leadership, Minister of the Interior Vadim Bakatin, was sacked. All this, as it turned out, was only the beginning of the new 'strong' policy. Incidentally, what astonished many was that the West, despite its constantly proclaimed allegiance to the cause of democracy in Russia, did not even seem to notice these changes in the official policy of the Soviet Union; perhaps their leaders were at this moment too much in love with Gorbachev and too busy with their own concerns.

Thirdly, further radical changes in Gorbachev's close political environment began. He distanced himself from his real political and personal allies and tried to make an alliance with people who in reality (and in many instances he must have realized) were bitter enemies of his policy and of himself personally. He also started to rely more and more on the army, on the police and on the KGB.

Fourthly, these latter forces received unprecedented access to power. An attempt was made to build a kind of police state, a garrison society. One cannot exclude the possibility that Gorbachev had hopes of making it serve his policy (including the defence of *perestroika*), but in reality it was used for opposite goals. This was first seen during the bloody events in the Baltic States in January 1991, then in the attempt to scare the Muscovites and deter them from protest against the planned demotion of Boris Yeltsin in March and finally during the August *coup* against Gorbachev himself. This obvious shift was so visible that Gorbachev himself found it necessary to explain his behaviour. On more than one occasion (once in my presence) he explained that all this was no more than a tactical manoeuvre, that his strategy as well as his loyalty to the ideals of *perestroika* remained unchanged. 'The mood of the public had shifted to the right,' he said, 'and the policy of the government has to follow.' A week later I sent him a personal letter, insisting that he had misread the mood of the public. I added that leadership does not always have to follow the mood of the crowd; sometimes it has to change it. Perhaps he even believed in what he was doing; but it was a self-delusion – an attempt to justify his retreat from former positions or even a betrayal of his own cause.

To be fair, it must be said that early in 1991 he again changed his policy, after some very visible and embarrassing defeats of his tactics. A truce with Yeltsin was concluded towards the end of March and, what was perhaps even more important, Gorbachev realized that he could not drag his feet any longer in concluding an agreement on a new Treaty of the Union. In fact, negotiations were started and seemed promising. From the very beginning, however, there was very vocal opposition against it, and a conspiracy against it was forged. Gorbachev demonstrated an absence of vigilance, will-power and simple sound judgement.

The price he paid for this misjudgement was the *coup* in August 1991. Although it ended in failure, it radically undermined his personal political position and he soon had to retire. But this was a very small and purely personal part of the total cost of mistakes and failures committed during this short 'transitional' period which followed the first, successful period of reforms. Incomparably greater damage has been wrought on the country as a whole: the chaotic breakdown of the Soviet Union, a deep economic crisis, serious social and political tensions, and a multitude of local conflicts, some of them rather bloody.

This leads us to the third period of recent changes (mainly in Russia), which are still unfolding, sometimes very dramatically, before our eyes. Avoiding generalizations and even attempts to give a name to this period, let us begin with a description of events from the first days after the defeat of the *coup* in August 1991. A 'grand euphoria' occurred among the 'democrats'. The identity of 'democrats' at that time was still very vague; anyone who was against the *coup* or at least said so, who was or had recently declared that he was against the Communist Party and supported Yeltsin, could claim to be a democrat. A mood of euphoria was also to some degree understandable for those who, perhaps to their own surprise, turned out to be the winners. They had managed in a somewhat miraculous way, almost bare-handed, to defeat the biggest army and the biggest secret police in the world. This was partially due to their courage and partially due to the mysterious, strange, if not outright stupid behaviour of the leaders of the *coup*, as well as to sheer luck.

As usual in such days of great triumph, a number of the victors almost immediately jumped into the stormy sea of struggle for the spoils of the victory. Alas, these included many rather well-known democrats; this did not contribute to their reputation, nor to the cause of democracy.

The Breakdown of the Soviet Union

Now let us turn to the most obvious changes which have occurred in the years since the *coup*. The Former Soviet Union was undoubtedly a unitary state which only pretended to be a federation of independent republics. It was an empire, a totalitarian empire, where even the 'imperial people', the Russians, were exploited and oppressed. It did not deserve salvation in its former shape. Nor would it have been possible to save it, at least without major bloodshed – which would have been counter-productive and in the end self-defeating.

But the suddenness of the collapse of the Soviet Union and the very clumsy way in which it happened left us, as well as the world at large, with a legacy of problems of tremendous dimensions: political and military, economic and financial, ethnic and ecological. Naturally, the problems soon started to burst forth, one after another. As it turned out, the dissolution of the Soviet Union not only failed to resolve many of the problems of the old empire, but seriously aggravated some of them or created new ones.

The immense Euro-Asian space of the Former Soviet Union is now undergoing not only reforms and changes but also a complicated process of further fermentation and disintegration, the ultimate outcome of which is not yet clear. There is the legacy of some unsettled and arbitrarily drawn borders. Many further problems have been created by the huge military heritage of the former superpower: how to divide it, how to retain control over it, how to prevent it falling into the wrong hands, and how to avoid the migration of scientists and engineers, crucially important to the production of weapons of mass destruction, into the arms of potential aggressors. Last but not least, we inherited a number of problems stemming from the multitude of national minorities. Many were caused by migration during the lifetime of the multinational Soviet state. But whatever their origins, the problems carry the seeds of serious conflicts. All these issues, national issues for Russia and other countries of the Commonwealth of Independent States (CIS), are also tending to become problems of vital interest to other countries, as they acquire international dimensions.

Economic Failures

At the moment of decisive victory for democracy after the defeat of the August *coup*, the leadership embarked upon a fundamentally erroneous course of economic policy. It was disguised as a market reform but in reality only discredited the whole idea of a market economy. The economic situation was certainly miserable, though much better than it is now, but, apart from a relatively small group of economic extremists, few informed people could believe in a miraculous salvation by means of 'shock therapy' to heal the fundamentally sick economy in a few months. So why did economic policy, something demanding many years of hard, clever and very consistent work, become for us immediately after the August *coup* a matter of the highest and urgent priority, so urgent that the essence and plan of reform was not properly discussed and instead irresponsibly improvised? At the same time the Russian government missed a unique chance of concentrating on the real priority – the democratic political reform which could have been a great success immediately after the defeat of the *coup*.

Only in such a situation of post-revolutionary chaos was it possible to turn away from all the experience that already existed in the world, from all the failed attempts at 'shock therapy' or from successfully working models. We ignored the American model (with its 'welfare state' and 'Reaganomics'), the German *Soziale Marktwirtschaft*, the Swedish model and the French or Italian economies, with their large government-owned sectors, and the Japanese or South Korean models, where the government plays a vital role in managing the economy. And we ignored the experience of countries like China, Mexico and Argentina, which have achieved visible success after rejecting many of the same recommendations proposed to Russia (many think imposed on Russia) by the International Monetary Fund (IMF) and similar organizations. Instead, we made the worst possible choice, opting not for more or less working real models (and of course carefully adjusting them to the concrete conditions of Russia), but giving preference to a kind of 'dead economic language', a model of 'classical' nineteenth-century capitalism, which would be unacceptable not only in Russia but also in any modern Western country.

It might be that one of the main motives of this choice was a futile hope by some Russian leaders that all the immense work of economic reform and orderly transition to a working market economy could be done without any special efforts by the government: it would be achieved by the 'invisible hand' of Adam Smith. They forgot that it was precisely this kind of 'Manchester capitalism', so vividly described by Charles Dickens, Karl Marx and Friedrich Engels, that led to Marxism, the Bolsheviks' October Revolution, and to Fascism and the Second World War. Do we have to repeat this cycle again and again? Or could we go along a less disastrous path?

In a world saturated with weapons, including nuclear weapons, there is clearly great international danger if one persists in the wrong economic course. Though I am not a professional economist, I have been rather deeply involved in economic policy in Russia, as well as studying foreign economic policies and theories, so I shall therefore venture to express my views on this crucial subject. What are the results of two years of the so-called 'Gaidar reforms'? These were in reality borrowed from the IMF and from some of its consultants, such as the American Professor Jeffrey Sacks and his Swedish colleague Andreas Oslund, who created this model principally for 'Third World' countries for the primary purpose of debt repayment. The practical results are: runaway inflation (in two years prices increased from a hundred to a thousand times); a constant decline in production (17–20 per cent a year); and the pauperization of the majority of the population against a background of conspicuous consumption by the very few. And, of course, in addition, we face corruption and a swiftly growing crime rate.

A ruinous result of this ill-conceived economic 'reform' has been a virtual collapse of education, fundamental science, the arts, culture and health care. For the first time since the Second World War the death rate in the country is higher than the birth rate, and the population is declining. The 'brain drain' has acquired threatening dimensions and will become even worse in the event that artificial obstacles to travelling abroad are removed. A major threat of all these developments is a catastrophic de-intellectualization of Russian society, which will mean a loss not only to the Russians, but to civilization as a whole. It would be a great tragedy, and at the same time a great paradox, if Russian culture, literature, art and science, and social and technical thought, having survived all kinds of difficulties, severe persecution and a ruthless censorship under the tsars and totalitarian Communism, should perish in an encounter with the economic and social system we are now trying to create under the guise of a 'democratic market reform'.

Hand in hand with this de-intellectualization of the country has also gone the inevitable process of an ugly moral degradation of society. We can already see many alarming signs of it. As well as the rising crime rate and unprecedented corruption, there is the deformation of many values and the creation of an intellectual vacuum. This vacuum cannot exist for long without being filled by all sorts of 'trash ideologies', such as rabid nationalism and racism, even witchcraft and religious fundamentalism of different kinds. And most usual and seemingly harmless, though only at first sight, is the idolization (even deification) of money, personal wealth and greed, which has already seriously affected not only the personalities of millions, but also the very fabric of society. As we are dealing here with a huge country, all this can also have global consequences, adding to the destabilization of international life.

This picture of economic disaster and its political consequences has been unfolding gradually, and the same has been happening to our perceptions of it. By early 1992, however, there was growing concern and later alarm. Some who had the opportunity decided to share their concerns directly with Yeltsin, but were not successful. Thus for two years living standards declined and there were moves away from democracy, which had to have political consequences.

Such concerns were confirmed by the elections to parliament in December 1993, following Yeltsin's apparent victory over the former parliament in the White House confrontation. Because of economic difficulties, the absence of any prospect for improvement and (though this is another topic) the national humiliation of a significant part of our population, the democrats lost. The extreme nationalists (to speak without euphemism, the fascists) were the biggest winners, followed by the Communists. Furthermore, a new constitution giving authoritarian rights to the president and providing for a very weak parliament was adopted. In the case of a presidential victory for the fascists this could serve as a basis for the legitimization of dictatorship.

The Forces of Disorganization and Disarray

My life has led me to work more or less closely with six governments and officially or unofficially to serve as an adviser to five leaders in Moscow.[1] Here permit me to make only one observation: never have I seen an administration and a bureaucracy so undisciplined, disorganized, unprofessional and influenced by very strange perceptions about ethical standards of business behaviour as that presently in office.

Of course, this can be partially explained by the sheer fact that we are considering a post-revolutionary government, lacking experience, education and sometimes even an elementary political upbringing. It has within it a number of new people, often only recently living in remote provinces and holding jobs far from anything even closely resembling a more or less serious governmental activity, lacking elementary professional training and civic experience, coming *en masse* into many different branches and to different levels of responsibility within the government.

The hope remains that with the accumulation of experience, as well as the process of natural selection among the bureaucrats, sooner or later things will start to improve. But the situation in Russia hardly gives us much time. If these things only improve slowly, even the better plans and programmes could fail.

Two Scenarios Affecting International Security

One can envisage two basic scenarios on the basis of the foregoing analysis. Let us begin with the worst possible case scenario, that could become a reality in the event of a complete destabilization of Russia (and the CIS states), leading to a collapse of the Russian state and society. There would be complete political chaos in the immense territories of the former Soviet Union, saturated with weapons and aggravated by multiple local armed conflicts. There is no need to stress that the implications of such developments for global security would be extremely negative; such chaos could hardly be localized within the borders of Russia or even the CIS. It could lead to a 'Yugoslavization' of Europe or at least of a significant part of it. Nor should one fail to consider a spread of the conflicts to other areas – in particular the Middle East, South Asia and parts of Africa. In the event that the situation in Russia develops into a full-fledged civil war which ends with a new nationalist and fascist military or civilian dictatorship, one could not exclude attempts at resurrecting the empire, possibly not limited to the former borders of the Former Soviet Union. Adventures of this kind would in the end almost certainly fail. Until September–December 1993 even an attempt to go in this direction looked highly improbable. Events since then, however, have changed our perceptions, showing that almost anything is possible. The existence of substantial amounts of nuclear weapons in the region underlines the importance of applying 'preventive medicine' policies designed to exclude the risks of further destabilization and chaos in Russia.

There are at least three major factors of danger that will need to be addressed. The first is that there will be a complete breakdown of the national economy as a result of the 'shock therapy' so enthusiastically supported by the West as a 'democratic market reform'. Regrettably this risk, with its unavoidable social and political consequences (like increasing the power of extremists), will remain high, at least until there is a very radical change to purge Russian economic and social policy of Gaidar's 'reforms' and traditional IMF prescriptions. Naturally, there also needs to be a change in the position of the West, and in particular that of the United States, whose support for 'shock therapy' has encouraged this suicidal course. A second danger is that the fragmentation of Russia will occur because of grave mistakes in national, regional and economic policy. A third risk arises from the weakness of democratic mechanisms and institutions (such as parliament, political parties and the courts) and from the tremendous over-militarization of the country. These factors still make the whole political system very vulnerable to breakdown and to incidents triggered by personal incompatibilities and the ambitions of its leaders. The outcome could be personal dictatorship and even fascism of some kind.

A second scenario we need to consider is that there will be a safe and successful resolution of the present crisis. There is, of course, no place for dreams about miracles or gimmicks which could liberate Russia from the long, difficult and arduous work that is needed. Indeed, it seems that the people themselves neither expect nor believe in miracles. What they want to see is a change in direction, a halt to the negative trends, and a beginning (if even a very modest but persistent one) of positive, visible and consistent changes. Bearing in mind the wealth of the country, its natural resources, its intellectual and industrial potential, one can hardly consider such a prospect as too optimistic. Indeed, it looks realistic enough to many in Russia and gives strength and stamina to those fighting for a better future. Such a scenario will demand, however, serious political efforts from both Russia and the West, as well as from other CIS states.

As to the policy of Russia, the first task for its leaders is to signal a radical departure from 'shock therapy' and servility to the IMF and the World Bank, and to reject the advice of Western well-wishers who may be sincere but if so are ignorant. A realistic economic course must be adopted. This will consist of viable industrial, agricultural and social policies and will really lead the country towards a socially-oriented market economy.

The other important task for Russia is to beware of any temptation to resurrect the former empire. At the same time it should persistently seek to improve and strengthen the economic and political ties between the CIS states. The aim should be to create smoothly working mechanisms that could transform the CIS into an active working body whose purpose would be to build a framework for an economic and political union, which in turn could become a foundation for peace, stability and co-operation within the whole territory of the former Soviet Union. It is quite possible to achieve this. We are already seeing an increasing interest of many CIS states in such an alliance – at least in economic terms – and some formal agreements have recently been concluded or prepared.

Meanwhile, the most important issue today remains, as already stated, Russian economic policy. In this connection one has to say a few words about what happened in 1993. On the surface this was a year overburdened with political battles and confrontations, which hardly left any time for any serious work on industrial, agricultural and social policy. But this picture might be a little misleading. It may be that the whole course towards political confrontation and a power struggle started because of rationally understood or instinctively felt economic purposes. In the autumn of 1992, when this tendency started, there was an awareness that 1 December 1992 was coming closer, and with it the end of the president's emergency powers, which included his right to appoint and dismiss all members of the cabinet, the prime minister included. In addition, the next Congress of People's Deputies had to be convened, and the first item on its agenda had to be a report on the state of the economy. But nobody wanted to be responsible for it and for the results of the reforms – neither the executive (though initially it had accepted full responsibility for the reforms) nor the legislature (which, though formally it had given all the rights and responsibility to the president, could not consider itself free of responsibility for the destiny of the country). These considerations were probably the real reason why, for a year from the autumn of 1992, very few in the leadership cared about the real business, about the economy, and became engulfed in a power struggle. Such 'games' could not last for ever. A price had to be paid in October 1993: the bloody tragedy that followed the unconstitutional dismissal of the parliament by the president. This was a tragedy of such dimensions that it cannot be calculated even now. One thing is clear: it will have far-reaching and long-term consequences.

The Next Steps for Russia and the West

The most obvious adverse result of the disintegration of the Soviet Union was and remains the fate of the Soviet nuclear arsenal. In particular, there are the weapons deployed outside of Russia, in Ukraine, Kazakhstan and Belarus, some of which have ambiguous positions as to their non-nuclear status and their attitude towards the whole issue of nuclear non-proliferation. Nevertheless, since the agreement reached by Russia, the United States and Ukraine in January 1994, one may feel more optimistic on this issue. The second concern (also a legitimate one) of the West is the possible proliferation of nuclear and some other especially sophisticated and dangerous weapons to third countries. For example, former Soviet republics could sell essential technology and materials, and there could be migration of specialists and the export of 'know-how'. In the case of nuclear weapons such problems are partially regulated and managed by international treaties and agreements, and hence in this sense they are recognized by the world community as international issues. That legitimizes international concerns and policies which are aimed at avoiding such developments. Russia shares such concerns, and welcomes such policies. The dominant opinion is that Western participation in an early solution of these problems is essential. And if the West has in mind not tactical but long-term interests, its involvement can be effective. All new independent states consider it absolutely crucial for their existence and their future to become fully accepted members of the international community. And if not only Russia but also other governments make it clear to the other CIS states that an essential condition for their international acceptance is adherence to the basic international norms of political behaviour and to the most important treaties and agreements, including those which cover the issues of non-proliferation and arms control in general, respect for existing borders between states and for human rights (including the rights of national minorities), there will be a much greater chance that the message will be received and understood. This position is not an attempt by the largest of the former Soviet republics to shift its responsibility on to the shoulders of other states and governments. Thoughtful and fair Russians consider Russia's responsibility to be a special one, and this is a topic to which I shall return, but because of certain historical and political reasons Russian efforts may turn out to be insufficient and this makes the influence of the West of particular importance.

Russia, without a doubt, has certain special responsibilities *vis-à-vis* other former Soviet republics. In Soviet times Russia suffered along with the other republics from oppressive and arbitrary rule by the totalitarian centre. But what for Russians was cruelty and oppression by the totalitarian regime often appeared to other republics as national oppression and exploitation by

Russia. And Russians cannot deny that there were good reasons for this interpretation – the historical roots of the relationship between Moscow and the republics were founded upon national oppression. The Russian empire, as well as the subjugation of other nations by Russia, is a sad historical reality. That is why Russia cannot escape her duty to persuade other former Soviet republics, not by words alone (who trusts them nowadays?) but by deeds and actual policy, that Russia has no imperial ambitions and does not threaten their sovereignty. In principle this probably corresponded to the initial goals and strategy of Russian foreign policy after August 1991, but it would not be the whole truth if Russian nationalism and chauvinism were not also mentioned. It is a reality, it exists and is sometimes very vocal, though it does not (at least as yet) determine official policy and mostly represents the opposition. It could, however, become a serious force in the future, if there is a complete disintegration of the economy, an acute political crisis, an explosion of ethnic conflicts or some other condition favourable to its nurture.

The highest interests of Russia prompt her to pursue an internationalist policy. Of course, being the largest and strongest of the republics of the Former Soviet Union, with a wealth of natural and intellectual resources and great industrial and agricultural potential, Russia could 'go it alone' – attempt to guarantee its own security, prosperity and well-being. Yet even a huge country like Russia could 'go it alone' only in a friendly environment. If it came to be surrounded by hostile nations we could have another cold war, but probably more vicious. On the other hand, if the Russians succeed in removing the lingering suspicions, complaints and grudges of other former republics, the ground could be cleared for the natural trends and forces of integration which already have shown their strength in Europe and some other regions. Such a policy is the more important because it confronts not only the openly imperialistic views of Vladimir Zhirinovsky and people like him but also the 'kind, paternalistic imperialism' that has a following in the establishment. In the latter context, for instance, some political ideas have recently emerged which stress 'special' and even exclusive rights and responsibilities of Russia to 'care' about 'law and order' throughout the whole territory of the Former Soviet Union – a kind of 'Monroe Doctrine' (or, as some joke, 'Monrovski Doctrine') for Russia which could hand over to the United States responsibility for the rest of the globe. This would be not only immoral but would constitute a direct route to a new cold war, involving as it does first-step attempts to resurrect the Russian empire.

The major preoccupation of most Russians are at the moment, it seems, not with the long-term future. The immediate prospects are a cause for serious concern. On them depend the costs and the amount of time which progress in Russia will take. The failure of the economic and political reforms in Russia, not to speak about a victory, even a temporary one, of the extreme nationalist, fascist or quasi-fascist forces would mean a real disaster for Russia and have serious negative international, indeed global, after-effects. We saw the first rehearsal for it in October and December 1993. Today we can easily assess not only the economic results of a possible failure – the death of a modern economy, the misery of the overwhelming majority of the population – but also a catastrophic decline of culture, science, education and the health service, a depressing decline of intellectual life, rampaging crime and corruption and other symptoms of the degradation of society. This could last for a substantial time: years, perhaps decades. This alone is already a reason for grave concern, at least for every Russian. I think, however, that there are even more reasons for alarm. First of all, a failure of the reforms will have a deeper impact on the mentality of the Russian and possibly other peoples for decades, if only because it will discredit in their eyes the whole idea of the reforms, democracy and a market economy. Too much was promised from the beginning, too many commitments were given not only by our not too experienced politicians, but also (what is in my view especially disturbing) by foreign political leaders respected by the greater part of our public and our politicians.

'Approved abroad' was almost synonymous with a mark of highest and indisputable quality. One should ask oneself: how could it happen that such a man as Yeltsin, initially not too experienced and sure of himself in economics (not to mention macroeconomics), could so easily entrust the economic fate of such a gigantic land to a group of young economists who at that time were almost unknown in the country and had no practical experience, and who in addition he had not even once seen personally before the day the decree was signed? The most important if not the only explanation may be that they possessed the stamp 'approved abroad'. They were approved, that is, by the major international financial organizations and by the respected world leaders of the Group of Seven.

As the disastrous results of the 'Gaidar reforms' were becoming more obvious, a theory was born in Russia which won approval not only in the ranks of the extremists, but also among a part of the moderate opposition, to the effect that all this was a conspiracy intended by the West to ruin the Soviet Union and then Russia. No doubt there are some Western politicians who could nurture such plans for 'doing away with the enemy for ever', but most people in Russia are not paranoid enough to take these scenarios too seriously. In any case, some of them know personally too many sober-minded Western politicians who understand clearly enough that chaos and disaster in Russia would create for the West and for the whole world tremendously dangerous problems. At the same time, the concern remains that the failure of the economic reforms proposed or imposed by the West could seriously undermine confidence and strengthen the positions of fanatically anti-Western factions in Russian political life.

Russians are often asked by their counterparts in the West: How can we help you? The first answer, it seems, should be: Do not give us any more wrong advice, in particular about our economic policy. We have had more than enough of them from people like Sacks and organizations like the IMF. And the second answer is: Be absolutely honest, tell us the whole truth and nothing but the truth. Do not make promises of help which you cannot deliver. Tell our people the truth: that the Western governments do not have enough money to save a huge country like Russia (which, incidentally, does not give an impression of a country in a hurry to save itself). Of course, some assistance is possible and one hopes that it will be given – for such needs as help in destroying nuclear or chemical weapons, in the building of apartments for demobilized soldiers, in projects for conversion of the defence enterprises and, in extreme cases, humanitarian help.

But though it can be very welcome, such help will be of no more than marginal importance. The main thing is not to foster any illusions among the Russian public and leaders. This approach will also make it easier for the Russian people to understand that, in terms of co-operation with foreign countries, they have to rely more not on governmental assistance but on private investments. And in order to get them Russia will have to make the country attractive for investors, which will demand serious changes in the legal system, the creation of appropriate guarantees and the provision of services.

Recently the Russians have begun to see some signs that the real situation with respect to the 'Gaidar reforms' is becoming more obvious in the West. For example, there was the 1993 Annual Report on Trade and Development from the United Nations Conference on Trade and Development (UNCTAD), and there have been statements by US Senators Robert Dole and George Mitchell. But the supporters of these 'reforms' immediately launched a counter-attack, making statements to the effect that their favoured policy failed in Russia only because it was not pursued strongly and persistently enough. If such a point of view should become dominant in American policy, the possibility cannot be excluded that President Bill Clinton will have his next summit in Moscow not with Yeltsin, but with Zhirinovsky. There is one additional comment to be made concerning the Western attitude towards events in Russia and other CIS states. One can understand only too well that leading personalities in the West are also human – they too can have their personal sympathies and antipathies, but these should not grow into interference in the internal affairs of another country. Official support should be rendered as a rule not to concrete personalities but to concrete political causes or policies.

The Russians have to rely for their economic recovery first of all on their own resources. This does not mean that some assistance and some money cannot or must not be given, but above all the Russians themselves have to have a correct economic policy and follow it persistently. As to relations with the West, removal of any remaining obstacles to trade and co-operation are even more important than money. So much can be done by both Russia and the West to prevent a dangerous course of events.

My final message to the reader is that many people in Russia are seriously concerned about the autocratic trends in political life in view of the tragic events of October 1993 and the draft of the new constitution. In short, at the time of writing (1994), the development of democracy remains the core question. There will be no decent future for Russia as a non-democratic country. Without democracy there will be neither market reforms, nor a safe and stable life for Russia's neighbours. Given the size, military might and international influence of the country, it is vital that Russia becomes not only a great power but a great democratic power.

Note

1 The more fundamental impressions and some generalizations are described in a book of memoirs: Georgi Arbatov, *The System: An Insiders Life in Soviet Politics* (New York, 1992).

2   Economic Instability in Russia: The Price of Peace?

Derek Braddon

Introduction

At the London Summit in July 1990, which formally signalled the end to the Cold War, President George Bush commented that the events of the preceding year would alter the way we think about defence. At the time, the wave of political and economic liberalization that was sweeping through the Former Soviet Union (FSU) and Eastern Europe was welcomed as an unprecedented catalyst for systemic change, offering the potential for both a more peaceful world and renewed economic prosperity. Recent developments, however, particularly in the Russian Federation, suggest that such optimistic expectations failed to recognize the destabilizing impact of the conflicting economic forces being unleashed.

To expect a major command economy to adjust rapidly and smoothly to the changes required to transform that system into a world-class market economy with only minimal support from the West was undoubtedly optimistic. To believe that it could do so while simultaneously undergoing transformation to a post-Cold War economy, requiring the rapid reduction of its highly significant military–industrial complex, was simply unrealistic.

Russian Economic Reform

The first half of the 1990s has seen the relatively stable, if declining, superpower command economy of the FSU transformed into an unstable, fragmented and economically weak group of increasingly market-oriented economies. Particularly within the Russian Federation, the key indicators of economic instability have been prominent over this period: rampant inflation; unsustainable budget deficits; unprecedented levels of unemployment

15

(rising from 2 per cent to 10 per cent between 1992 and 1995); industrial bankruptcies; sharply falling living standards; and significant losses of both domestic output and trade. While some of these economies are slowly beginning to respond to the stimuli of market forces and may well recover some of their lost economic potential, there is little evidence that they can, under present conditions, successfully undertake the economic transformation required of them. Without a genuine and significant increase in external support, internal political and economic vested interests, fundamentally opposed to the market experiment, may well use deteriorating economic conditions to bring economic and political liberalization to an end.

In common with most transition economies, Russia adopted a wide-ranging approach to economic reform after 1990. This strategy combined planned limits on monetary expansion; targets for a reduced fiscal deficit; price and wage deregulation; extensive privatization and property rights reforms; the fragmentation of state monopolies; enhanced social provision; and progressive steps towards wider currency convertibility.[1] At the heart of the strategy was an attempt to create at the earliest opportunity a degree of macroeconomic stability, coincident with a major transformation of the economic base along more competitive, market-driven lines with increased emphasis on civil rather than military production.

Without question, the transformation of the massive, resource-hungry Russian military–industrial complex was central to a successful outcome. By the late 1980s, it had become increasingly clear that, against the background of a long-term decline in Russia's economic growth rate which commenced at the end of the 1950s, the burden of maintaining such a vast military–industrial complex was no longer economically feasible. The economic condition of Russia, already causing concern in the late 1980s, deteriorated sharply after 1989 due to the impact of economic reforms in dislocating the process of state management of the economy, replacing the inefficient but functional bureaucratic decision-making process with initially chaotic market forces. At the same time, the potential benefits of reform may well have been delayed by deliberate obstruction from the very bureaucracies overseeing their implementation. Over this period, about one-third of Russia's national income was eliminated, effectively matching in proportion the economic depressions experienced in the United States during the period 1929–32.[2]

Exacerbated by the collapse of foreign trade with its former command economy partners and dislocated further by the August 1991 *coup*, the economic contraction continued and estimates for 1994 suggest a further loss of some 10 per cent of national output.[3] Unlike the situation elsewhere in the transition economies, the output collapse in Russia preceded the full implementation of market reforms and is viewed primarily as 'supply induced', originating from the fragmentation of domestic inter-enterprise and external trading relationships, exacerbated by sharply declining demand for defence production.[4] Nevertheless, throughout this immensely difficult period, the reform process continued under Prime Ministers Yegor Gaidar and, somewhat against expectations, under his successor Victor Chernomyrdin, with particular emphasis being placed on the privatization process in ultimately generating a market-based, competitive economic and business environment. At the end of 1993, it was estimated that in Russia some 60,000 smaller factories with less than 200 employees had been privatized, together with about 5000 large factories, placing some 50 per cent of the national product in the market sector.[5] The sheer scale of the economic crisis confronting Russia in the early 1990s and the reluctance of the West to commit sufficient resources to support the transition process (due principally to political and strategic uncertainties) required a degree of economic adjustment of 'unique proportions'.[6]

The Russian Military–Industrial Complex and the Approach to Conversion

Recent estimates suggest that the defence industries in the FSU, much of it concentrated in the Russian Federation, employed in 1991 about 4.8 million workers (12.6 per cent of industrial employment), contributed some 12.3 per cent of gross national product (GNP) and absorbed about 45.9 per cent of central government expenditure. This was supplemented by a further 3.8 million members of the armed forces.[7] Dismantling such a politically sensitive and economically significant industrial sector under the established mechanisms of a command economy would have been a difficult enough task. Attempting to do so in the volatile conditions generated by sudden and simultaneous exposure of the economy to newly released market forces and political liberalization was inevitably a much more formidable challenge.

At the start of the 1990s, the military sector of the Russian Federation employed as much as one-fifth of the country's industrial labour force. Over 3000 industrial enterprises were believed to be involved in military production, many of them also contributing significantly to the production of consumer goods. Military industries tend to be geographically concentrated, contributing over 30 per cent of industrial employment in north-west Russia and in the Urals region, and over 20 per cent of industrial employment in at least five other regions. It has been estimated that between one-half and three-quarters of such employment in and around the major cities of Moscow and St Petersburg could be defined as defence-dependent. Converting the military–industrial base of the Russian economy, therefore, has more than national macroeconomic significance; it has serious regional implications which take on an important political dimension when the disproportionately high numbers of expatriate Slavs currently employed in the military–industrial complex is noted. With the Russian military–industrial complex intended to decline from a 12 per cent share of gross domestic product (GDP) in 1990 to just 6 per cent by the end of 1995, the implications for unemployment, output and income loss, and severe regional decline, are clear and unavoidable, unless a successful conversion programme can be delivered over the next few years.

The disintegration of the FSU left Russia with approximately 80 per cent of the its defence industrial assets.[8] This gave it the potential both to produce most kinds of defence equipment and, more critically, to undertake conversion strategies in the widest possible industrial context. Furthermore, much of the bureaucracy that managed the external defence sales of the FSU was retained by the Russian Federation in the form of the General Engineering and the General Co-operation Departments of the Ministry of Foreign Relations. Transformed into the General Defence Export Corporation (or *VO Oboronexport*), the corporation enabled Russia to achieve relative success in pursuing an export drive in weapons, securing important contracts with Malaysia, India and Turkey. But this relative success must be set against the background of a dramatic collapse in Russia's arms export earnings between 1990 and 1992. In 1990, foreign arms sales contributed about 8 per cent of the GNP of the FSU. By the end of 1992, the share accruing to Russia's GNP amounted to just 1.6 per cent. As a share of total industrial output (which itself fell by one-fifth in the first two years of this decade), defence products declined from 49.7 per cent for the FSU in 1990 to just 22.6 per cent for Russia in 1992.

In common with most other major arms-producing nations, Russia's defence industrial base experienced a deep and sustained reduction in demand for its output in the early 1990s. The apparent end of the Cold War, bringing with it fundamental changes in military strategic requirements, produced a sharp reduction in the defence goods required for Russia's armed forces and removed the necessity to supply former Warsaw Treaty Organization members with subsidized weapons. Although the available data on military production in Russia is recognized as being somewhat suspect, it appears that output of the most important weapons declined sharply during the first two years of the decade. The output of tanks, artillery, military aircraft, submarines and surface fighting ships fell by between one-half and two-thirds over this period. At the same time, Russia's evolving military strategy (and, therefore, perceived defence requirements) increasingly had to take into account new areas of political tension and actual conflict (such as the apparently ill-fated venture in Chechenia), as well as threats to future stability (such as territorial disputes in Abkhazia, South Ossetia, Armenia and Tajikistan).

To resolve both the deepening economic crisis and to address the changing requirements of the post-Cold War world, Russia thus had little choice but to attempt a radical downsizing of the defence sector and a rapid expansion of civil production. The conversion process, unavoidably, lay at the heart of an effective economic recovery programme. Conversion plans were aligned closely with strategies to enhance Russia's economic growth rate with specific targets set for the elimination of shortages in supply of many consumer goods by the mid-1990s. For example, the output of refrigerators, freezers, televisions and radios was intended to increase by one-half, while that of vacuum cleaners would double, together with a 33-fold increase in the output of video-recorders. The conversion plans envisaged television ownership within Russia increasing by 3 per cent per annum and refrigerators/freezers by 4 per cent per annum. Even then, it was expected that this would represent ownership levels within Russia three to five times lower than in the United States, with additional concern about product quality. It has been noted that:

> More than Rb40bn in capital investments are requested for the respecialization of existing production facilities, for the large-scale creation of new capacities for the production of goods and other civilian products, and for the mothballing of specialized production facilities in 1991–1995. However, the extraordinarily strained balance of investment resources today makes it impossible to allocate this sum.[9]

Despite the problems constantly encountered with recent conversion strategies, it is important to note that the process of defence conversion has been actively pursued by the governments of both the FSU and, more recently, Russia, for several years. The conversion programme was formally launched by President Mikhail Gorbachev in December 1988. Under President Boris Yeltsin, the strategy continues with somewhat mixed results. As one writer noted:

> The new Russian government inherited a Soviet defence conversion policy, but in circumstances of acute budget stringency lacked resources to implement it. To a considerable extent, defence enterprises were left to their own devices. Some have shown remarkable initiative in finding foreign partners and organizing new civilian production; others have been paralysed, capable only of begging for state budget support or credit on preferential terms.[10]

Transforming the most successful and politically powerful sector of the Russian economy was always going to be an essential but formidable challenge. The defence sector has always had a priority claim on managerial, labour and material resources. It differed from other sectors of the economy in that it could offer employees incentives in terms of higher salaries, bonuses and fringe benefits, and was the only part of the economy to face genuine international competition through the arms race. The gap between research, innovation and eventual production that has been damaging to the civil sector of the economy is not a feature of the military sector.[11] Unfortunately, these strengths have, in the past, been offset to some extent by the absence of incentives to economize on the use of capital, labour and material inputs in military production.[12] Given its critical strategic role within the economy, now significantly reduced, and its unquestioned political influence, the military–industrial complex in Russia seems certain to remain a key player in facilitating or, perhaps, obstructing the process of overall economic transformation. For example, one writer noted that:

> the fruits of the conversion efforts over the past three years must be seen as extremely discouraging. Yet it is important to emphasize that the lack of progress is attributable not to technical obstacles, but to political, bureaucratic and managerial ones.[13]

Another commentator makes this critical point:

> the defence complex is itself a principal actor in the unfolding drama of Soviet development in post-Communist times. It has the power and influence to undermine progress towards a market, mixed economy. ... Decisions adopted during recent years have also put the defence industry into a position where it can determine the success or failure of efforts to improve the living standards of Soviet citizens.[14]

Economic Reconstruction, Military Conversion and Market Forces

For those economists who retain a healthy scepticism regarding the efficacy of market forces in reaching desirable economic outcomes in conditions of severe economic contraction, the results so far have not been particularly surprising. The evidence of the last five years suggests that, without substantially greater involvement by Western companies, financial agencies and international institutions in facilitating the transition of the Russian economy in the future, deep and sustained economic instability in the Russian Federation will be the inevitable and ultimately self-destructive price of peace.

Crucial to the eventual success of the economic reform strategy in Russia was the extent to which newly-unleashed market forces could cope adequately and rapidly with the resource reallocation process so essential to the regeneration of a modern industrial economy. Economic history provides us with clear lessons about the degree to which the market mechanism can facilitate the process of economic adjustment, even in less demanding circumstances. Where economies operate at or near to the full-employment level of national income, encountering only modest and occasional deviations, the equilibrating power of market forces can be extremely effective. In such conditions, the market appears able to correct, rapidly and smoothly, temporary movements away from full-employment equilibrium. Market forces appear to operate most effectively where the deviations to be absorbed and corrected are marginal in scale and originate in the context of a prosperous, expanding economy. In such circumstances the market mechanism can be extremely efficient in its role as a powerful allocator of resources, if not always equitable in its redistributive function.

The situation is very different, however, where major systemic changes are concerned. Evidence suggests that market forces can fail abysmally where the scale of change required and the associated expectations of consumers and producers extend beyond what would normally be experienced in the 'corridor' around full employment. In such circumstances, the equilibrating mechanism of the market cannot adequately deal with major and sustained deviations from full employment (or even from an equilibrium level of national income below full employment). Markets abhor conditions of extreme risk and prolonged uncertainty, particularly in an environment where the established *modus operandi* of political and economic life has been virtually demolished. Deviations from equilibrium on a major scale tend not to be responsive to correction through minor price adjustments and, indeed, are more likely to be accompanied by significant adjustments in output and employment, long before the price mechanism can respond. For a major economy in conditions of political turmoil, confronting significant economic contraction and the urgent need for fundamental industrial reconstruction, the unleashing of powerful market forces are likely to exacerbate the economic situation for a considerable period of time rather than improve it. The market mechanism will still attempt to secure equilibrium but, with prices no longer truly reflecting economic conditions, its co-ordination role is constrained and false signals will be transmitted to the economy.

Furthermore, in the 1990s, the majority of markets have a critical international dimension and, with so many economies undergoing the process of economic and political transformation simultaneously, market signals are likely to become increasingly confused worldwide. Equilibrium may be achieved in due course but at much lower levels of income and employment. More likely, a state of long-term disequilibrium will persist, generating economic instability and, potentially, weakening the economic base until it confronts the possibility of critical mass collapse.

Such a critique of the efficacy of market forces, by no means universally accepted by economists, has been well documented in the literature and remains the subject of intense conjecture.[15] The debate, however, provides an important backcloth against which to examine the experience of Russia in the 1990s, for, in addition to experiencing deep economic contraction in the domestic economy, partly attributable to the dramatic reduction in demand for the output of the military–industrial complex, that economy had to address the total or partial elimination of many of its established international trading relationships, further fuelling the slide into economic disequilibrium.

Military Expenditure Reduction and the Market

By far the most important systemic change required in the transformation of the Russian economy is the rapid and smooth reallocation of resources from the military to the civil sector. In this process, for a genuine economic recovery to take place in Russia, and in similar transition economies, resources must be channelled by rapid and smooth market adjustment from the defence sector into the production of goods and services required by both the domestic consumer and the global market. The military–industrial complex in Russia certainly consumes a vast range of resources that could be released for alternative use, particularly important in an economy where the consumer goods and services requirements of the domestic population are almost unlimited. Furthermore, many Russian military enterprises have been heavily engaged in civil production, yielding both experience of the sectors requiring expansion and suggesting the capacity for exploring and exploiting potential new market opportunities. In addition, reduced military expenditure should, in theory, provide the potential for a substantial 'peace dividend' with which to regenerate sectors of the economy designated as critical components for economic reconstruction and recovery.

Unfortunately, at least in the medium term, the scope for acquiring such a 'peace dividend' in practice appears to be very limited. There are two principal reasons which constrain the immediate acquisition of positive economic gains from declining military expenditure. First, while reductions in defence budgets clearly provide resources that could finance conversion activities, evidence suggests that such resources will be severely eroded (if not fully depleted) by the new costs arising from military contraction. Following a significant decline in defence expenditure, these additional costs are likely to be associated with the decommissioning of weapons systems (especially nuclear); maintenance and safety costs for those weapons taken out of service and held in reserve; environmental recovery costs to make good the damage associated with former defence-related production and military-related activities; and extensive governmental and corporate redundancy costs in terms of income protection, retraining and job creation. Second, in the current situation confronting the Russian economy, considerable priority would need to be attached to the policy objective of further reducing the budget deficit. Overall, the scope for economic expansion based upon the notion of a realizable and significant 'peace dividend' must be treated with extreme caution.

Furthermore, the experience of attempts to reallocate resources from military to civil production in NATO countries where the market system is not only established but, under the macroeconomic policies of the last 15 years has been considerably strengthened, is hardly encouraging. This experience suggests that, in market economies, the adjustment to sustained reduction in military expenditure often yields results in a sudden, uncoordinated and frequently damaging way for both national – and, more particularly, for regional – economies. To understand the problems of military conversion in Russia under a new market-force adjustment mechanism (and the associated tensions likely to be created as a result), the experience of other market economies needs to be briefly considered.

Within major arms-producing market economies such as the United States or the United Kingdom, the damaging impacts associated with sustained reduction in military expenditure are only too apparent and are principally attributable to corporate strategic response to perceptions of a 'permanently' lower level of military requirements. Expectations of future worldwide defence expenditure cuts of up to 40 per cent became almost the 'conventional wisdom' of the early 1990s, and action was taken by major defence supply companies to address the problem. In general, defence supply companies have responded to the situation by a drastic reduction in the workforce and a streamlining of their operations. In some instances complete divestment of defence operations occurred, while in other cases new specialist avenues within the smaller defence market were identified and explored.

The emerging response from defence contractors seems to be one of long-range market positioning while also targeting realistic short-term opportunities. The range of strategies being pursued in corporate restructuring in response to declining defence expenditure includes the pursuit of collaborative ventures in order to share the burden of costs and risks horizontally; the enhancement of civil business, harnessing and transferring technology and other operational aspects; and the spreading of risks and costs associated with research and development vertically, by persuading their suppliers and subcontractors to bear a greater proportion of the research and development burden.[16] For the most part, prime contractors in the defence industry have pursued corporate restructuring by a combination of rationalization, international industrial partnering, the reorganization of supplier networks, conversion and diversification, together with determined attempts to increase foreign military sales.

In addition, recognizing the need both to attain and maintain world market competitiveness, the corporate restructuring process for both defence and non-defence companies in the 1990s has had to recognize the importance of three key developments. First, in Western economies, civil technology now often leads defence technology and, in areas such as electronics and new materials, achieves lower costs with higher quality. Second, to attain 'world-class' business performance, Western enterprises have had to move away from mass production operations towards a 'flexible manufacturing' approach, allowing low-volume, multi-product output with more specific market focus and enabling the potential of dual-use technology to be pursued more rigorously.

Lastly, increasingly in the West, there is considerable overlap between the critical technologies (such as advanced electronics, new materials, software, advanced manufacturing equipment and advanced information systems) required for an effective defence industrial base to operate and those necessary to maintain international competitiveness in the whole economy. In the future, it seems certain that very few business sectors will be totally defence-specific; most will feature fully integrated civilian and military production activities. The shift towards increased civilian production by defence companies in the United States was identified and analysed more than two decades before the end of the Cold War,[17] yet, in a study of 46 major US defence contractors surveyed in 1989, it was observed that only 5 per cent had redirected a significant share of their production from military to civilian production over the previous 15 years. However, almost half the sample was planning to do so in the period 1989–94. Similarly, a study of defence supply companies in the defence-dependent southwest region of the United Kingdom confirmed the renewed interest in the opportunities offered by defence conversion.[18] Only 15 per cent of the defence supply organizations surveyed had been pursuing a conversion or diversification strategy over the previous five years. A further 60 per cent confirmed, however, that a planned shift from military to civilian production would be a key element in their evolving corporate strategy for the future. Critically, perhaps, the study also found evidence that both those companies with existing diversified activities and those planning to expand into the civil sector were encountering formidable difficulties in the transition process, confronting technical, cultural, managerial, financial and other significant barriers. Studies of the defence conversion process in the West have identified three requirements to make a diversification or conversion strategy potentially successful. First, and perhaps most significant, there is the need for cultural change within the organization, both in respect of the shift from military to civil markets and also in recognition of the rapid changes currently taking place in those civil markets. Second, priority needs to be given to the provision of adequate financing for conversion, both because that process is likely to be long term, high risk and expensive to pursue, and because evidence suggests that successful diversification examples often originate in companies where access is possible to the financial resources of a major parent organization. The problem of financing conversion and diversification strategies adequately will be exacerbated in a market economy as financial institutions recognize that business conditions confronting defence supply companies are deteriorating with declining defence expenditure and as easily accessible market opportunities in the civil sector become congested by new entrants.[19] Finally, successful diversification or conversion requires complete understanding of the newly targeted market and its specific requirements, together with the capacity to meet those requirements swiftly and efficiently. Without question, the defence industrial base of market economies such as the United States and the United Kingdom is undergoing a dramatic and rapid transformation, similar to that experienced somewhat earlier in the non-military sectors of those economies. To acquire genuine international competitiveness and fully regenerate the Russian economy, the process of economic transformation must also encompass many of the developments outlined above and confront many of the same barriers to progress.

Military Conversion in Russia

To date, Russia has experimented with two approaches to the conversion of military industry. The 'physical' conversion approach, prominent between 1988 and 1991, aimed to retain some 30 per cent of military production capacity while converting the remainder to civilian production. Successful transition was expected in five to six years, or earlier if economic conditions were favourable. Failure with this approach has been attributed to the 'absence of clear-cut programmes, the wrong choice of priorities and directions of the use of the released potential'.[20]

A second approach – 'economic' conversion – utilized the income-generating capacity of the military sector through the arms trade to provide the financial resources to underpin conversion. In this approach, conversion is seen not merely as a transfer of resources from military to civil production but as a process of wider diversification, coincident with simultaneous expansion in both military and civil sectors. The inherent conflict in this approach is best demonstrated by the example of sectors such as aviation and space technology, where the income-generating capacity was high and the conversion process, consequently, was terminated in order to maximize potential earnings from the export market.

During 1992 senior Russian economists and industrialists became increasingly concerned about the poor progress being achieved with defence conversion. Vitaly Shlykov, a defence ministry adviser, demanded an end to the excessive production of armaments in Russia, whether for internal or external customers, and argued that 'reliance on the export of armaments will only deepen the domestic crisis and reduce the prospect of genuine reform'.[21] The enormous financial burden of the conversion process was also made clear in 1992 with estimated costs of Rb150 billion for a seven-year conversion programme affecting 70 per cent of Russia's defence complex being proposed.[22] By the end of 1992 it was estimated that, while defence production at some 600 plants within Russia had declined by almost one-half in the previous two years, the conversion programme had been 'largely unsuccessful, with only a 9 per cent rise in civilian output. Of the 900,000 workers shifted out of defence work, 300,000 are unemployed.'[23]

Furthermore, the experience with the conversion programme had yielded very few successful transfers of production from military to civil sectors 'except for ... foreign contracts for various civilian products from formerly military shipyards and various optical products'.[24] Under the twin impacts of declining military budgets and conversion strategies, the structure of the defence sector in Russia changed considerably during the early 1990s. By 1993, over 460 defence plants were undergoing specific conversion to civil production; 21 defence enterprises had been closed; a further 130 were about to be closed, and another 400 defence enterprises were operating on the basis of a reduced working week.

Under the 1993 Budget, some Rb250 billion were earmarked for military conversion projects in Russia, coincident with a new approach to the conversion priority. This new approach, designed to avoid a further disintegration in Russia's defence industrial base, reoriented 'conversion efforts from a strategic imperative to a more pragmatic view ... plants that ensure Russia's own armaments supply will be subsidized together with those converted plants producing civilian goods previously imported'.[25] To date (and in general), the conversion strategy within Russia has yielded few significant benefits and, with time at a premium, a new approach is clearly required.

Is there a Solution?

The successful transformation of Russia's economic system to the requirements of a post-Cold War international business environment requires enhancement of critical factors of production. First, improvements in the quantity and quality of important materials (such as rolled ferrous metal and copper) are required, together with extensive retraining programmes for redundant labour to facilitate the acquisition of new skills in, for example, marketing and contract negotiation. Second, more substantial and carefully focused capital resources are required to ensure a rapid and successful transition of defence-related industry to civil production. The absence of a realistic 'peace dividend' precludes a simple switch of resources from military production and, at the national level, the dire problems with the Russian budget deficit – and the associated risk of explosive inflation – will constrain any significant funding from government.

The only real sources of capital enhancement to facilitate economic transition are from foreign governments, international agencies and, of particular importance in the current situation, from foreign companies. Despite promises of support from Western governments and international agencies estimated at around $24 billion by 1992, the actual amount of external financial support received by Russia is believed to range from $1.5 billion to $8.5 billion, offered principally as short-term loans at market rates. By 1995, initial interest payments of at least $2.5 billion have accumulated. Western economic advisers to the Russian government as well as the leaders of the International Monetary Fund (IMF) and the World Bank have requested that Western governments reduce military expenditure further in order to free resources to supplement aid for the reconstruction of the Russian economy. The announcement of increased financial commitments from the IMF for Russia (and of the possibility of new conditional support from the European Union (EU)) in March 1995 represents a welcome recognition of the need for external assistance in transforming the economy.

However, if the Russian experiment with market liberalization is to be wholly successful, it will be necessary for external involvement in the reform process to be forthcoming from *within* the market system itself. That is, while foreign governments and international agencies clearly have a role to play, the most important and potentially productive gains are likely to be acquired at the corporate level. Foreign companies have, for some time, been involved in joint ventures with Russian enterprises and have enjoyed considerable success. Joint ventures such as East–West Technology Partners, established in 1993, bring together Russian scientific expertise and Western business acumen with the objective of marketing Russian technology in the West, while facilitating the flow of Western technology into Russia.[26] Frequently, however, joint ventures have been in primary sectors of the economy where foreign investment and expertise have been utilized in, for example, the extractive industries. For successful regeneration of the Russian economy and, with it, the preservation of international peace, it is essential now to build upon such modest beginnings and to create an environment in which Western capital investment and marketing expertise works in a genuine partnership with Russian enterprise.

To achieve this desirable end requires recognition of a 'mutuality of need' on both sides. Virtually all defence supply companies, wherever they are located, are struggling to accommodate defence cuts and to remain viable. Almost all are finding the process of defence conversion difficult. Almost all require access to new markets such as that of Russia where demand is virtually unlimited and where, with appropriate macroeconomic policies and sufficient external financial support, constrained potential can be fully realized.

Recognizing this mutuality of need, a pooling of common interests would enable sufficient resources to be deployed over the long term designed to build effective industrial partnerships between foreign and domestic companies in the key sectors of Russian industry. All the ingredients for success are present: high and rising demand levels, enormous supply capacity, leading-edge technology and significant reserves of skilled labour. Furthermore, if they can overcome the current economic malaise, Russian consumers will, in the future, offer a lucrative and almost limitless market for well-positioned Western companies. These companies need to recognize the barriers they will need to overcome in the future and take appropriate action now. As was noted in 1993: 'The Russian market is in effect closed. Demand exceeds production. We can make and sell at a profit a vacuum cleaner for 8000 roubles. Electrolux cannot compete with that.'[27]

To encourage Western corporations to participate further in this fusion of common interests in the complex international business environment of the 1990s, however, powerful incentives will be required to help overcome natural risk-aversion. A combination of policy measures at governmental level, designed to encourage international industrial partnership formation, will be essential. Such measures could include allocating to collaborative ventures preferential future access to the expanding Russian market; devising profit-sharing reward mechanisms for international technology 'pooling'; making the award of additional funding from international agencies conditional upon proof of successful international partnership formation; and underwriting joint initiatives aimed at resolving issues of common concern to governments worldwide, such as environmental action programmes.

While evidence suggests that few governments are good at devising such facilitating mechanisms, it is encouraging that often market players lead governments in the transformation process. For example, while member nations in the EU continue to debate the merits of full integration, many industrial companies have already taken the necessary steps towards full corporate restructuring and integration on a European basis. Governments can assist this natural tendency towards transnational integration with respect to the requirements of Russian economic transformation by agreeing a regime for, say, the international protection of intellectual property rights in collaborative ventures and by accepting a share of the burden of additional costs frequently associated with partnership arrangements in industry.

Five years after the end of the Cold War, there remains a real price to be paid for the preservation of peace. The current price being paid in terms of Russian economic and political instability cannot be sustained. The attainment in 1994 of the 'Partnership for Peace' agreement between North Atlantic Treaty Organization members and some countries in Eastern Europe clearly defines an important moment in recent political history. At the present time, however, a 'Partnership for Prosperity', encompassing the Russian Federation, may prove even more critical.

Notes

1   Henry S. Rowen, Charles Wolf, Jr. and Jeanne Zlotnick (eds), *Defence Conversion, Economic Reform and the Outlook for the Russian and Ukranian Economies* (London, 1994), pp. 1–8.
2   G. Khanin, 'The Economic Situation in Russia', in ibid., pp. 39–65.
3   Economist Intelligence Unit, *EIU Country Report on Russia*, 3rd Quarter, 1994.
4   Peter Southwood and Steve Schofield (eds), *The New Militarism Briefings: The Triumph of Unilateralism* (Leeds, 1993).
5   Rowen, Wolf and Zlotnick, *Defence Conversion*, p. 6.
6   World Bank Report, *Russian Economic Reform: Crossing the Threshold of Structural Change* (Washington, DC, 1992).
7   A. Izyumov, 'Conversion in the Soviet Union and Possibilities for Co-operation in the Baltic Region', *Bulletin of Peace Proposals*, vol. 22, no. 3 (1991), pp. 276–9.
8   International Institute for Strategic Studies, *The Military Balance 1994–1995* (London, 1994).
9   A. Ozhegov, E. Rogovskii and L. Iaremenko, 'Conversion of the Defence Industry and Transformation of the Economy of the USSR', *Problems of Economics*, vol. 34 (1991), pp. 79–94.
10 J. Cooper, 'Transforming Russia's Defence Industrial Base', *Survival*, vol. 35, no. 4 (1993), pp. 147–62.
11 G.C. Weickhardt, 'The Soviet Military–Industrial Complex and Economic Reform', *Soviet Economy*, no. 2 (1986), pp. 193–220.
12 Hannes Adomeit and Mikhail Agursky, *The Soviet Military–Industrial Complex and its Internal Mechanism* (Kingston, Ontario, 1978).
13 M. Leitenberg, 'Non-Conversion in the Former Soviet Union', *The New Economy*, vol. 3, no. 2 (1992), p. 11.
14 J. Cooper, *The Soviet Defence Industry: Conversion and Reform* (London, 1991), p. 96.
15 Axel Leijonhufvud, *Information and Co-ordination: Essays in Macroeconomic Theory* (Oxford, 1981).

16   D. Braddon, P. Dowdall, A. Kendry and S. Reay, *Defence Procurement and the Defence Industry Supply Chain* (Bristol, 1992).

17   J.S. Gilmore and D.C. Coddington, 'Diversification Guides for Defence Firms', *Harvard Business Review*, May–June 1966, pp. 144–50.

18   D. Braddon et al., *Positioned for Recovery? The Future of South West Business* (Bristol, 1993).

19   P. Dowdall and D. Braddon, 'Puppets and Partners: The Defence Industry Supply Chain in Perspective', in A. Latham and N. Hooper (eds), *The Future of the Defence Firm* (Dordrecht, 1994).

20   Military–Industrial Complex Newsletter, no. 1, January 1993.

21   V. Shlykov, cited in *Aerospace Daily*, 19 November 1992, p. 274.

22   M. Maley, cited in ibid., 19 November 1992.

23   S. Zaloga, 'Russian Reports', *Armed Forces Journal International*, March 1993, p. 23.

24   N. Koutznetsov, from a statement presented at the North Atlantic Assembly Seminar, Foundation for Conversion, Moscow, January 1992.

25   *International Defence Review*, no. 3 (1993), p. 189.

26   *Defence News*, 14–20 June 1993, p. 50.

27   K. Martirosov, cited in *The Economist*, 16 January 1993.

3 Russia and NATO Enlargement

David Carlton

It is frequently said, though rarely written, that the aim of the founders of the North Atlantic Treaty Organization (NATO) was to keep the Americans in, the Russians out and the Germans down. Even today these priorities still have relevance as the issue of the enlargement of NATO refuses to go away. For the fact is that only those who wish to see the total emasculation of the Alliance want the remaining 100,000 American forces in Europe to go home or want Russia to be admitted to full membership or want Germany to play as powerful a role in European military matters as it does in economic terms. Calls for such an emasculation have so far come from few influential Americans and from even fewer influential Germans. And even some influential Russians acknowledge that the continued US presence in Europe may serve the general interest and that such a presence would probably not long survive Russian entry into NATO.

Russia under President Boris Yeltsin has actually behaved so far with great statesmanship with respect to NATO. It has shown no notable nostalgia for the defunct Warsaw Treaty Organization (WTO), and has recognized without rancour that it cannot possibly be admitted to full NATO membership in the foreseeable future. It has instead settled for an associated status under the Partnership for Peace initiative.[1] What is understandably causing alarm in Moscow is the prospect of ever larger numbers of its neighbours in the former WTO and even in the Former Soviet Union (FSU) applying for and being granted full membership. Isolation and encirclement could thus be the ultimate result. Good relations between Russia and the West will not long survive if this comes to be seen as an unstoppable evolution.

How, then, should the present members respond to the potentially destabilizing clamour that is coming from Eastern Europe for NATO enlargement? So far NATO's leaders have played for time – inventing the North Atlantic Co-operation Council in 1991 and the Partnership for Peace in 1994 – and President Bill Clinton has stuck to the vague line, enunciated in Prague in January 1994, that it is 'no longer a question whether NATO will take on new members but when and how we will do so'.[2] But clarification cannot be indefinitely avoided.

What NATO first needs to do is to spell out to all concerned that membership is a privilege and not a right. It should also stress that the security it is able to provide will not be on a global scale nor even on a Europe-wide basis. Other organizations exist for these purposes, namely the United Nations and the Organization for Security and Co-operation in Europe (OSCE) – though the amount of security they may be able to provide may in some circumstances amount to very little, as some former Yugoslavs have discovered. What is special about NATO is that it is not primarily a European collective security organization but rather that it embodies what are in all essentials the unilateral security guarantees provided by the United States to a select number of European states for more than four decades. The fact that these guarantees are perceived in the United States to have proved splendidly effective during the Cold War is the principal reason, together with inertia, why they are likely to remain in place into the indefinite future. NATO, in short, is a gift from history to its present European members. It is not, however, a gift that can be safely shared, other than in rather exceptional cases, with other OSCE states not currently enjoying a US guarantee, for any very considerable further sharing would run the risk that the US guarantee would be stretched so far as at some point to lose all credibility for old and new members alike. Our principal guide with respect to NATO enlargement, then, must surely be what will be broadly acceptable to the politicians and the people of the United States. The endorsement of a controversial candidature by a particular president or by a narrow affirmative vote in the Congress should if possible be avoided. Near-unanimity in the United States is what is needed. And the willingness to deploy US troops in the country concerned should be a *sine qua non*, for NATO has surely no need of semi-detached members.

How, then, should NATO's European members proceed in deciding which candidates to recommend to Washington? They should first elaborate a number of criteria that may help to place possible applicants in categories denoting varying degrees of suitability. Six such criteria might be as follows:

- The paramount need, as already stated, to avoid any weakening in the perceived credibility of the existing US guarantees, under Article 5, to 14 West European states
- The need to avoid undue provocation of Russia.
- The desirability of ending Germany's role as the most easterly of NATO's members in Central Europe.

- The undesirability of unnecessarily creating further intra-NATO disputes along the lines that have applied with respect to Turkey and Greece since 1952; and the undesirability of recruiting new members which have actual or potential disputes with non-NATO states unrelated to the central perceived threat to NATO which would appear, as in the past, to come if at all from Moscow.
- The desirability of maximizing the overlap between NATO and European Union (EU) membership not least because of the risk, however remote it may now seem, that the United States may eventually disengage completely from Europe, leaving the EU, with the Western European Union, to take over principal responsibility for present NATO missions.
- The desirability that new members meet broadly acceptable standards in terms of democracy, human rights and respect for ethnic minorities.

With these criteria in mind we may now consider the case for admitting various actual or possible applicants to NATO, and an attempt will be made to place them in some kind of ranking order. Seven tiers seem to this writer to suggest themselves (see Table 1).

Table 1:   Suggested Ranking Order of Possible NATO Applicants

Tier 1   Republic of Ireland
Tier 2   Sweden, Austria
Tier 3   Finland, Switzerland
Tier 4   Czech Republic, Poland
Tier 5   Hungary, Slovakia, Romania, Bulgaria
Tier 6   Baltic States, Ukraine, Belarus, Moldova, Former Yugoslavia, Albania
Tier 7   Russia, the Caucasian and Central Asian Members of the Former Soviet Union

In the first tier the Republic of Ireland stands in glorious solitude. Should it wish to join NATO it is difficult to see how serious objection could be raised, least of all in the United States. Such a move would clearly make no meaningful difference to Russian security and it would end the anomaly of Ireland being the only long-standing member of the EU not to belong to NATO. The reason for Ireland's original self-exclusion from NATO was, of course, the dispute with Great Britain over the future of the Six Counties, but it would now appear that London, Dublin and, for that matter, Washington are now in broad agreement about the manner in which they hope gradually to resolve that conflict. Certainly a direct confrontation between London and Dublin is now unthinkable, and hence the United States does not need to fear a replication of the Turkish–Greek relationship which has been so disruptive to NATO.

Sweden and Austria are located in tier two. Both are now EU members and accordingly strong candidates for admission to NATO, and it is clearly in the interests of most European NATO members to press for their inclusion. This will be especially the case if the process of EU integration is to proceed further. For that will mean that foreign and security policies will be increasingly harmonized – something which was not given central attention at Maastricht. Nor would Sweden and Austria have the demerits of most other candidates. For they have excellent relations with states to which they are contiguous. And Russia can have no strong grounds for objection. For neither Sweden nor Austria belonged to the WTO. The latter, it is true, was subject to four-power partition until the agreement of 1955 which formally required it to remain neutral between the two blocs, but today it is very remote geographically from Russia and should surely be entitled to join NATO if it so desires without serious complaint from Moscow.

In tier three Switzerland and Finland are to be found. They are actually very different cases, but what they have in common is that they have only one shortcoming, if a serious one. Switzerland is clearly so remote from Russia as to constitute no security threat to it whatsoever, whether or not in NATO, and it has excellent relations with all its neighbours. Its demerit is that its people recently voted against applying for EU membership or even for closer association. Clearly a second Norway – in NATO but not in the EU – is undesirable. (Iceland and Turkey are the other European NATO members not in the EU, but the former is of no economic importance and the latter will clearly be vetoed as an EU member for the foreseeable future.) Switzerland's candidature for NATO membership, if ever put forward, should be conditional on that anti-EU vote being reversed. If, however, such a reversal took place it could at once join Ireland in our first tier. Finland has a different and more intractable weakness: it has a long frontier with Russia and hence acceptance of any application to join NATO might be seen as provocative in Moscow. It is for this reason that the present writer is inclined to regret that it was recently allowed to join the EU. Despite its long post-war history of cultivating a special relationship with Russia, however, it was not a member of the WTO, and it is unlikely if allowed into NATO to become more of a threat to Russia than its neighbour Norway (which, despite being a founder member of NATO and despite having a land border with Russia, kept a low profile throughout the Cold War). But perhaps Finland is the first case we have considered about which the Americans may have serious doubts concerning the wisdom of extending the NATO guarantee. If so, it may be better to leave Finland in an anomalous situation, particularly given its extremely small population and its good relationship with Moscow.

In the fourth tier are the Czech Republic and Poland. Here we have to consider for the first time in this analysis eager applicants for membership of both NATO and the EU who were formerly members of the WTO. At the outset it must be conceded that they have some advantages that do not apply to other former WTO members. First, they have acceptable relations with all their immediate neighbours, with irredentist conflicts involving them seemingly unlikely. Second, they happen to be the two countries lying immediately to the east of Germany. If admitted to NATO they would thus end the Federal Republic's long-standing role as the NATO front-line state on the crucial Central Front facing Moscow. Many might welcome such a change – including some nervous Russians aware that if confrontation unfortunately returned to Central Europe a cushion would exist that might enable NATO's largest West European member (in economic and population terms) to feel relatively relaxed. And, seen from the point of view of NATO's military planners, the inclusion of Poland and the Czech Republic would reduce the importance of the anomaly that exists with respect to the territory of the former German Democratic Republic – which, under the terms of the unification agreement made with Moscow, cannot host NATO forces. (Presumably the Poles and Czechs would only be admitted to NATO on the understanding that, if deemed necessary in a future return to confrontation, they would host forward-based NATO forces and theatre nuclear weapons.) Another argument supportive of the Czech and Polish candidatures is that they are the only former members of the WTO, with the exception of the Hungarians, who have undergone a sufficient economic transformation to make them suitable for relatively early admission to the EU. In addition, American opinion might be persuaded to be relatively sympathetic to their candidatures – especially in the case of the Poles, given the lobbying potential of the Polish American community. None of these points, however, serves to disguise the fact that many in Russia are bound to be unpersuaded that it is in their interest to see *any* former WTO members enter NATO. Above all, they may reasonably fear that NATO will accommodate ever more East European applicants in salami fashion over the longer term – a reversal of the pattern of step-by-step Soviet expansion of control over East-Central Europe between 1944 and 1948. We shall return to this concern in due course.

In our fifth tier Hungary, Slovakia, Bulgaria and Romania are located. These states constitute the remainder of the former WTO region, but they lack most of the advantages possessed by Poland and the Czech Republic.

They are geographically nearer to Russia and were all allied to Nazi Germany during the Second World War; with the exception of Hungary they have made little economic progress and could not possibly enter the EU in the near future; and they have little or no 'clout' in the United States. But, above all, they are all on relatively poor terms with at least one neighbour. Bulgaria contains a Turkish minority which would complicate relations with an existing NATO state; Slovakia has tense dealings with Budapest over its Hungarian-speaking minority; and Romania may clash in the future with Hungary over Transylvania and with Russia over Moldova. As for Hungary, it is surrounded by potential adversaries: Romania and Slovakia, as already mentioned, and in addition Serbia, which continues to dominate Hungarian-speakers in Vojvodina. For Hungary, in particular, one may feel sympathy, for it would be economically qualified for early EU membership and it has forged useful links with Prague and Warsaw in the so-called Visegrad Group. Moreover, Hungary has shown exceptional restraint in championing the cause of Hungarian-speaking minorities in Romania, Serbia and Slovakia. But the hard fact is that it is a less attractive candidate for NATO membership than Poland and the Czech Republic and would probably, through no fault of its own, involve NATO in Balkan complications. For example, great numbers of Hungarian-speaking political or economic refugees might begin to try to enter NATO–EU territory if Hungary is not excluded. What also cannot be lost sight of is the extent of the opposition in Washington to seeing US ground forces being drawn into Balkan civil wars, the case of Bosnia-Hercegovina amply illustrating this. All in all, then, the group of countries in this tier seem ill-suited for NATO (and hence EU) membership. And it might be a good idea if this was openly proclaimed by Western leaders at an early date, possibly after some bargaining with Moscow.

In the sixth tier are to be found the countries of the former Yugoslavia, Albania and most of the non-Islamic states of the FSU. None has much realistic hope of admission to NATO (or the EU). In the case of the Balkan states the ultimately insoluble problem is the chronic instability between and within them. In addition, some of them do not meet reasonable standards relating to democracy, human rights and respect for ethnic minorities. With regard to the states of the FSU, most of which are currently members of the Moscow-led Commonwealth of Independent States and in theory at least defended by the former Red Army, the principal difficulty is that Russia would strenuously object to transfers into NATO and, in this writer's view, rightly so. And in the case of all these states (except perhaps for Slovenia and the Baltic States) economic progress has been so limited that EU membership is surely unthinkable at any early date.

In the seventh tier we find Russia itself as well as the Caucasian and Central Asian states of the FSU. These are in effect the absolute no-hopers as far as NATO is concerned. In the case of Russia the objection ultimately is, of course, that it is the potential adversary against which the US guarantee is really directed – despite some rather unconvincing efforts by Mediterranean-facing NATO states to draw Washington into a long-term crusade against Islamic Fundamentalism. This need not imply any particular animosity if Moscow stays with its present type of leadership and continues to head in the direction of market economics. But the possibility clearly exists that other forces, symbolized so far by Vladimir Zhirinovsky, could emerge victorious, and in this eventuality Russia just might become a serious threat to West European security. It has, after all, a larger population than any European state and it has a nuclear-weapon capability matched only by the United States. So Russia simply cannot be allowed to join NATO. Nor should NATO even consider admitting FSU states in the Caucasus and Central Asia, even those that may meet reasonable standards with regard to democracy, human rights and respect for ethnic minorities – any US guarantee, under Article 5, of these geographically remote states against Russian aggression would be utterly incredible. Clearly the Americans could not send their own conventional forces to assist these states any more than they were able to do so for Afghanistan. So the only alternative, if a guarantee needed to be honoured, would be to threaten first use of nuclear weapons. That, for the sake, say, of Kyrgyzstan, would simply not play in Peoria.

If NATO's leaders come to see the merits of the possible applicants in something like the variegated fashion set out here, how, then, should they proceed? One option would be to adopt a purely pragmatic approach, reacting in the light of circumstances as each application comes to the fore. Thus, if Russia is temporarily convulsed with internal strife and unable to bring much immediate pressure to bear, that might seem a good moment hastily to admit several East European states to NATO and the EU. But the long-term risk to good relations with Moscow could be extremely serious. It would be far preferable, in this writer's opinion, for the United States now to attempt to draw up a comprehensive and long-term plan for NATO enlargement and then to put this to its European allies and finally to Moscow. What, in short, is desirable is another Yalta-like deal – and one if possible more clearly elaborated than that managed by Franklin Roosevelt, Winston Churchill and Joseph Stalin in 1945. The West could offer a long-term European settlement, rather on the lines of the 50-year Chinese–British equivalent but less one-sided in character. Essentially, Russia could be asked to give its blessing to some enlargement of NATO (and the EU) in return for solemn pledges that the West European security (and integrated economic) system would then be considered finalized for an agreed period – say 20 years or even longer. This would not, of course, preclude a continuation of the Partnership for Peace or of economic and cultural co-operation among states belonging to different groupings (hopefully not adversarial blocs in the Cold War tradition).

Many states, though probably not Russia, would nevertheless strenuously object to such a bargain in principle – particularly those discriminated against. They would claim that the West was creating a divided Europe. The rejoinder would have to be that Europe is divided now and is doomed to remain so for many years, whatever is decided. For example, a single trading bloc involving a common currency, freedom of movement and total mobility of labour stretching from Lisbon to Minsk (let alone Vladivostok) is just not practical for the foreseeable future. V.I. Lenin and his followers have ensured this by irretrievably impoverishing large areas of the Eurasian land mass. Again, the same fanatics have also made the early creation of one vast European security zone impossible, for they have left economically-stricken Russia simultaneously the foremost European military power. Of course, this makes for a balance of power of a kind in that it ensures that the EU does not become a regional near-hegemon as the United States is in North America. Whether this is actually desirable is rather questionable. After all, who would seriously think it helpful to the cause of world security if Third World Mexico were to become a nuclear superpower with First World United States having to rely for military balance on a transatlantic guarantor? However, for good or ill, such a bizarre balance between Moscow and Western Europe is what we must now learn to live with for the foreseeable future. So the Leninists' legacy inevitably means that it is not a question whether Europe will be divided, but how and where and with how much mutual agreement between Russia and the West. It is equally inevitable that there will be marginal losers who fall just the relatively impoverished and relatively insecure side of any line that emerges. The writer would tentatively see Hungary as such a loser, though he is quite aware that a deep sense of grievance would in that case prevail in Budapest. But if the Hungarians did succeed in creeping under the portcullis – possibly as a belated tribute to their behaviour in the more-or-less free elections in 1945 when as many as 85 per cent voted against the Communists despite the intimidatory presence of the Red Army – the sense of grievance would merely be shifted elsewhere – say to Sofia or Bratislava.

Russia's present leaders are surely realistic enough to recognize the force of the foregoing arguments and hence, in the writer's estimation, they would probably be delighted to be invited to bargain on the basis long ago set out by Otto von Bismarck, namely that when the eagles agree the sparrows must be silent. The problem with the Russians, then, will presumably lie not with the principle of a new division into spheres of influence to replace that which emerged after Yalta. For, as Foreign Minister Andrei Kosyrev stated on 22 June 1994, Moscow has 'no fundamental objection to NATO enlargement'.[3]

Rather, the difficulty will arise over the detail. And probably at the heart of matters will be the question of whether Poland and the Czech Republic are to be admitted. For NATO itself will presumably be grateful to be able to cite Russian hostility as a barrier to any generalized Eastern enlargement.

Of the two the Czech Republic is surely a lesser problem for Moscow as its presence in the WTO was after all something of an accident. Prague was assumed by Stalin and Churchill in 1944 and later by the Big Three at Yalta to be destined for the Western camp, and hence the Soviets withdrew from Czechoslovakia soon after liberating it from the Germans – in contrast to their insistence on keeping the Red Army in all the other states that later formed the WTO. What effectively delivered Prague to Stalin, then, was the action of the Czechoslovak people themselves who, in striking contrast to the Hungarians, saw fit to give 38 per cent of their votes in a free election to pro-Moscow Communists – after which the *coup* of 1948 followed. Also taking into account most influential Russians' bad conscience about the invasion of 1968, we may reasonably hope therefore that Moscow will eventually give its blessing to a Czech move into NATO and the EU.

Poland will presumably cause greater concern to the Russians, given its central strategic position and considerable population. The West may hope, however, that the Russians can be won over to accepting the various arguments already set out here about the broad desirability of NATO having an eastern cushion beyond Germany. In addition, the Russians should be asked what will happen if NATO does finally agree decisively to exclude the Poles. Would not Poland become an aggrieved and embittered 'loose cannon' in Central Europe? Might it not attempt to create a third military force in Europe led from Warsaw but including such other Visegrad states as felt similarly insecure? Might it even try to recruit to this combination Ukraine and perhaps other states in Eastern Europe which might have or develop fears of Moscow? On the other hand, without Poland no such robust anti-Russian alliance could possibly emerge. So perhaps Moscow could be brought to see that Poland could be tamed most effectively by inclusion in NATO – as in a certain sense the potentially revanchist West Germany was similarly tamed during the Cold War. A corollary of this argument could be that if the Russians gave way over Poland (and the Czech Republic) they could have a formal assurance that no further eastern expansion by NATO would take place for an agreed number of years (or even decades). The Russians would thus have something of a free hand in the FSU and in the rest of the former WTO area. Paradoxically, this knowledge might well lead at least moderate Russian leaders to favour the emergence of a genuine neutral belt between the Russian and NATO frontiers rather than lead them to a brutal reassertion of Muscovite authority. Of course, nervous Hungarians, Lithuanians, and others might not see it that way at the outset, but they may need to be reminded that NATO is probably in no position to guarantee their security in any case, given the quasi-isolationist nature of much of US public opinion. Some Western-led appeasement of Moscow may thus be their best hope.

Some readers will blink at the deliberate use of the word 'appeasement' in this context. But, many specialist historians of the 1930s are now increasingly persuaded that there was much to be said for Neville Chamberlain's opposition to drift in security policy and much to be said against the view that Great Britain and France alone could, at least by the late 1930s, have acted as effective policemen for all of Europe. (A.J.P. Taylor, for example, asked the cruel question about the events of 1938–9: 'Which was better, to be a betrayed Czech or a saved Pole?' He pointed out that 'less than one hundred thousand Czechs died during the war' but that 'six and a half million Poles were killed'.)[4] True, in the end Chamberlain's policy was widely deemed to have failed and somewhat despairing guarantees were given by London and Paris to Poland and other East European countries. But perhaps this was because Nazi Germany behaved with a complete absence of reasonableness or, in the end, even minimum sanity – as evidenced by the decision gratuitously to go to war in 1941 with both the Soviet Union and the United States. Today's Russia shows no signs of being a second Nazi Germany, but the surest way of increasing the chances of it becoming so would be for the West now to deny any measure of appeasement to a beleaguered Moscow in the matter of NATO enlargement. Such appeasement must, however, have its limits. For if Washington is wholeheartedly supportive, Poland and the Czech Republic should be admitted to NATO and the EU even in the face of Russian hostility. But a far better outcome, if Moscow can be persuaded, would be for their admission to take place in the context of a new and more civilized version of Yalta.

Notes

1 Hannes Adomeit, 'Russia as a "Great Power" in World Affairs: Images and Reality', *International Affairs*, vol. 71, no. 1 (1995), p. 63.
2 The International Institute for Strategic Studies, *The Military Balance, 1994–1995* (London, 1994), p. 34.
3 Ibid., p. 107.
4 A.J.P. Taylor, *The Origins of the Second World War* (2nd edn, Harmondsworth, 1963), p. 26.

4 Demobilizing and Disarming Formerly Soviet Nuclear Weapons

Victor Gilinsky

During the Cold War, the United States and the Soviet Union produced staggering numbers of nuclear warheads, perhaps as many as 75,000. To provide the nuclear explosives for these warheads, the United States and Soviet Union created huge industrial complexes which produced about 1.5 to 2 million kilograms of such explosives. Each kilogram of this material – mostly highly enriched uranium (HEU) and the rest plutonium – is capable of releasing nearly 20 kilotonnes of fission energy, roughly the energy released in each of the Second World War nuclear explosions.[1] In many warheads, the fissionable material is designed to trigger even larger thermo-nuclear reactions. The magnitude of this destructive energy, and the extent to which it captivated military thinking, suggests that we were lucky to survive the period of hostilities. The end of hostilities does not, however, bring an end to our concerns with nuclear warheads.

The United States and Russia are now engaged in a huge nuclear weapons demobilization. It is a complicated process, technically and politically, and an expensive one, too. The demobilizations are codified in a series of formal and informal agreements reached over the last few years. The practical effect of these, if they are carried out, would be to leave the United States and Russia, about a decade from now, with about 5000 deliverable warheads. This would still leave them as the most powerful nuclear weapon states by far, but it would involve perhaps a fivefold reduction from current levels.

These reductions, dramatic as they are, will not, however, automatically lead to comparable reductions in nuclear warheads, and certainly not to reductions in the stocks of nuclear explosives. The various strategic arms

41

agreements, for example, deal not with warheads, but with *deliverable* warheads. As a consequence, they leave the surplus warheads in the hands of their current owners.

Even if the warheads are dismantled – and that is neither simple nor cheap – the explosive material remains and cannot easily be destroyed. One cannot simply set it off as one might with high explosives in conventional warheads.[2] It is no longer acceptable to dispose of the nuclear materials in an uncontrolled manner, say, through underground explosions, even if that were practicable. Fortunately, in the case of HEU, which forms the bulk of nuclear explosive stocks, there is a convenient way to both disarm the material and make economic use of it as nuclear fuel. For this purpose, HEU is worth more than its weight in gold. By contrast, weapon-grade plutonium, while usable as a fuel, is not an economic fuel, and its use for this purpose raises security problems to which so far there are no adequate answers. Even if both explosive materials were turned into fuels, it would still take many years, perhaps decades, to consume them. This means that, in any case, the demobilized nuclear explosives will have to be protected for a very long time. In these circumstances, two objectives stand out: first, to make the nuclear demobilization irreversible, that is, to make it extremely difficult for the owners to put the warheads back into the weapons from which they emerged; and second (and this is the more important one) to make the warheads and their nuclear explosives inaccessible to other would-be bomb-makers.

It would not take much of this material to create a major security problem. We have been speaking of tens of thousands of warheads. At the same time we know that a few nuclear bombs, perhaps even one, in the hands of Iraq would have radically transformed the Gulf War. The possibility that North Korea may have one or two nuclear bombs is said to pose the most serious security challenge now faced by the United States. Clearly, if even a tiny fraction of the demobilized superpower warheads, or the material they contain, were diverted to illicit use, we would face a very difficult situation. Hence, the demobilized material has to be well protected.

The demobilized warheads in Russia and the other post-Soviet republics will presumably first be put into storage. Many questions arise. How will the warheads be stored? Who will control them? What kind of protection will they have? To what extent will they be dismantled? What will happen to the explosive material of dismantled warheads? Will it be kept in its original metallic form? Will it be converted into bulk form to be used as fuel? On what time-scale? How will the conversion be protected? Will the process be verified by outside parties? In most cases we can only get partial answers to these questions in view of the secrecy that continues to surround nuclear weapon matters in all countries.

We do not even know how many warheads the Russians have. In the early 1990s Viktor Mikhailov, the Minister at Minatom, the Russian Ministry for Atomic Energy, mentioned a peak figure of 45,000 warheads in 1986.[3] He was also quoted in 1992 to the effect that the Soviet stockpile had declined 20 per cent from its peak, which would have put it at about 36,000 warheads.[4] At about the same time, in mid-1992, the CIA presented an estimate to Congress of 25,000 to 35,000 warheads, with a best estimate of about 30,000.[5]

It is equally uncertain how much actual nuclear explosive material the Russians have. The amount of explosive material per warhead is not a fixed constant and depends on design. Some warheads use HEU and others plutonium, and some use a combination.[6] Some of the explosives may be in unfabricated stocks. President Boris Yeltsin, in a September 1992 interview with Japanese TV, mentioned a figure of 1200 tons of Russian nuclear explosives.[7] That is about double what the United States is said to have. More recently, in October 1993, Mikhailov gave an even higher figure when he mentioned 500 tons of HEU which Russia has agreed to sell to the United States as about 30–40 per cent of Russian stocks.[8] US observers regard these numbers as high, and perhaps put out for commercial reasons, but they are consistent with the high warhead numbers the Russians cite.

There is no public knowledge of what happened to the several thousand Soviet (and now Russian) warheads that have been demobilized up to now. Have they been removed from the active warhead reserves? Have they been dismantled? Or have the Russians just put them aside in a storage facility? It would be interesting to know.

The Russians have said that all the tactical nuclear warheads (which form the majority of warheads) have been moved to Russia. These include nuclear bombs, rocket warheads, artillery shells and mines, altogether probably several thousand deliverable warheads. All were returned from non-Soviet territory in 1990–1. The last train carrying such then-Soviet warheads is said to have returned from the German Democratic Republic (GDR) in the summer of 1991 (there had apparently been about 500 such warheads in the GDR). The very last train from non-Russian territory returned in May 1992 from Ukraine. (About 1500 tactical warheads were returned from Ukraine and disassembled and reportedly 'destroyed' with Ukrainian verification.)

There are still, at the time of writing, strategic warheads in Belarus, Kazakhstan and Ukraine. About 1800 strategic warheads remain in Ukraine, and these pose a special problem. The warheads are apparently under Ukrainian physical control with no Russian troops involved. Ukraine, in the person of its president, Leonid Kravchuk, has more than once agreed to the removal of these to Russia and perhaps eventually an agreement of this kind will actually stick.

The situation in Belarus and Kazakhstan is more favourable to a transfer of all warheads to Russia. The Belorussian warheads are apparently under Russian control and are expected to be returned to Russia soon.

These new republics were not, of course, involved in negotiating the initial arms control agreements under whose umbrella current warhead demobilizations are taking place. The Strategic Arms Reduction Talks (START) Treaty I was signed by Presidents George Bush and Mikhail Gorbachev on 31 July 1991. This was followed by informal agreements, which came soon after the August 1991 attempted *coup*, on reductions in tactical nuclear weapons. These agreements were announced by Bush on 27 September 1991 and by Gorbachev on 5 October 1991. After the Soviet Union broke up, it was necessary to convert START I to a five-party agreement (thereby including Belarus, Kazakhstan and Ukraine), which was done through the Lisbon Protocol of 23 May 1992. This was soon followed by START II, essentially agreed to in June 1992 and signed by Presidents Bush and Boris Yeltsin on 4 January 1993.

START I involves about a one-third reduction in strategic nuclear warheads. Under the Lisbon Protocol, the Soviet successor states agreed that Russia would remain the only nuclear successor to the Soviet Union, that nuclear warheads in the other republics would be returned to Russia, and that the other three republics would acede to the Non-proliferation Treaty as non-nuclear states 'in the shortest possible time'. In view of this, START II, which builds on START I, is an agreement only between the United States and Russia. The imprecision of the Lisbon Protocol made it difficult, however, to achieve compliance in the case of Ukraine, although, after the mid-January 1994 visit of President Bill Clinton, Ukraine may have finally accepted non-nuclear status.

START I and II require the reduction of US and Russian strategic forces from a level of about 11,000–12,000 deliverable strategic warheads to about 3500 warheads each over the next ten years. If these agreements are carried out, together with the agreement to demobilize the majority of tactical nuclear warheads, perhaps 25,000–30,000 Russian nuclear warheads presently in their stockpile will have lost their military role over the next ten years.

A vital point about these demobilization agreements, at least the strategic ones, is that they do not involve any obligations with respect to the demobilized warheads. START I and II basically deal with deliverable warheads, and leave it up to the owners to decide what to do with the redundant warheads. The rationale for this was that without rapid means of delivery the warheads were of little significance in terms of US–Soviet nuclear stability. But the same warheads and their nuclear explosives are of enormous significance if others get their hands on them.

These excess warheads in the Russian case presumably first go into storage at military installations. To avoid any future temptation to redeploy the warheads, it would help if they were dismantled, or at least rendered unusable. But warhead dismantlement turns out to be about as difficult as initial assembly, perhaps even more so. It is certainly expensive.

The Americans and Russians have separately said that they would not only demobilize, but also dismantle many, perhaps most, of the tactical nuclear warheads. In his 5 October 1991 statement on nuclear weapons, Gorbachev said the Soviet Union would 'destroy' all nuclear artillery shells, land-mines, and short-range missiles. In addition, some of the surface-to-air missiles, naval tactical weapons and nuclear weapons on ground-based naval aircraft would be destroyed.[9]

Russian officials have spoken of dismantling their nuclear mines by 1998; their tactical nuclear warheads in missiles and shells by 2000; about half their anti-missile warheads by 1995; about a third of their sea-based missiles, presumably tactical ones, by 1995; and about half their gravity bombs by 1996. It is difficult for outsiders to know at what rate the Russians are actually proceeding with these activities.

The common estimates of Russian dismantling rates are about 2000–2500 warheads per year, although the capacity of the facilities is said to be larger. Dismantling 25,000–30,000 warheads in about ten years is therefore within the capacity of Russian plants in the original nuclear weapons assembly complex where the warheads were produced in the first place. The work will involve a great deal of careful and expensive effort and could presumably be expanded with additional resources.

To help overcome the resource limitations on demobilization, the US Congress has appropriated funds for this purpose. Unfortunately, so far the money does not seem to have been translated into much actual help. The so-called Nunn–Lugar funds, named after the two sponsors, Senators Sam Nunn and Richard Lugar, were intended to help Russia to 'destroy nuclear weapons, chemical weapons and other weapons', to 'transport, store, disable and safeguard weapons in connection with their destruction', and to 'establish verifiable safeguards against the proliferation of such weapons'. Congress voted $400 million in the fiscal year 1992 defence appropriation, another $400 million for 1993, and there is additional money for 1994. All four post-Soviet republics with nuclear warheads are eligible for this money. But, as of summer 1993, which marked the end of the first fiscal year of aid, only about 5 per cent of it had actually been spent.[10]

The initial difficulty with providing aid seems to have been that it was Congress's idea and not that of the Bush Administration. As a result, the Administration had no enthusiasm for carrying it out, especially as the legislation did not provide new funds but required the reprogramming of military funds. Moreover, the grant of money was conditioned in many ways that allowed bureaucratic foot-dragging in the United States.[11] There have also been problems on the other side. Russia has apparently not been very impressed with the aid that the United States was proposing to supply and wanted to use the funds for purposes only indirectly related to dismantlement. On the other hand, the Clinton Administration seems to be trying to make the assistance process work.

Fortunately, economics provides a strong incentive for dismantling Russian warheads: to mine them for their HEU. The HEU in the warheads, which is enriched to more than 90 per cent uranium-235, can be diluted (or 'blended') with natural uranium or slightly enriched uranium and used to produce common reactor fuel of about 4 per cent enrichment.[12] This has the potential of solving both a security and economic problem. The blending disarms the material as the 4 per cent fuel is far below explosive concentrations, and, once blended, the HEU is not recoverable without an enrichment facility, so the material is protected from most would-be bomb-makers. The commercial value of the HEU for this purpose is more than that of gold, which makes the HEU a valuable source of Western funds for the Russian (and other) owners.

The United States and Russia have signed a contract to blend down and transfer to the United States 500 tonnes of Russian HEU from warheads over about 20 years.[13] Under the agreement, blending of the HEU to produce lower enrichment material would be done in Russia. This would avoid international transport of large quantities of bomb-grade material. It would also allow Russia to obtain additional payment for this part of the process. The total price comes to about US$12 billion, which is roughly, possibly somewhat higher than, the commercial fuel value of 500 tonnes of HEU. It should help Russia with funds needed for warhead dismantlement.

The contract was held up mainly by problems related to the inability of Russia and Ukraine, which claims a share of the proceeds, to agree on suitable terms. Ukraine will apparently get about US$1 billion of the proceeds as credit for about 50 tonnes of HEU in strategic warheads destined to be turned over to Russia.[14]

Initially, Russia will annually supply to the United States a fuel blend containing about 10 tonnes of HEU. Each tonne of HEU when blended with natural uranium produces about 30 tonnes of low-enriched uranium (LEU) reactor fuel, so 10 tonnes of HEU is equivalent to about 300 tonnes of LEU. That is about 12 per cent of US annual requirements. After five years, Russia is supposed to supply annually the equivalent of about 30 tonnes of HEU.

In time, this approach can resolve the HEU problem. The time, however, is long from a security point of view. Put another way, the rate of blending and transfer of HEU contemplated under the agreement is fairly slow. After five years, the Russian stocks may only have been reduced by 5 per cent. It would be advantageous to get as much as possible of the surplus nuclear explosive material out of harm's way more quickly. One possibility would be to blend the HEU rapidly to below-explosive concentrations, say, to 20 per cent uranium-235. Once this has been done, the material would be much better protected against illicit use for bombs.

Another problem is that the conversion agreement does not cover the Russian surplus weapon-grade plutonium stocks, and there is no prospect for an arrangement analogous to that of the HEU. The difficulty is twofold: whereas HEU is commercially valuable as power reactor fuel, plutonium is not. More importantly, there is no satisfactory way of disarming plutonium by blending it with other materials the way HEU can be blended with natural uranium. A fuel mixture of plutonium and natural uranium can easily be separated into its components by chemical means. The security of the Russian surplus plutonium stocks, as well as that of the United States, will evidently require a different approach than that of HEU.

The reason that weapon-grade plutonium does not have any commercial value is that it costs more to fabricate plutonium fuel than can be gained in using it to generate energy. That, at least, is the case for recycling plutonium in current generation reactors.[15] In other words, it does not make economic sense to burn plutonium fuel in current reactors even if it comes free.

The real difficulty is not so much economic as related to security. If it were just a matter of subsidizing the consumption of weapon-grade plutonium stocks as fuel, and if this could be done in a secure manner, it would be well worth the money. But it is not at all clear that security would be satisfactory. Because there is no technical 'fix' for plutonium security analogous to blending of HEU, it would be dangerous to put large quantities of weapon-grade plutonium into commercial channels. Commercial security is not likely to be equivalent to military security.

In addition, any move in the direction of converting military plutonium to fuel has to be seen against the background of civilian nuclear power reactors around the world. These are producing plutonium at a rate in excess of 50 tonnes a year. The total world stock of plutonium produced in civilian reactors is approaching 1000 tonnes. Most of this material is still unseparated from the highly radioactive spent fuel in which it was produced and so is self-protected. But once separated for use as fuel, the civilian power reactor plutonium, while not optimized for military use in the manner of the weapon-grade material, is nevertheless useful for warheads and poses a serious security problem. Despite this, and despite the unfavourable economics, several countries are still committed to the use of plutonium fuel. The economic case for this looks increasingly inauspicious, and the proponents of civilian plutonium use are increasingly on the defensive.[16] In these circumstances, it would not be helpful if the weapon-grade plutonium were used in a way that encouraged the further separation and commercial use of the much larger stock of civilian plutonium.

An alternative to burning the plutonium is to make it inaccessible for weapon use by changing its form, say by mixing it with radioactive reactor waste products. This would probably be the cheapest option and would make the plutonium about as secure as that in radioactive spent fuel. It would also make the plutonium inaccessible for fuel use, and this generates resistance in some circles. Plutonium has for so long been lauded as the fuel of the future, and it costs so much to produce, that nuclear establishments see it as valuable material. That seems especially the case in Russia. As Mikhailov said recently: 'Two opposite point[s] of view on plutonium may be singled out presently. One considers it as a radwaste, another – as a national asset.'[17] It is clear where the minister and his scientists stand, and one has the impression that in Russia the nuclear technical community has more influence than their counterparts do in the United States.[18]

Mikhailov estimated there was 'about 250–300 metric tonnes of weapons plutonium around'.[19] Subtracting about 100 tonnes for the United States, this would leave Russia with about 150–200 tonnes. (No other country has comparable amounts.) He said:

> In our quest for applications for this material, we must look for ideal applications that justify the high costs that go into its creation. The cost of producing plutonium is six times higher than that of producing HEU.... . The full commercial use of weapon plutonium probably won't be achieved until the year 2010. This is very important because the labour that has gone into this production was colossal and to just use it today in ways we currently can is simply irksome or *obidno* as we say in Russian.

This is a natural reaction of people who were responsible for producing the plutonium. At the same time, one does not have to be an economist to know that the value of the plutonium does not depend on the cost of production.[20]

Russia expects US help in the construction of a plutonium storage facility – it is one of the projects identified for Nunn–Lugar money. The minister says, 'Russia will pay back this money once plutonium is used commercially.'[21] There are storage facilities, obviously, in Russia, but there is an important security advantage in a central storage facility built to the latest standards of safety and security. US support would entitle the United States to a role in the continued oversight over the material.

The best storage option – whether the nuclear explosives should be stored in their original shape, or in bulk – is not immediately evident. The further the metal is from its bomb configuration, the less the chance that it will resume its former role. At the same time, the more handling and processing that takes place, the more the chance that some of the material will disappear. Furthermore, the closer the warheads are to their original form, the more likely that they will be subject to military protection. The same nuclear explosives in bulk form and labelled as 'fuel' is likely to be subject to a lesser level of civilian protection. That, at least, has been the traditional pattern around the world. Ironically, this may argue at times for leaving the warheads as they are.

Because we are all going to have to live with the presence of Russian nuclear explosive stockpiles (as well as those in the United States) for some considerable time, it would ease worries around the world if there could be more information to verify the security of these stocks. Other countries should have access to such information, particularly as it no longer affects the owner's security. Without verification of dismantlement and destruction of the material, an appreciable uncertainty remains about the amount of nuclear explosives and their security. At a minimum this feeds suspicion. The United States, which has insisted on verification as a condition of military agreements in the past, seems to be taking less interest in this matter recently. It appears that the United States is less concerned about verification of the disposition of Russian warheads than it is to avoid precedents for similar verification of US operations.

In ratifying START I in October 1992, the US Senate adopted unanimously a condition proposed by Senator Joseph Biden, the so-called Biden condition, which promotes exchange of data on nuclear warheads and explosives. It states that in connection with any further agreement on reducing strategic arms the president shall seek reciprocal arrangements to monitor the numbers of nuclear stockpile weapons and the location and inventory of facilities capable of producing or processing significant quantities of fissile materials.[22] Nothing much seems to have happened on this point. There is a feeling in some US quarters that 'we won the Cold War' and that there is no longer a need for reciprocal verification.

If there is to be verification, everyone seems immediately to think of the Vienna-based International Atomic Energy Agency (IAEA). Indeed, it seems to be actively lobbying for the job. In late 1993 the United States proposed making HEU and plutonium that was in excess of military needs subject to inspection by the IAEA.[23] This is a very small step intended to fortify the IAEA shortly before the 1995 Non-proliferation Treaty Review Conference. The idea is that the United States is making the offer under the USA–IAEA voluntary safeguards agreement.

The IAEA may be a natural choice, but it is not necessarily the right choice. It has some troubling characteristics that suggest that a new approach is needed for the serious work of monitoring nuclear explosives. The IAEA has not distinguished itself in doing its current 'safeguards' job – monitoring civilian nuclear facilities and materials to make sure they are not used for illicit purposes. Like all international bureaucracies, its staff is very much interested in not offending its member states, which in this case are also the states whose programmes the IAEA inspects. Of special concern is that it has been willing to play down the security significance of civilian plutonium programmes and to exaggerate its ability to protect the material. It would be worrying if the same thing happened in connection with protection of warhead plutonium.

Another, no less significant, problem is that as long as one is talking about monitoring warheads, it is difficult to devise a verification scheme that does not in some way compromise design information. The IAEA, which is a collection of citizens of its many member states, seems ill equipped for coping with such issues.

As we are going to have to watch over nuclear explosives from warheads for some considerable time, we need to find an approach which maintains disciplined oversight for the indefinite future. A serious worry is that when explosive materials become military surplus, there will be a tendency to relax security. It would be wise to find technical means to pull the teeth of the explosives as soon as possible. Fortunately, there is an excellent solution for HEU – blending to produce low-enriched uranium fuel. But the US–Russian HEU deal only involves part of Russia's HEU, even of its surplus HEU, and the contemplated rate of blending is slow. We should think about speeding this up and expanding it to include more of the HEU in the Russian (and US) stocks.

Unfortunately, there is no such technically and economically satisfactory solution for disarming weapon-grade plutonium. Ultimately, to deal with this we shall have to confront the legitimacy of the use of plutonium in civilian industry.

Solutions to these problems are going to cost more, and the United States and others should be prepared to contribute more, than is now contemplated. The amounts of money involved, perhaps several billions of dollars, which now loom large in economic calculations, are not large compared with defence expenditures of lesser consequence. They would not have been thought large only a few years ago as the price of eliminating a large portion of the Soviet nuclear explosive stockpile. Nor are they large compared to the havoc that could follow even a small part of the explosive stocks getting into the wrong hands. That is now the greatest concern.

Notes

1 Henry D. Smyth, *Atomic Energy for Military Purposes* (Stanford, 1989, reprint of 1945 edn), p. 43, cites a figure of 20,000 tonnes of TNT. This was the motivation for the Manhattan Project.

2 Consider that 50,000 conventional bombs containing on average 500 kilograms of high explosive (a large amount), or 25,000 tonnes of high explosives in all, have an energy content of about 100 terajoules, or the equivalent of about 10,000 tonnes of coal – the amount burned by a single large coal-fired electric station in one day.

3 Remarks at a meeting in Washington, DC, hosted by the Committee on International Security and Arms Control of the National Academy of Science, 17 February 1993. Cited in Thomas Cochran and Christopher Paine, 'Nuclear Warhead Destruction', paper prepared for a workshop at the Carnegie Endowment for International Peace, Washington, DC, 16 November 1993.

4 Viktor Mikhailov and Evgeniy Mikerin, remarks at the International Symposium on Conversion of Nuclear Warheads for Peaceful Purposes, Rome, 15–17 June 1992, cited in ibid.

5 Testimony of Lawrence K. Gershwin, National Intelligence Officer for Strategic Programs, House Committee on Appropriations, 6 May 1992, cited in ibid. By comparison, Cochran and Paine report the US stockpile as having reached about 32,000 warheads in 1967. It is now apparently about 17,000, or about the 1958–9 level.

6 About three times as much HEU is required per warhead as plutonium. The nominal figures used by the IAEA are 25 kg HEU and 8 kg plutonium. Actual amounts could be much less.

7 *New York Times*, 11 September 1992.

8 Elizabeth Martin, 'A Conversation with Viktor Mikhailov', *NUKEM Market Report*, October 1993, p. 24. This would put Russian stocks at between 1250 and 1667 tonnes. Later he used the lower number, and also said this amounted to 'more than 1000 tonnes of HEU and about 100 metric tonnes of plutonium, both in stockpile and in warheads'. Mikhailov also put the Russian figure at between 1.5–1.7 times that of the United States and all other nuclear-weapon states combined. If one accepts the common estimate of about 500–600 tonnes HEU for the United States, and adding a modest amount for other countries, this would give the Russian total at about 900–1000 tonnes.

9 See Robert S. Norris and William M. Arkin, 'Nuclear Notebook', *Bulletin of Atomic Scientists*, December 1991, p. 49. See also 'Factfile', *Arms Control Today*, October 1991, p. 37.

10 Dunbar Lockwood, 'Dribbling Aid to Russia', *Bulletin of Atomic Scientists*, July/August 1993, p. 39. The negotiations on the disbursement of these Nunn–Lugar funds are conducted under the rubric of talks on Safe and Secure Dismantlement of Nuclear Weapons. Umbrella agreements have been signed with Russia (17 June 1992), with Belarus (22 October 1992), and more recently with Kazakhstan and Ukraine. These umbrella agreements require further 'implementing agreements' for specific forms of aid. See 'Interview with Gen. William F. Burns', *Arms Control Today*, September 1993, p. 3.

11 The US Defense Department interpreted the law, at least initially, to require payment only to US entities and to require competitive bidding, a lengthy process of Byzantine complexity.

12 The idea, in the context of Soviet warhead demobilization, was first suggested by Thomas Neff, a professor at Massachusetts Institute of Technology. See Thomas Neff, *New York Times*, 24 October 1991.

13   15 January 1994 Contract. This arrangement follows an agreement of a year before: Agreement between the Government of the United States of America and the Government of the Russian Federation concerning the Disposition of Highly Enriched Uranium extracted from Nuclear Weapons, 18 February 1993.

14   Considering that Ukraine has about 1800 warheads, this comes out to a credit of 28 kilograms of HEU per warhead.

15   For a discussion of this point, see V. Gilinsky, 'Russian Swords into American Ploughshares', in D. Carlton et al. (eds), *Controlling the International Transfer of Weaponry* (Aldershot, 1995), pp. 157–72.

16   Taking into account the cost of separation (reprocessing), the cost of plutonium fuel for ordinary light water reactors is about 5–10 times as great as that of normal LEU fuel of comparable energy content.

17   V.N. Mikhailov et al., 'Plutonium in the Nuclear Power Industry', paper presented at the National Resources Defense Council Washington Seminar, 15–17 December 1993.

18   Interestingly, in the latest (January 1994) agreement with Ukraine over the transfer of strategic warheads to Russia, Ukraine does not apparently get its plutonium back, nor does it get credit for its value. This suggests that the parties recognize that it is a dangerous substance with no commercial value.

19   *NUKEM Market Report*, October 1993, p. 28.

20   The strong Russian interest in plutonium use may come into conflict with US official views. The 1994 Defense Authorization Act places a plutonium-related condition on any expenditure of US funds to assist the Russian Ministry of Atomic Energy in building a storage facility for surplus plutonium. Basically, it requires Russia to cease separating any more weapon-grade plutonium from spent fuel, which it is apparently still doing. See the National Defense Authorization Act for Fiscal Year 1994, Conference Report to accompany H.R. 2401, 18 November 1993.

21   *NUKEM Market Report*, October 1993, p. 29.

22   'The START Treaty', Report of the Committee on Foreign Relations, US Senate, 1992, p. 101: 'Nuclear Weapons Stockpile Arrangement – in as much as the prospect of a loss of control of nuclear weapons or fissile material in the former Soviet Union could pose a serious threat to the United States and to international peace and security, in connection with any further agreement reducing strategic offensive arms, the president shall seek an appropriate arrangement, including the use of reciprocal inspections, data exchanges, and other cooperative measures, to monitor: (a) the numbers of nuclear stockpile weapons on the territory of the parties to this Treaty; and (b) the location and inventory of facilities on the territory of the parties to this Treaty capable of producing or processing significant quantities of fissile materials.'

23   'Fact Sheet on US Excess Fissile Materials and Safeguards', The White House, Office of the Press Secretary, 11 September 1993; and 'Fact Sheet on Non-proliferation and Export Control Policy', 27 September 1993, which states: 'the United States will ... submit US fissile material no longer needed for our deterrent to inspection by the International Atomic Energy Agency.'

5 The Issue of Non-proliferation and its Implications for the Foreign and Security Policies of the Commonwealth of Independent States

Yuri Pinchukov

One of the major consequences of the end of the Cold War was a shift in international security concerns from the global nuclear confrontation between two military blocks to the dangers of global proliferation of weapons of mass destruction. For Russia and several other former Soviet republics this new focal point of international security relations has had its domestic dimensions in addition to more traditional concerns about nuclear proliferation threats.

The problem of securing the management of nuclear assets inherited from the Former Soviet Union (FSU) was between 1991 and 1994 a major task for the foreign affairs and security policy decision-making communities within the Commonwealth of Independent States (CIS). This chapter in the dynamic history of non-proliferation was closed, however, at the end of 1994 with the Ukrainian accession to the Non-proliferation Treaty (NPT). Meanwhile, the Western countries' efforts to help Russia, Ukraine, Belarus and Kazakhstan to find a mutually acceptable solution to this problem also became a new and valuable vehicle for military and economic co-operation between the former adversaries. Efforts to cope with a new pattern of proliferation threats in this area encouraged a sequence of intense negotiations among the highest authorities of many states and fostered healthy relations between the West and the CIS. The results of the non-proliferation dialogue between East and West thus exceeded its immediate aims of bringing to an end the 'nuclear disputes' within the CIS by providing them with the rational political and institutional mechanisms for the elimination of surplus nuclear weapons located on the territory of the former Soviet Union. A major task was to enable the 'newly independent states' to feel members of the global community, each having its fair share of global and regional responsibility.

The collapse of the Soviet Union created a variety of nuclear proliferation risks, and the NPT regime faced a major challenge posed by its dissolution – one of the world's two nuclear superpowers – into 15 new independent states. The largest of them, Russia, inherited the nuclear status of the former Soviet Union and three others, Ukraine, Kazakhstan and Belarus, have had Soviet nuclear strategic weapons and other important nuclear assets and infrastructure stationed on their territory since the dissolution. Some other former Soviet republics also inherited a number of facilities dealing mainly with the initial phases of the nuclear fuel cycle.

The proliferation risks with respect to the management and disposal of nuclear weapons and fissile materials are now often categorized in terms of: the emergence of many nuclear-armed states where previously there was only one; the erosion of government control over nuclear weapons and materials within a particular state; the repudiation of arms reduction agreements and pledges; and the reconstruction of a larger nuclear arsenal.[1]

In the immediate aftermath of the Soviet Union's disintegration the major proliferation concerns were: the prospect of the emergence of new nuclear weapon states; the danger of a loss of command and control over the dispersed arsenal of many thousands of strategic and tactical nuclear warheads, as well as of their safety and security; the danger of a chaotic spill-over of fissile materials, nuclear weapon components, equipment, technology and know-how across the borders of the FSU, since the Soviet export control system virtually ceased to exist; and the threat to the implementation of the first Strategic Arms Reduction Treaty (START I), since a substantial part of the former Soviet strategic arms were deployed outside Russia.

By the end of 1994, the CIS states had managed, on the whole, to cope with most of these problems despite all the hurdles presented by economic decline, domestic political disputes, social unrest and local conflicts. But the road had not been easy. It could not have been achieved without the help of the international community. First, the world community was not slow in recognizing Russia as the only legitimate heir of all former Soviet nuclear weapons. Almost immediately after the signing of the Belowezh agreement Russia took the place of the Soviet Union as a permanent member of the United Nations (UN) Security Council. Then, to ensure centralized control over the nuclear arsenal deployed across the FSU the leaders of the four 'nuclear republics' hastened to issue a joint statement. Signed in Minsk on 30 December 1991, the 'agreement between the member states of the CIS on strategic forces' instituted a joint command of the strategic forces and established the form of political control over the nuclear weapons. In accordance with this document, 'the decision on the need to use these weapons is taken by the President of the Russian Federation in agreement with the Heads of the Republics of Belarus, Kazakhstan and Ukraine and after consultation with the Heads of the other member states of the Commonwealth'. This system for control over the CIS/ Russian nuclear arsenal has clearly given to Russia an executive role in the use of strategic nuclear weapons.[2]

In January 1992 the Russian Federation notified the International Atomic Energy Agency (IAEA) and the UN that it was the successor to the Soviet Union's nuclear arsenal and accepted all its international obligations and commitments. This was not challenged by the other former Soviet republics, and Russia was accepted on to the board of the IAEA and became one of the three nuclear weapon states (NWSs) that were the depository states for the NPT. On 10 July 1992 ten CIS states (including Ukraine) endorsed Russian participation in the NPT as the only NWS successor of the Soviet Union and pledged their will to accede to this treaty as a non-nuclear weapon state (NNWS).

Until very recently the main problem was caused by the vacillations of other members of the 'post-Soviet nuclear club' – Ukraine, Belarus and Kazakhstan – over nuclear weapons deployed on their territories. In May 1992 the foreign ministers of the Ukraine, Kazakhstan and Belarus signed the Lisbon Protocol to START I in which they assumed an obligation to adhere to the NPT and eliminate by the year 2000 all strategic nuclear weapons deployed on their territories. By the summer of 1993, however, only Belarus had ratified the Lisbon Protocol and announced its adherence to the NPT.[3] The ratification of the Protocol by Ukraine and Kazakhstan was repeatedly delayed by the parliaments of these states.[4] Moreover, many Ukrainian leaders have often stated the view that they were mistaken in giving their agreement to the transfer of tactical nuclear weapons to Russia. Ukraine and Kazakhstan had common positions in that they denied the right of Russia to own all the nuclear weapons of the FSU. They compared the treatment of nuclear weapons with that of conventional armaments and other property of the FSU located on their territories.[5] Neither the new Ukrainian parliament nor its new president, both elected in 1994, changed the basic principle of so-called 'administrative control' over nuclear weapons deployed on Ukrainian soil.[6]

The contradiction in the situation of 1993–4 was underlined by Russia's internationally recognized status of being a NWS with certain rights and obligations as one of the three depository states of the NPT. In accordance with Article I of the NPT Russia has assumed the obligation not to transfer nuclear weapons nor control over them to anyone, nor to give technical assistance to a NNWS or incite such a state to acquire nuclear-explosive devices. Technically, Russia has already violated the NPT by having partly or fully surrendered control over the strategic nuclear weapons deployed on the territories of Ukraine, Kazakhstan and Belarus. However, international recognition of Russia's nuclear status could encourage its leadership to bring political and other pressure to bear on the governments of these states in order to force them to abandon any claims to the 'nuclear' property of the former Soviet Union.

The choice of levers available to Russia was not large. The use of force was absolutely excluded. The imposition of economic sanctions upon states which were until recently economic partners and with which existing links still remained extremely close would not only have been ineffective but quite counterproductive.[7] In 1993, however, it became evident that the 'nuclear ambitions' of Ukraine were largely being dampened by its worsening economic situation. This has forced the Ukrainian leadership, in the persons of the president and the prime minister, to make a series of important concessions over the division of the Black Sea Fleet and the elimination of strategic nuclear weapons. In September 1993 Ukraine agreed to dismantle the nuclear warheads on 130 of the 176 'Ukrainian' ICBMs which were subject to reduction under START I. According to the Russian interpretation, the warheads should be transferred to Russia to be dismantled at the appropriate facilities. In compensation Ukraine would receive fresh fuel for its nuclear power stations in the form of low-enriched uranium (LEU), obtained from the highly enriched uranium (HEU) extracted from the dismantled warheads. Ukraine was also hoping for help from the United States in the dismantling of missile launchers.

By that time the United States administration and the European states were applying pressure on the Ukrainian leadership to relinquish their position. Their combined efforts resulted in the trilateral Russian–Ukrainian–US statement of 14 January 1994. Under this agreement, signed by three presidents, there was a Ukrainian commitment to remove all strategic nuclear warheads located on Ukrainian territory to Russia without delay for eventual dismantling and to accede to the NPT as a NNWS in the shortest possible time, in return for compensation, additional financial aid and security guarantees. Ukraine agreed to ensure the elimination of all nuclear weapons located on its territory in accordance with the relevant agreements and during the seven-year period, as provided by START I. The presidents recognized the importance of compensation for Ukraine, Kazakhstan and Belarus for the value of the HEU within the nuclear warheads located on their territories (Ukrainian representatives insisted on compensation for weapon-grade plutonium as well), and they decided to transfer nuclear warheads from Ukraine while simultaneously delivering fuel assemblies for nuclear power stations to Ukraine. It should be noted that Russia and the United States agreed to promote the adoption by the IAEA of an agreement placing all the nuclear activities of Ukraine under IAEA safeguards, thereby allowing the unimpeded export of fuel assembles from Russia to Ukraine for nuclear power plants.[8]

In addition to financial compensation the Ukrainian political leaders made accession to the NPT as a NNWS conditional on Ukraine being provided with security assurances. These were given to Ukraine by the members of the nuclear club. They were: to respect the independence and sovereignty and the existing borders of member states of the Organization for Security and Co-operation in Europe; to reaffirm their obligation to refrain from the threat or use of force against the territorial integrity or political independence of any state; to reaffirm their commitment to Ukraine to refrain from economic coercion; to seek immediate UN Security Council action to provide assistance for Ukraine if it should become a victim of an act of aggression or an object of a threat of aggression in which nuclear weapons are used; not to use nuclear weapons against any NNWS party to the NPT, except in case of an attack by such a state in association or alliance with a NWS.

Ukraine duly began the process of removing the warheads from all its SS-24s, and finished it within ten months. The agreement did not, however, establish a formal timetable for transporting the warheads to Russia (calling for completion within 'the shortest possible time'). Nevertheless, by the end of 1994 not less than 160 nuclear warheads had been transported to Russia. Russia had arranged the transport while Ukraine provided security for the warheads while they were within her boundaries. If this agreement is complied with by the Ukrainian authorities, Kiev is due to get US$ 1 billion worth of LEU for its power plants over a nine-year period, starting with US$ 60 million in the first ten months, and an initial influx of US$ 300 million in World Bank import credits and the promise of some additional billions in trade and investment from international lending agencies during the years ahead.

The withdrawal of strategic nuclear weapons deployed in Belarus and Kazakhstan went more smoothly. Both Belarus and Kazakhstan acceded to the NPT in 1993 and 1994 respectively as NNWSs. There are still some nuclear warheads on the territories of these states, but they have never been out of Russian control. In spite of some speculation about the possibility of these governments changing their positions towards the remaining nuclear warheads, the chances of this happening are low, though one could envisage some difficulties in implementation, however, if compensation from Russia is delayed.[9] One must nevertheless take into account the complexity of the economic relations between members of the CIS, where the Russian influence as the main oil and natural gas producer in the region is considerably stronger.

The whole process of removing nuclear weapons and their further dismantlement has been made conditional on the sales of the HEU extracted from nuclear warheads from Russia to the United States. The relevant agreement between the governments of the Russian Federation and the United States was signed on 18 February 1993 in Washington. It stipulated the principles of the economic and technical co-operation between the two nations on the processing of HEU and LEU for use as fuel in nuclear reactors. The United States became committed to purchasing LEU from Russia, obtained from the processing of HEU or (by specific agreement of the two sides) an equivalent quantity of HEU. This material is to be sold to users in the United States for commercial purposes. In its turn, Russia assumed the obligation to reprocess no less than ten tonnes of HEU annually over the following five years and, subsequently, not less than ten tonnes per year. Altogether Russia would have to reprocess a total of 500 tonnes of HEU extracted from dismantled nuclear weapons. All these agreements mean that the 'Ukrainian' nuclear weapon stockpile is regarded as a uranium source for nuclear fuel material to be sold to the American utilities.

As the question of ensuring effective control over the nuclear weapon arsenal of the former Soviet Union is being successfully solved, other types of potential nuclear dispersal are moving to the top of the non-proliferation agenda in the CIS countries. Ukraine and some other CIS states possess other aspects of a nuclear infrastructure, such as power plants, other civilian nuclear facilities, nuclear research establishments and qualified personnel. There are 42 civilian nuclear power reactors in operation in the former Soviet republics: Russia has 25 power units; Ukraine 14; Lithuania 2; and Kazakhstan 1. In Armenia the decision has been taken to reopen its nuclear power plant. Uzbekistan and Tajikistan are among the chief producers of natural uranium in the CIS.

Nuclear export control and emigration regulation systems in many CIS states are embryonic or non-existent. Russia, the United States and the appropriate international structures such as the IAEA need to address this problem and make arrangements to close these worrying loopholes in the non-proliferation structure. This is an example of the more traditional non-proliferation activities designed to deal with proliferation threats on the basis of international law and international co-operative efforts.

Russian and CIS policy is to strengthen the non-proliferation regime. This regime was constructed during the Cold War in the 1960s and formalized in the NPT, and was designed to satisfy the various objectives of the superpowers as well as the interests of the international security system. During the Cold War two major factors played a crucial role in dampening proliferation incentives: first, the global bipolar security structure (the ability of the superpowers to offer to their allies and friends 'extended deterrence' and 'nuclear umbrellas'), and second, the existence of technological barriers to obtaining nuclear weapon production capabilities. Both these pillars of the NPT regime have been weakened in the post-Cold War political and technological environment. The task of strengthening this regime has emerged as a priority in world policy. Its urgency has been confirmed by: the discovery of a clandestine nuclear weapon development programme in Iraq; the nuclear crisis in the Korean peninsula; the failure to reverse Indian and Pakistani acquisition of a nuclear capability and persuade them to join the NPT; and the remaining nuclear proliferation issues in the Middle East. The basic elements of the Russian non-proliferation policy can be summarized in the following way. First, Russia sees the existing non-proliferation regime based on the NPT as playing a key role in ensuring global stability. One of the goals of Russian foreign policy in the first half of 1995 was thus to ensure a successful outcome at the 1995 NPT Review and Extension Conference, with the hope that it ensures an indefinite and unconditional extension. Then the Russian government believes that the existing international regime should be strengthened through a combination of agreed measures of nuclear disarmament, first through a comprehensive nuclear test ban treaty (CTBT) and then a global prohibition on the production of fissile materials for nuclear weapons.[10] Russia values the role of the IAEA in ensuring compliance with the NPT and supports the efforts taken by the agency in perfecting the system of safeguards. Russia intends, moreover, to continue to play an active role in the global non-proliferation effort, while pursuing her national interests and priorities. In terms of a national defence posture, Russia's position derives not so much from any sense of direct immediate threat from any potential proliferator, as from concerns about ensuring global and regional stability, in particular around the borders of the CIS.

A new Russian military doctrine, adopted in November 1993, has important potential implications for the non-proliferation effort. Its general tenor is favourable to the objectives of the NPT. According to the doctrine, local wars and armed conflicts pose the main threat to national security and international stability, and hence there is less of a focus upon nuclear forces in military strategy than in the past. The stated mission for Russian nuclear forces is to serve as a means of war prevention. Nuclear weapons have been relegated to a category of 'last resort'. The new military doctrine contains the important recognition that any use of nuclear weapons, including a limited one, may provoke a massive reaction and cause catastrophic consequences. This statement reflects an acknowledgment of the need to lessen the reliance upon nuclear retaliation. The document contains provisions for the improvement of international mechanisms to control the spread of weapons of mass destruction and their delivery systems; encouraging the indefinite extension of the NPT; a ban on nuclear weapon testing; and opening of multilateral negotiations for further nuclear disarmament. As far as NNWSs are concerned, the doctrine contains a pledge not to use nuclear weapons against NNWSs that are parties to the NPT, 'except in the case of an attack upon it, its territory or armed forces, or its allies, by such a state allied to a NWS by an alliance agreement or acting jointly with a NWS in carrying out or sustaining the attack'. The new Russian military doctrine has ended the Soviet Union's commitment not to be the first to use nuclear weapons and not to use nuclear weapons against NNWSs without nuclear weapons stationed on their territory; this reverses a long-standing Soviet policy, which was never reciprocated by the Western nuclear powers. It has reserved the right to use all the means at Russia's disposal to repulse aggression, and places fewer restrictions on the use of nuclear weapons. This may be interpreted as an implicit recognition of the need for a stronger nuclear deterrent posture and for an extended deterrent policy. The shift is alleged to strengthen deterrence and to bring Russian doctrine in line with the positions of the United States, Great Britain and France.

In addition to substantial nuclear arms reductions (down to a level of a few thousand deployed or stockpiled weapons or less), an important contribution to implementing Article VI of the NPT would be made by a verifiable ban on the production of fissile materials for nuclear weapons. In September 1994 President Boris Yeltsin presented an initiative to the UN General Assembly for a treaty among the five permanent members of the UN Security Council to halt the production of fissile materials for weapons. A fissile material cut-off, which has been an item on the UN agenda for many years, would help to curb the proliferation of nuclear weapons both by NWSs and NNWSs. Its achievement would signal the determination on the part of the NWSs and other nations with advanced nuclear capabilities to exclude the possibility of any resumption of a nuclear arms race and proceed at a global level to reduce the emphasis on nuclear weapons. Russia also confirmed the proposal they had made to the United States on a monitored cessation of the production of military fissile materials. Russian production of HEU for weapons purposes had been halted earlier. Thus there now seems to be a favourable opportunity for a joint US–Russian agreement leading to a worldwide verifiable cut-off agreement. A cut-off agreement should provide for the safeguarded disposal of all plutonium and HEU through an international storage regime. This would permit the release of fissionable material for eventual civilian use under appropriate international procedures that would provide additional assurances concerning non-diversion and exclusively peaceful use. The use of plutonium is plagued by security, safety and environmental problems. An international plutonium storage (IPS) regime appears today to be the only viable option. The original concept of IPS, unsuccessfully addressed by an IAEA group of experts some ten years ago, was intended for plutonium retrieved from civilian reactors of NNWSs. Naturally enough, it should apply in the first instance to plutonium extracted from the nuclear weapons of NWSs, as well as to the plutonium accumulated by other nations with advanced nuclear technology. The IAEA is uniquely qualified to be the monitoring agency for a cut-off agreement. The safeguarding of enrichment and reprocessing plants is a task which is already one of the agency's duties. As for an IPS regime, it is already authorized by the IAEA's statute.

A cut-off of production of fissionable material for weapons purposes should be given top priority on the international agenda. Agreements on this burning issue would greatly enhance the possibility of achieving universal adherence to the NPT and might lay the groundwork for a more ambitious scheme of international control of atomic energy in the future. For verification purposes it would require a clear separation of the civil and military nuclear sectors in NWSs. This would facilitate the requirement to verify that no transfer of material was made from one sector to another.

To a more considerable degree than in the past Moscow's non-proliferation policy is driven by economic considerations, that is, by the need to ensure fair access to foreign markets for the products of the nuclear industry. It should be noted that incentives to export high technologies and sensitive products (as well as arms) have been growing in Russia and in other former Soviet republics. Efforts are made within the framework of the CIS bodies to handle this problem. Thus eight CIS states concluded an agreement on 26 June 1992 on the basic principles of co-operation in the field of peaceful uses of atomic energy. The parties agreed to abide by the IAEA guidelines for nuclear export (INFCIRC/254) and conduct regular consultations on the issues over the implementation of the agreement. The document contains provisions for the establishment of appropriate institutional structures. In another agreement, also signed on 26 June 1992 by the same states, the parties agreed to carry out co-ordinated action to this effect, to create national export control systems, and to co-operate with other countries on the elaboration of harmonized lists and on the standardization of the rules of export control. Russia, as the only CIS state with a well-developed export control infrastructure, has a special role to play. Russia is providing assistance to other CIS members as well as to the CIS collective bodies in charge of nuclear export control matters, particularly in harmonizing the lists of materials, equipment and technologies subject to controls. Since March 1992 the Russian Government has been applying in its nuclear export policies IAEA full-scope safeguard principles as a condition of nuclear supplies to other states. It has established a system of national export control, and the governmental commission on export control has been given a mandate to ensure a single state policy in this field. The Russian Government has adopted a list of controlled items and introduced a criminal code over the illegal export of these items.

Russia supports the idea of an international organization involving states with developed scientific–technical potential and those interested in obtaining access to leading-edge technologies. This would permit the modernization of the international non-proliferation regime and help remove suspicions of a strengthening monopoly on the uses of results of scientific–technical progress by a restricted 'club' of industrially developed states.

Notes

1   This classification of proliferation threats is given in the '1994 Report on Management and Disposition of Excess Weapons Plutonium', Committee on International Security and Arms Control, US National Academy of Sciences.

2   All former Soviet tactical/non-strategic nuclear weapons were withdrawn to Russia by July 1992. It should be pointed out here that the concern of the world community in respect of the nuclear weapons of the Soviet Union preceded its disintegration. In the course of 1991 and even earlier, many experts and statesmen of various countries expressed their worry about the loss of control over the Soviet nuclear arsenal as a result of the growing political crisis in that country. The unsuccessful *coup d'état* in August 1991, when for a few days there was virtually no central control over nuclear weapons, considerably added to this concern.

3   Strategic nuclear weapons (54 SS-25 ICBMs), located in Belarus and controlled by the appropriate Russian authorities, are being withdrawn in accordance with the agreed schedule. They will probably have left Belarus by 1996, although this was not required by the terms of either START I or START II.

4   The Lisbon Protocol committed Ukraine, Belarus and Kazakhstan to acceding to the NPT in the shortest possible time as NNWS (Article V). The protocol has been ratified by all the signatory states (although the Ukrainian parliament initially ratified it with reservations, leaving out the commitment contained in Article V, but later reversed this position and expressed a willingness to accede to the NPT without a deadline).

5   According to this logic, the Lisbon Protocol could not be interpreted as recognizing the right of Russia to own the nuclear weapons of the Former Soviet Union, since it was taken in the context of an international agreement. Russia was regarded here as a technical executor, while the whole weapons elimination process is subject to control by the United States, as another party to START I.

6   Silo-based 130 SS-19 and 46 SS-24 ICBMs carrying 1240 nuclear warheads, and 36 heavy bombers equipped with about 500 nuclear gravity bombs and short-range air missiles.

7   One possible means of putting pressure on Ukraine could be to restrict or prohibit

access to Russian radio-chemical plants, reprocessing spent fuel from Ukrainian nuclear power stations, and access to the storage sites of radioactive waste produced by
Ukrainian nuclear facilities and power plants. Such means have already been resorted
to spontaneously by the administration of Russian radio-chemical plants, hoping to
hasten payment by Ukraine for these services.

8   Trilateral Statement by the Presidents of the United States of America, the Russian
Federation and Ukraine, 14 January 1994, *Programme for Promoting Nuclear Non-
Proliferation Newsbrief*, no. 25, 1994.

9   Belarus, Ukraine and Kazakhstan from time to time raise the question of compensation
for weapon-grade plutonium, but Russian officials totally reject this idea.

10   Joint Statement on Strategic Stability and Nuclear Security by the Presidents of the
United States and Russia, 28 September 1994.

6   Russia and Central Asia

Alexei Vasilyev

An expression widely used by both politicians and political analysts is that 'the Soviet Empire has collapsed', and the present writer occasionally refers to the 'Soviet Empire', though feeling a little ashamed every time. What, then, should one understand by the word 'empire'? It seems to include several elements. First, there is the existence of a metropolis that dominates weaker and subjugated parts, that is a certain element of centralisation is implied. A second element is that there is a dominating ethnicity or two ethnicities which occupy a privileged position in the subjugated parts so-cially, culturally and politically. A third feature is that there is exploitation of the imperial periphery by the centre in various forms. Given this defi-nition, an imperial structure could be discerned in the case of the Soviet Union, but surely only partially.

There was, indeed, centralization and firm political control by the centre, and there was a certain dominance of the Russian language. But the problem was that the Russian people, like all other peoples of the Soviet Union, were victims of the Communist regime and suffered, perhaps, greater losses than all other large nationalities, with the exception of such smaller peoples as the Chechens, the Crimean Tatars, the Volga Germans and others who faced especially intolerable treatment. The centralized system also existed in mili-tary and economic construction, in foreign policy and in security matters. But another question arises. Did the Russians occupy privileged positions in any sphere to the extent that the English or French did in their former colonies? The answer is a categorical no. Who were the privileged strata of population in Central Asia? First and foremost, there was the party–state *nomenklatura* who occupied the highest posts in the state hierarchy and used them to enjoy legal privileges and to enrich themselves through cor-ruption. The Russians in those republics, when they entered the élite, never occupied leading positions. The only exceptions – the Russians and Ukrain-ians sent from the centre as second secretaries to the local party organiz-ations – did not change the general picture. The second stratum who were materially privileged were the people who worked in the trade system. Their privileges were anything but legal, based on theft and corruption, and Russians were extremely few among them. The Russian population of the republics in question were mainly workers, including those engaged in hard and non-prestigious labour, from mines to environmentally-harmful industries. The Russians were also numerous among the local technical community and partly among scientists. True, the Russians were absent from the most deprived sector of the local population, the rural cotton growers. But, as stated, they were also under-represented in the highest echelons.

A final question concerns exploitation. Who exploited whom? Formally, only three republics – Russia, Ukraine and Azerbaijan – had positive balances of trade with other republics, that is they gave more than they received. However, the statistics of the Soviet period are completely unreliable, and hence nationalists now claim that their republics were exploited by Moscow. This writer does not share their opinion and holds that Russia gave more than it took; the republics' budgets repeatedly received subsidies from the centre, that is mainly at Russia's expense. However, the truth in this dispute will become clear only later, when inter-republic economic and trade relations will be based on world prices. Then we shall learn who gave to whom.

Thus, the Soviet Union may hardly have been described as an empire in a strict sense. Another point concerns the case of Ukraine, which was the second largest component of the Soviet Union. While a part of it was gradually Russified linguistically and culturally (for example, teaching in the Kiev State University was in Russian and that was nothing but an insult to the Ukrainian nation), on the all-Union level the Ukrainians occupied notable positions. In any case, among the army officers they were over-represented compared with the Russians.

Moreover, when there are references to the 'collapse of the empire' as in the title of Hélène Carrère D'Encausse's famous book,[1] it should be remembered that, strangely enough, the empire did not collapse at its periphery. Central Asia retained its Communist regimes to the very end (and retains them now). And it did not sever ties with Moscow before the empire collapsed from inside as a result of the decades-long Communist experiment, the tiresome arms race and the confrontation with the powerful West. Yet when the forces that earlier united the empire disappear, especially Communist ideology, what remains? What replaces them? In the Central Asian republics, alias states, it is first and foremost nationalism and Islam. This is but natural.

It is a mode of national being with its own ideology, culture and civilization; it is a return to the roots from which Communist pseudo-civilization tried to cut off the peoples. Both to the popular masses and to intellectuals, an appeal to nationalism and Islam is an appeal to self-identification, a search for their own authenticity, while to old and new political élites it is a form of legitimization of their power. Thus, relying on Islam and nationalism, they must move a few steps away from Russia and counterpoise themselves to it. It is a quite natural process. True, many people are extremely cynical in their behaviour when following that course – former Communist Russifiers portray themselves as ardent and extreme nationalists and avid former propagandists for atheism attend mosques and demonstrate their deep devotion to Islam.

To move away from Russia, then, is a must for Central Asia at the current stage. Hence its leaders are turning their eyes outwards in search of allies and protectors. Among the new actors in the Central Asian theatre Turkey and Iran are mentioned most frequently. To Turkey the policy of protection of younger Turkic brethren is a form of struggle in the field of home policy, a form of placating the attitudes of the country's population, or rather those of Turkish intellectuals and the political élite. Turkey is claiming a leading role in the Turkic world with pretentious declarations to the effect that the twenty-first century will be the century of Turkic nations. The former Communists who rule Central Asia are attracted by the Turkish socio-political model thanks to its secularism, pro-Western tendencies, and strong authoritarian elements allied to a degree of democracy. In return, Turkey makes generous gestures by organizing summits of Turkic states (thereby claiming a new geopolitical role), allotting scholarships to Central Asian students and promising loans.

Iran for its part is striving to spread its political influence to the territory that was traditionally (for almost 2500 years) in its sphere of interest and then was cut off first by Russian conquest and then by the Communist regime. Iran relies on Islamic propaganda, appeals to believers' feelings and claims that the socio-political problems of the region may be solved using the models of an Islamic society such as that under construction in Iran.

In this context, it is often considered that Turkey is backed by the United States and Western Europe and is confronted by a hostile fundamentalist Iran. Both countries' influence is, however, restricted mainly by their economic potential. Both Turkey and Iran are too weak to influence substantially the economic development of the newly independent states. Turkey is separated from them geographically and this prevents any real growth in trade. Iran is closer but the question is, what can they trade in? Dry fruits are an export item of Turkey, Iran and Central Asia. The same holds true of cotton. Azerbaijan or Turkmenistan will hardly export petrol or gas to oil-rich Iran, while Turkey is too far away.

Another point deserves attention. Whatever negative emotions the former Communist regimes may evoke, some of the achievements of the Central

Asian republics are beyond any doubt. Their literacy level and number of students per thousand of population are higher than in Turkey or Iran. Some industries in Central Asia are developed far better than in Turkey or Iran. Thus, after the first period of euphoria, when the nations in question enjoy the warmth of emotions produced by the restoration of historical ties with their brothers and cousins, a period of cold sobriety will come; economic necessity and the restored local pride of Uzbeks or Azerbaijanis will rise to the forefront, when the role of being someone's little brothers will become intolerable to them.

In that sense Russia's relations with those countries do have a future, though they are remote enough particularly with respect to economic matters. Nobody would deny, however, that the Soviet Union was a country with a united economic system and transportation ties, and the rupture of these links is among the causes of the present crisis. There is nobody and nothing to replace them or substitute for them in the near future. The most characteristic example is Uzbekistan, the most populated state of the region, with 20 million people. The only good highway connecting it with the regions beyond the former Soviet Union leads to Afghanistan. It is ridiculous to suggest that the country can develop its foreign economic ties by relying on that highway. In this connection it is worth recalling the case of Algeria, with its favourable location and free access to sea routes connecting it with the rest of the world and with its immense petrol and gas deposits. After 30 years of experiments, that country came to the conclusion that it could not do without close ties with France. It is thus obvious that after moving three or four steps away, Central Asia and Russia will take one, two or three steps closer to each other and build their relationship on a new foundation.

An important role in future relations will belong to the Russian-speaking population forming minorities of various strengths in the republics of the region and a majority in Kazakhstan, and to the section of the national élite sharing Russian education and Russian values. Again, while speaking of the Communist regimes, it should not be forgotten how much was done by them for the emancipation of women. To the local intellectuals, acceptance of the Iranian model would thus mean a return to a much older state of affairs.

There are several rival trends at work in the shaping of future Russian policy in the region. One is of complete neutrality towards internal conflicts and implies indifference towards the destiny of the Russian-speaking population. Another calls for an active policy and eventual interference in the conflicts in order to settle them, maybe even by violent means, including the setting up of a Russian brand of rapid-deployment forces. The destiny of the Russians in the 'near abroad', as Central Asia is referred to now, is also becoming an object of home policy struggle in Russia. The rise of nationalist feelings makes the Russian leaders issue more and more serious statements in support of the Russians outside Russia and may prompt them to take action.

The situation differs in various republics. In Turkmenistan, the former Communist *nomenklatura* persists. The former regime has, however, slightly changed its name and character, old tribal and regional ties have become overt and the old dictatorship is preserved under the guise of new parties. Huge gas deposits and their profitable sale are proving helpful in supporting stability in the republic. An interesting feature of the situation is that the Russian troops guarding the Turkmen frontier have obtained a status close to dual citizenship.

Tajikistan is being torn apart by civil war. The labels of Communism, anti-Communism, democracy and Islamism mask the struggle for power and influence among various tribal and regional clans. The country is in chaos, with the Russian population leaving it *en masse*.

The events in Tajikistan are viewed with considerable fear in Uzbekistan, which is also ruled by a reconstructed Communist regime devoted to a policy of harsh control of the opposition. However, potentially strong Islamist opposition and the presence of a Tajik minority in Bukhara and Samarkand makes the situation dangerous and explosive. An important factor is that the Tajik–Uzbek border passes through mountains and is hardly amenable to control.

The only leader lacking a Communist *nomenklatura* past is the Kyrgyz President, Askar Akaev. This pro-Russian, pro-Western and pro-democratic leader rules a country possessing powerful regional clans that are split ethnically and nationally. Uzbeks have been traditionally engaged in irrigated land cultivation; Russians in non-irrigated cultivation and industry; and Kyrgyzians worked nomadic pasture in the mountains and later some became involved in urban administration. A collision among these forces may be disastrous to the country.

At first glance, the situation in vast Kazakhstan is relatively favourable, thanks to the approximate numerical equality between ethnic Russians and Kazakhs, though Russian-speakers outnumber the Kazakhs. That is why President Nursultan Nazarbaev pursues a cautious policy of balance between different trends in order to prevent conflicts and is using the colossal mineral resources of the country for development of Kazakh society.

Russia's problem is how to find means of coexistence with its Muslim Turkic neighbours. If one takes the Turkic states as a single entity, their frontier with Russia is the longest in the world, and the question is whether the frontier zone will be a zone of co-operation and coexistence or of bloody conflicts devastating to both Russia and Central Asia.

Note

1　Hélène Carrère D'Encausse, *l'Empire éclaté: la révolte des nations en URSS* (Paris, 1978).

7 Inter-ethnic Conflicts of the 'New Generation': A Russian View

Alexander Ivanov

The ending of the Cold War and the disintegration of the bipolar global structure mark a qualitative change in world politics. In the previous periods relations between states were regulated by means of coalitions and blocs of coinciding interests and balances between them. Today, attempts to cling to bloc structures are senseless.

A main feature of the present transitional state of world affairs is the contradiction between a wide spectrum of possibilities in global and regional interaction on the one hand, and on the other the remaining old and new challenges to peace, security and stability. This contradiction needs to be reconciled. Achieving this end is possible by the collective efforts of the international community in realizing new possibilities for co-operation between states in opposing modern threats.

Inter-ethnic conflicts have a special place among these threats. It would not be an exaggeration to say that their settlement is as important as developing further efforts in confronting the nuclear threat. They are the most difficult political, military and diplomatic tasks which the international community has faced lately. Unlike arms control issues or problems of maintaining stability in the 'old' conflict zones, such as the Middle East and Cambodia, the 'new generation' conflicts have inherently dangerous elements to which the world community has been unable to respond adequately.

This phenomenon can be explained to a large extent by the nature of the new conflicts, which are rooted in the breaking down of the bipolar confrontation. This system had certain balances and controls which prevented open conflicts between different ethnic groups, and at the same time drove inter-ethnic conflicts deep underground. Within the Former Soviet Union the ideological doctrine and the antidemocratic governmental mechanism played the same role. It is no coincidence that the collapse of this doctrine and the disintegration of the bipolar global structure have coincided with an outburst of separatism and inter-ethnic conflicts that have taken especially violent forms on the territory of the former socialist countries.

There are forces in the Newly-independent Countries (NICs) which put forward a slogan of nationalism to seize political power or break the state to pieces. In doing so, they exploit the current ethnic explosion caused by the legacy of Soviet domination and by the hardships of the current process of transformation in society. Imposing an ideology of internationalism and ignoring ethnic development, the leaders of the Soviet Union caused grave imbalances in inter-ethnic relations. The inferiority complex formed as a result and the feeling that the interests of many ethnic groups, including the Russians, were infringed, created a fertile ground for the activities of modern separatists and national extremists.

In confronting economic hardships, political destabilization, the ideological crisis and the social disruption, people have lost their bearings in life and are seeking solutions in ethnic identity, which allows national chauvinists and separatists to exploit such disaffection. These trends took place while new systems of government were formed in many NICs, and help to explain why ethnic tensions grow so readily into conflicts, posing a threat to the integrity of the fledgling state.

One prominent feature of the contemporary social processes is nationalism, widely believed to be the main cause of inter-ethnic conflicts. It is often interpreted as hostility to another ethnic group in the same country, but at the same time it is also understood as a love for one's own culture and people and a struggle for national revival. Thus nationalism, as a phenomenon of social life, has a dialectical nature.

Under the influence of demographic shifts and social and political upheavals, a simple awareness of ethnic differences can develop into a negative and hostile attitude to other ethnic groups and, as a result, aggressive nationalism emerges. After the Cold War aggressive nationalism has become one of the major challenges to security and stability in Europe. One should not underestimate the danger of such aggressive nationalism in Russia itself. However, overestimating the danger could also lead to wrong conclusions, and, in particular, could engender a desire in European circles to isolate Russia. This would be an unfortunate response which could also be detrimental to the Europeans themselves.

In assessing the extent of the risk posed by radical nationalism in Russia, the following should be taken into account. First, nationalist sentiments are not shared by the majority of the people. The population is more concerned with social and economic problems and changes in living standards. Nationalism can cause anxiety among the population in so far as it poses a threat of armed conflict and violence, and can worsen the economic situation. Second, it would be wrong to equate extremist groupings with a natural growth in Russian national self-consciousness. The idea that the Russian revival is rooted in xenophobia and anti-Semitism has also proved unfounded. Ultimately, the experience of 1994 shows that 'the Russian issue' arises only when pressure is exerted on Russians.[1] It happens mainly outside Russia, in other countries of the Commonwealth of Independent States (CIS).

The Russian issue has acquired a new external dimension following the disintegration of the Soviet Union. Some 150 million people, the biggest nation in Europe, have become divided. About 25 million people, or 17 per cent of the Russian population of the Former Soviet Union, now live in the newly-independent foreign states. Some of them witness a trend in these states towards ethnocratic regimes and discrimination against the Russian-speaking population, provoking ethnic tensions. Many Russians living outside Russia have felt that their future was threatened. The more they are discriminated against, the more stormy and radical is their response. It is precisely among those Russians who have become ethnic minorities in the 'new abroad' that radical nationalist movements are being formed, and these movements directly affect Russia itself. Discrimination against ethnic Russians in these countries actually nourishes attempts to restore totalitarian order in Russia itself; that would by no means meet the interests of the Europeans nor Russia's neighbours.

A normal national revival of the NICs will not be achieved unless other ethnic groups, including Russians, are included within this process. The problem has become particularly serious in Russia's relations with the Baltic States. It is widely acknowledged that Russia made every effort to support their drive for independence. Moscow is interested in promoting widespread co-operation, especially in the economic field, with these countries. However, to be successful, the 'abscess' in relations between Russia and the Baltic States needs to be cured. This can only be done by rejecting radical nationalism and guaranteeing legitimate rights for ethnic minorities on the basis of relevant international standards and norms. This would enable Russian's relations with the Baltic States to be integrated with the rest of Europe, thus strengthening European security and stability.

There is also the danger of separatist trends and the disintegration of Russia, which could undermine stability in the entire Eurasian space. What will happen if Russia becomes weaker or even disintegrates? Would Europe be able to shoulder such additional Russian burdens when it faces its own problems as urgent as the Balkan crisis? It seems doubtful. Totalitarian nationalist regimes may emerge if the Russian Federation disintegrates.

Some of them will find alliances with countries such as Iraq and Libya. New conflicts are likely to arise, provoked by border disputes, divided nations and ethnic minorities. A new problem of nuclear weapon ownership will appear. Such a disintegration would be fraught with the most dangerous consequences for European and global security. A famous Russian philosopher, Ivan Ilyin, wrote in 1948 that 'the division of the Russian "besom" into small twigs would be an adventure unprecedented in history'.[2]

The peculiarities of separatist trends and the 'new generation' conflicts were not taken into account during the Cold War period. Now *ad hoc* policy-making responses are being worked out case by case as new 'hot spots' appear. Theoretical and legal analysis fails to keep pace with activities on the ground. The international legal basis of conflict resolution has evolved mainly in the sphere of interstate relations, whereas many of the new conflicts are internal. The basic principles of international law and the United Nations (UN) Charter prescribe fundamental limits to interference in the internal affairs of states. The concept of modern peace-keeping and peacemaking operations is still fluid. All these and other factors which influence international stability in the transitional period demand urgent further codification of international law within the framework of the UN and regional organizations. The most delicate and pressing problem is the marriage between the principles of territorial integrity of states and self-determination of nations; such a resolution would strengthen the legal basis in the collective management of world stability. Favouring one of these principles to the exclusion of the other often leads to bloodshed and the violation of human rights. Such principles need to be considered in the light of other aspects of international law. Each needs to be measured against the welfare of the peoples involved, including the neighbouring nations, and the observation of human rights.

The self-determination of a nation is often understood as the creation of a nation-state corresponding to this nation. This is, however, too simplistic; the main thing is to ensure free development of the nation and its equality with other nations. Self-determination of one nation should not infringe the rights of other nations and peoples. Equal rights should be respected for all ethnic groups and national minorities. Other approaches to this problem will lead to inter-ethnic strife and threaten territorial integrity.

The legitimacy of new states should be determined primarily by the consequences for self-determination. If the actions that promote the new state provoke threats to regional and international peace and security or the mass violation of human rights, they cannot be justified. Besides, a new state's ability to survive and bear the burden of independence may be considered a prerequisite for its right of existence.

Of course, each situation needs to be examined in detail case by case. Historical, cultural, political and other peculiarities militate against universal recommendations. Recent trends in this delicate sphere demonstrate on the one hand the growing determination of the UN Security Council to curb the claims of small ethnic groups for state independence (on the grounds that their corresponding activities lead to serious challenges to regional and international security), and on the other hand the reluctance of 'Third World' countries to compromise their control of internal affairs by allowing mediation and peace-keeping.

In maintaining regional and global stability 'soft' political decisions without territorial recarving seem to have more chances of yielding positive results in the longer run than the use of force or economic sanctions (though in some urgent cases there may be no alternative other than prompt and resolute actions by the UN and regional organizations). The organizational emphasis in society needs to be shifted away from national-territorial structures to national-cultural networks, broadening the notion of self-determination to include self-governing status (or national-cultural autonomy).[3]

Stability and security has in a broad sense many aspects, such as: sovereignty; independence and territorial integrity of states; military–political security; economic security; and ecological security. Each of these aspects is influenced by modern inter-ethnic problems and vice versa: inter-ethnic stability depends on different aspects of state, regional and global security. The complex of inter-ethnic problems has come to dominate mankind's progress and as such it has two principal dimensions: theoretical and practical. The failures to find solutions to the minorities problems in the former Yugoslavia are caused not only by 'political flaws' but also by lack of successful theoretical research and analysis. Such theoretical 'black holes' are related to the need for modernizing international peace-keeping. Thus the recent development towards a multipolar world raises the issue of the role of the UN as the key peace-keeping instrument within the framework of a new collective security system. Without the domination of the two military blocs, the development of the UN peace-keeping potential is no longer hampered by their conflict, but still needs to become more effective.

First, the roles of the UN and regional security structures need to be determined, along with their interaction. They should be mutually complementary, taking into account the widening gap between present UN capabilities and the increasing demands on its resources, without encroachment upon Security Council prerogatives. Prior to 1988 the UN authorized 13 peace-keeping operations; since then it has initiated a further 17 such operations, with a budget of US$3.3 billion, and now employs more than 70,000 troops and military observers in the field. The most reasonable way to increase the effectiveness of peace-keeping operations is to involve influential regional organizations in the prevention and settlement of conflict situations. On this basis a broad and relatively decentralized network of collective security could form, provided that the UN and its Security Council are guaranteed the leading political role.

Traditional peace-keeping operations were usually started after a consensus on the issue had been reached. Peace-keeping forces are now often employed in the regions where conflicting sides cannot reach agreement on deployment. The parameters of peace-keeping activities are not clearly outlined in the UN Charter; in practice, peace-keeping forces are involved in a wide range of activities, such as providing humanitarian aid, mine-clearing operations, observing human rights violations, assisting in the holding of elections, policing and re-establishing democracy.

In addition, the neutral status of peace-keeping forces needs to be protected. Building up a UN military presence, protesting against human rights violations and staffing peace-keeping contingents with soldiers from countries neighbouring the conflict area, are sometimes perceived as undermining this principle. On the other hand, some politicians and diplomats, including the UN Secretary-General Boutros Boutros-Ghali, propose to revise the grounds for UN intervention in conflict situations; they point out that a situation 'threatening international peace and security' as grounds for intervention, mentioned in the UN Charter, is insufficient.

All this clearly demonstrates the significant institutional and organizational shortcomings of the UN in its peace-keeping operations. UN peace-making capabilities need to be enhanced and the prerequisites and demands of peace-keeping operations adjusted for different conflicts, with further improvement in planning and executing such operations. There needs to be a closer connection with political dispute-settlement efforts. These ideas are actively discussed in international circles. New approaches have been already tested in practice; for example, by France in Rwanda and the United States in Haiti. While supporting these and similar non-traditional operations by the Western powers, some circles in Europe and in the United States criticize such peacemaking efforts by Russia in the former Soviet area under the pretext that they do not correspond to international standards. On the other hand, neither international organizations nor Western states are yet ready to shoulder the burden of peacemaking in the Former Soviet Union. Further aggravation of inter-ethnic conflicts in the territory of the Former Soviet Union could thus pose a real threat not only to Russia but to pan-European security. This would undermine the efforts of the whole world community towards the construction of a secure and stable world.

In spite of its economic crisis and internal difficulties, Russia is doing its utmost to settle these conflicts. The international legal base for responses in conflict settlement was laid down in the agreement about peace-keeping which collective forces of the CIS signed in 1992, along with protocols to this agreement on the procedure for the formation of collective forces and principles governing their actions. Ratification of the agreement by the CIS parliaments took more time than was expected, however. Meanwhile, conflicts near Russia's border posed a great threat to its vital interests. Russia could not ignore requests from the conflicting sides and started peace-keeping operations on the basis of trilateral agreements between the governments of the corresponding republic and the Russian Federation, and the leadership of the region. These three sides together formed peace-keeping contingents. Such were the operations in South Ossetia, the Dniester region and Abkhazia. The decision to carry out these operations is in complete accordance with the UN Charter. The departure from international standards was motivated by specific conditions in these conflicts and the necessity to halt the conflict as soon as possible. The experience of peace-keeping operations in the Dniester region and South Ossetia proves that such measures can make it possible to re-establish and maintain peace for prolonged periods (more than two years). This experience could be built upon by the UN and the Organization for Security and Co-operation in Europe (OSCE).

A top priority of Russian peace-making activities is co-operation with the UN and the OSCE in the prevention and settlement of conflicts in the Former Soviet Union, where all peace-keeping operations are transparent. Russia's efforts at political mediation are co-ordinated with the activities of the UN and OSCE. Moscow regards co-operation with international organizations as one of the most important aspects of its peace-keeping concept, enshrined within the text of its new military doctrine. This doctrine creates the legal foundation for peace-keeping activities by Russian contingents on the basis of UN, OSCE and CIS decisions. Practical training of Russian contingents for peace-keeping operations corresponds to the standards and procedures of the UN and agreements within the OSCE and CIS. It is very important that international organizations reciprocate by rendering more specific assistance to Russia and the CIS.

Concrete spheres of interaction between Russia, the CIS, the UN and the OSCE have happened over the conflicts in Abkhazia, Tajikistan, South Ossetia and Nagorno-Karabakh. In this connection it is of great importance for Russia as well as for other CIS members that there is recognition of the CIS as a regional organization with rights to engage in peace-keeping operations.

One such operation is in a zone of the conflict between Georgia and Abkhazia. In June 1994 the CIS countries reached a decision to launch a peace-keeping operation in this zone on the invitation of both sides, based on Chapter VIII of the UN Charter. The peace-keeping operation of the CIS was unavoidable because of the critical humanitarian situation (250,000 refugees from Abkhazia is a heavy burden for Georgia's economy, weakened by civil war) and because for several months the UN Security Council had not reacted to the numerous appeals from Georgia and Russia on the issue of sending UN peace-keepers. We were told that 'standard' UN pre-requisites were 'not ripe' for a UN operation. It would be interesting to know how many lives can be lost before a situation 'ripens'.

At the same time the Security Council adopted a resolution on a French initiative regarding Rwanda which was not in the least ideal in UN peace-keeping practice (the consent of both conflicting parties had not been reached and most African states did not approve of the initiative). Naturally, many believed that 'double standards' were being applied. Russia did, however, vote in favour of the resolution on Rwanda, holding the opinion that the Security Council should react adequately and promptly to non-standard challenges.

Finally, after prolonged discussions, on 30 June 1994 the Security Council adopted the resolution welcoming the CIS operation in Abkhazia and Georgia. This was the first official positive example of the Security Council attitude towards peace-keeping operations in the CIS area. The first stage of the peace-keeping operation, involving the separation of conflicting forces and mine-clearing, over the period 15–26 June 1994, cost Rb2 billion.[4] In 1993 the Russian Ministry of Defence expenditure for peace-keeping operations on the territory of the former Soviet Union was Rb26 billion.[5] Russia alone bears the burden of peace-keeping operations in the CIS. It also helps to finance peace-keeping operations outside the CIS. If CIS forces in Abkhazia are granted UN status, it would partly relieve the financial burden. Although the UN does not oppose CIS peace-keeping efforts in Trans-Caucasus, it refuses to give UN status to the forces deployed there.

At the same time there have been demands for close UN monitoring over the CIS operation in Abkhazia. From the very beginning allegations have been levelled against Russia that Moscow would like to have an international cover for a free hand in Abkhazia. It is necessary to consider the following. First, the operation with the participation of 2500 Russian volunteers is being carried out in close interaction and co-operation with the UN mission in Georgia. Second, Russia proposed to include military observers from Ukraine, Belarus and Kazakhstan in its peace-keeping forces. Third, Russia's proposal to transform the CIS operation into a full-scale UN operation is still on the table.

Close co-operation between the CIS and the UN is developing in Tajikistan affairs. At the request of the Tajik Government the CIS states formed collective peace-keeping forces consisting of contingents from Russia, Kazakhstan, Uzbekistan and Kyrgyzstan. All the relevant documents were sent to the UN Secretary-General. These forces prevented infiltration over the border by armed groups from the Afghan side and protected important economic targets in Tajikistan. Strict neutrality was observed over internal Tajik issues. Protection of this border is in the interests of all CIS countries and European states, to prevent an explosion of terrorism, narcotics smuggling, Islamic extremism and instability over the whole Eurasian region. Russia, being the closest neighbour of the Central Asian republics and having 'transparent' borders with Tajikistan, is vitally interested in a stable situation there and recognizes a responsibility towards maintaining peace, but it needs assistance from the international community. Political dialogue and the creation of a congenial political climate for democracy is also of vital importance for Tajikistan. Russia is playing the role of honest broker, in co-operation with other interested parties including the UN. Talks on national reconciliation between the Tajik sides are being held under the auspices of the UN and the UN Secretary-General's special envoy, as well as observers from Afghanistan, Kazakhstan, Kyrgyzstan, Iran, Pakistan, Russia, Uzbekistan and the OSCE.

The conflict in Nagorno-Karabakh became more complicated in late 1994. Leading Western oil companies displayed a keen interest in exploration in Azerbaijan Caspian oil. A contract was signed in October 1994 between the Azerbaijani Government and Western companies. Baku seems to cherish hopes of Western political and economic help; Western states in return seem intent upon using the situation to increase their influence in the region. Sending OSCE multinational peace-keeping forces to the region may yield positive results if it does not cover the intention to force Russia back into a secondary role in the settlement. If the OSCE is indeed being used to widen others' spheres of influence at the expense of Russia's this could only lead to a short-sighted confrontation. Besides, the OSCE has practically no experience in peace-keeping operations. Launching an OSCE full-scale operation in such a difficult situation could be counterproductive both for the settlement of the conflict and the image of the OSCE. Practical results are needed at this critical stage. It would be helpful if a clear mandate for the OSCE is worked out. A useful model for the OSCE may be the close co-operation between the UN, Georgia, Abkhazia and the third party during the talks in Geneva.

The best option would be for the UN Security Council to take the leading role. Unlike the OSCE, it has accumulated the necessary experience and worked out the mechanisms for planning and carrying out peace-keeping operations. The OSCE could also become involved at some later stage. The formation and maintenance of peace-keeping forces will be impossible without close co-operation with the Russians.

It is obvious that the interests of Russia and the West within the range of peace-keeping activities are not identical. This factor creates a certain 'natural limit' to their developing partnership, and it is important that additional artificial limits are not encouraged. There are tendencies to look at Russian foreign policy activity, especially its peace-keeping actions in the territory of the Former Soviet Union, in the light of 'Russian neo-imperial ambitions'. If these tendencies permeate from the lobbies and scholarly disputes into policy-making circles, the mutual damage will have a long-term effect. It is time to leave orthodox stereotypes and work out realistic assessments. Making a dogma out of outdated conceptions is a senseless business. Dynamic development of peace-making is desperately needed as crises are aggravated and their settlement is becoming more complex.

Judged in the light of pan-European security, conflicts in the former Soviet area are not in the least of merely peripheral importance. The speed with which they are settled is more important than 'theoretical flaws' in the response, because such efforts are directed at establishing peace and alleviating suffering as soon as possible – the more so as Russia observes UN-recognized standards of peace-keeping. Russian efforts are motivated not by mythical 'neo-imperial ambitions' but by simple and tough calculations of Russia's security interests: without peace and stability on its borders, Russia will not be able to restore and develop its economic potential.

Political and material support from the international community for Russian peace-keeping efforts could encourage stability and a real partnership. It would also enable military–technical co-operation between Russia and the West to blossom under recognized UN standards, including activities in the context of Partnership for Peace. Such activities include co-operation in peace-keeping operations and working out compatibility between military potentials.

Russia's true national interests lie in the formation of a good-neighbourhood 'belt' around the Russian borders, not in 'neo-imperial' ambitions. The thesis of Russian 'neo-imperialism' appears to be poorly founded; strictly speaking, Russia has never been a classic empire, there being no enforced colonization of the peoples living on its territory. There was a process of 'bringing lands together', as a form of 'soft assimilation' under the influence of mutual security considerations rather than 'metropolis–colony'. There was a desire in the territories neighbouring Russia to use the Moscow shield to screen themselves from external enemies. This was especially true for the Ukraine and Georgia.[6] Russian military, political and economic patronage covered such territories for centuries under the influence of its own security considerations: it was always better to live together with allies than to wait until their territory was conquered and an enemy was at Russia's walls.

Close mutual historical ties, the survival of a number of states and the maintenance of stability dictate the need for integration of the newly-independent states. Russia plays a natural initiating role in CIS integration. As historical experience shows, the economic, political and cultural 'expansion' of Russia was in fact beneficial for the welfare of its peoples. The internal structure of Russia appears to have been an integral and interconnected organism; the centre has always worked for a periphery. Such a mass of internal ties has been accumulated that its rupture, with the disintegration of the Soviet Union, has resulted in painful consequences. Thus, the strengthening of the CIS and its peace-keeping activities, along with general reintegration within the CIS framework, requires a leading role from Russia. There are historical precedents elsewhere: Britain, France and Portugal have preserved minimum (but significant) ties with their former colonies. The extent of internal association in the case of the CIS, however, is much higher. The particular form of integration will be decided by the participants within a wide range of mutual interests and preferences.

The degree of understanding and assistance from the international community will influence the direction of CIS integration, the success in settling inter-ethnic conflicts and the character of the CIS ties with the external world and international organizations. One should not forget that empires consolidated and expanded mainly in unfavourable external environments. If the world community would like Russia and the CIS to be an integral part of the UN system of security and co-operation, it should encourage a constructive 'two-way traffic'. A powerful, stable, democratic and predictable Russia will not be a threat to Europe. Russia's main policy goal in the CIS area is stability, peace and co-operation under recognized European norms. The alternative – aggressive nationalism, inter-ethnic conflicts and economic chaos – would hardly enhance the stability and security of the Europeans. The strengthening of security and stability in Europe urgently needs the recognition of collective responsibility for peace-building in the CIS area.

Notes

1 See *Razdelit li Rossiya uchast Soyuza SSR* (Moscow, 1993) pp. 59–70.
2 I.A. Ilyin, 'Chto sulit miru raschlenenie Rossii', *Etnopolis*, vol. 1 (Moscow, 1992).
3 K.V. Kalinina, *Natsionalnye menshinstva v. Rossii* (Moscow, 1993) pp. 21–8.
4 *Rossiyskaya Gazeta*, Moscow, 18 June 1994.
5 Ibid.
6 See R.G. Abdulatipov, L.F. Boltenkova and Y.F. Yarov, *Federalizm v. istorii Rossii*, vol. 1 (Moscow, 1992).

8 Peace Support Operations on the Territory of the Former Soviet Union

Alexander I. Nikitin

Multilateral UN Peace-keeping: Second Generation

The current stage in international affairs is characterized by a rising intensity in regional and local conflicts. 'Deterrence' (with a reliance upon nuclear weapons) elaborated within the bipolar East–West confrontation of the former Cold War years cannot be applied to war prevention in many modern local 'hot spots', from the former Yugoslavia and Somalia to Tajikistan and Abkhazia. Ethnically-rooted conflicts, both international and intrastate, are tackled by the world community and regional powers with a spectrum of tools, involving such notions as 'peace-keeping', 'peace support' and 'peace enforcement' operations.

Though peace-keeping practices are rooted in the United Nations (UN) Charter (mainly Chapters VI and VII) and we have seen more than 45 years of UN peace-keeping operations in practice, currently we are witnessing a radical change in approach, creating and using multilateral international armed forces in conflict areas. The UN has convened 27 international peace-keeping operations since 1948, with a participation of more than 600,000 military and civilian personnel. More than 860 lives of peace-keepers have been lost. The total cost of operations has exceeded US$8.3 billion.

There are currently 13 operations under UN Security Council mandate in different areas of the globe. By 1993 about 52,200 men of military and police contingents provided by 67 countries were participating in active operations. Of the current operations, two are financed by the general purpose UN budget, one (on Cyprus) through voluntary donations from national governments and other organizations, and ten by separate specially created accounts proportionally supplied by UN member states.

All UN-based peace-keeping operations are characterized by certain important 'classic' principles and criteria born out of years of practice governing the activities of the UN Peace-keeping Operations Department and other organizations involved in the preparation and adoption of such operations. Such principles are outlined below.

First, all peace-keeping operations are carried out on the basis of a clear legal mandate represented by a Security Council decision (resolution). This defines the objectives and means of the operation, and the terms and rules of engagement. Funds are provided collectively. Operations are commanded by a nominated professional commander who is subordinate to the UN Secretary-General. The nomination is co-ordinated with the host nation(s) and participating countries.

Second, those involved in the conflict should express a readiness to search for a peaceful solution before any decision to send multilateral forces is taken. A cease-fire and mutual readiness for conflict resolution is crucial for 'classic' 'Chapter VI' operations. Recently, in more than one case, the forceful 'peace-enforcement' model of operation was used, however, when multilateral forces were sent to stop the violence before the opposing sides had expressed a readiness for reconciliation.

Third, it is crucial that the forces participating in the conflict resolution are impartial. The forces and personnel selected by the UN and provided by member states should not be from the conflict region, and preferably from countries with no direct interest in the zone of conflict.

Fourth, participants in the operation must observe comprehensive neutrality and an 'equal distance' between the sides engaged in the conflict. They should not be involved in any 'preferential' relations with any of the parties involved, nor provide direct or indirect support to any of the conflicting groupings in the realization of their interests at the expense of any other parties.

Finally, military force within the framework of peace-keeping operations can only be used for self-defence. With a broader implementation of peace-enforcement actions this principle has been interpreted with greater flexibility.

Currently, the United Nations is severely limited by its financial, structural and personnel resources in the simultaneous implementation of many parallel peace-keeping operations. This is why the criteria for new UN involvement in conflicts become increasingly severe. For the first time UN officials have recently openly admitted that some UN operations were unsuccesful (including, for example, those in Angola, Cyprus and the Western Sahara). Clearly 'pragmatic' criteria are progressively being taken into consideration by the UN; that is, whether or not involvement in any new crisis situation will obtain clearly visible results relatively quickly and inexpensively. Even in the unlikely event of a UN resolution to intervene in a conflict on the territory of the Former Soviet Union it would be extremely difficult to find any countries ready to send their military contingents to the area (with the exception of newly independent states – the former Soviet republics themselves). The conflicts in the region involve ethnically plural and complex situations.

While analysing current UN operations, especially taking into consideration the multidimensional, difficult experience in the former Yugoslavia, one might conclude that some important shifts have occurred in such operations in the 1990s. Some analysts have labelled them 'second-generation' peacekeeping operations.[1] The primary changes can be summed up as follows. Firstly, there has been a shift to earlier engagements in conflicts to prevent mass violence rather than stabilize a situation after bloodshed has already occurred. Experience has shown that operations started later are less successful. Secondly, there has been the introduction of 'peace-enforcement' operations to disengage forces that are still fighting. This has often happened without the formal consent of one or all sides: that is to say, the 'world community' in the guise of the UN Security Council has felt justified in imposing its will on the conflicting parties. Thirdly, force has been used not only for the self-defence of UN troops but also to clear the area of fighting troops, to stop the shooting or to enforce a cease-fire. The UN's experience in Somalia and the former Yugoslavia has demonstrated the phenomenon of 'surgical bombing' under the name of peace enforcement. Fourthly, there has been a move towards using heavy weaponry and advanced command and control for multilateral peace support forces (including, for example, tanks and certain artillery and air force support). This provides UN forces with 'diplomatic' and real combat capabilities. Finally, there has been the application of 'active diplomacy', pushing the conflicting parties into negotiations, instead of just providing favourable conditions for political settlement and leaving it to the sides themselves to take up the opportunity.

The US-initiated multilateral operation in Iraq and the use of North Atlantic Treaty Organization (NATO) forces under a UN peace-keeping mandate in former Yugoslavia have dramatically changed the traditional parameters of peace-keeping operations. The involvement of a professional multilateral military machine has set a precedent for more forceful, comprehensive and militarily developed 'warlike' operations where conflict participants start to perceive a 'world community' fighting against them and see peace-keeping forces as combatants. Non-traditional peace-keeping practices have been widely used in the 1990s in the peace-keeping operations of

Russia and other countries of the Commonwealth of Independent States (CIS) in the conflict centres on the territory of the Former Soviet Union.

Russia's Conflict Resolution Abroad

Modern Russia is currently in a period of transition, reshaping its foreign and security policy and adjusting to the creation of more than a dozen independent states. Though it began in 1991–2, this process is still far from completion. This transition is dominated by several factors. First, Russia's foreign and security policy is being shaped in a pluralistic political space: instead of a dominating Communist party, many political parties and movements and a 'multi-voice' Parliament (Federal Assembly) are trying to elaborate a shaky consensus. Second, the 'bloc' approach (involving an alliance between the Soviet Union and Communist Eastern European countries) has disappeared, and Russia faces the unusual situation of being forced to begin the search for allies from scratch. Third, the economic and military 'heritage' of the Soviet Union dictates a painful process in the division into republics; the newly independent states produce and reproduce unending frictions and contradictions. Fourth, about 25 million Russians or so-called 'Russian-speaking' people remain outside Russia in the other newly independent states; this Russian-oriented diaspora constantly applies to Moscow for the protection of their rights and creates real and potential ethnic and political conflicts. Finally, Russia's new neighbours, from the Baltic states to the Ukraine, from the Central Asian states to Transcaucasian Georgia, Armenia and Azerbaijan, are still shaping their own statehood, changing orientation and defining their national interests, creating an unstable and constantly moving 'Rubik's cube'. There is no doubt that that demands from Russia quick and lasting adjustment and the adaptation of its own foreign and security policy.

Defining Russia's national security priorities, President Boris Yeltsin, in his address to the Russian Parliament in February 1994 stated:

Recognized principles and norms of international law serve as a foundation for our foreign policy. For the first time for many years Russia has no military adversaries. National security priorities for Russia are the liquidation of armed conflict spots near the Russian border, the strengthening of the regime of non-proliferation of mass-destruction weaponry and new military technologies, and increasing the control of the international arms trade, combined with obeying Russia's commercial interests.[2]

Operations in the Caucasian Region

Introduction

The Caucasian region is not top priority for Russian security policy, competing for attention as it does with other geopolitical regions. The North Caucasus (belonging to the territory of the Russian Federation) and Transcaucasus (shared by Georgia, Armenia and Azerbaijan) is a 'melting-pot' populated by around 40 different small or large ethnic groups and nationalities deeply and historically interconnected. Polyethnicity is multiplied by polyconfessionalism: Christian and Muslim populations are quite intermixed. Stalin's repression in the 1930s and 1940s created artificial national borders, and people were forcibly moved from their native regions to other areas. A multidimensional problem of 'repressed nations' was created, and their current partial return to their native lands creates as many conflicts as it resolves. It should also be noted that, while the whole Caucasian area seems large, there is a shortage of appropriate land for living because of the mountains and rocky soils. Overpopulation in the valleys creates substantial territorial disputes. Deliberate decentralization in policy-making and the dramatic weakening of influence from the 'centre' (Moscow) have caused an explosion in the major 'old' conflicts in this region which were frozen during Soviet years; there have also been some new conflicts.

Moscow's 'Caucasian' policy in 1989–94 can be more or less obviously divided into three periods. The first ran from 1989 until the collapse of the Soviet Union in late 1991 and early 1992. Then Moscow was still interacting with the Caucasian regional forces as if they were 'satellites', and paid particular attention to control. The later *perestroika* years were thus characterized by attempts by many local forces and groups in the Caucasus to gain the upper hand by appealing to Moscow. From 1992 to the first half of 1993 there was an intermediate transitory period. The collapse of Soviet political and economic ties was accompanied by 'revolutions of independence' in the former republics, with a dramatic loss of Moscow's influence. The division of the 'Soviet heritage' and particularly of Soviet army resources and weaponry became a focus for debate. Certain quantities of weaponry fell into the hands of forces in Armenia, Azerbaijan, Georgia, Abkhazia and Ossetia, without any authorization from Moscow, as a result of local 'trade offs', with the participation of emerging political leaders, local military commanders and civil authorities. The third period began in late 1992 when, in different areas of the Caucasian region, Russia started to act as a 'mediating force' to freeze or resolve regional conflicts, trying to provide a policy of stabilization on its southern borders. Instead of its earlier practice of 'taking sides' in conflicts, Russia began trying to limit itself, to operate impartially in peace-keeping activities. This last stage is evoking major international attention and criticism. In some cases there are accusations that Russia just 'emulates' peace-keeping rhetoric but *de facto* projects its 'new imperial interests' into the Caucasus. This is why it is important to get to the legal and factual roots of Russia's operations in the area.

North Ossetia and Ingushetia

In the autumn of 1992 there was an explosion of hostilities between the Ossetian and Ingushetian populations of the North Caucasian area, in the territory of the Russian Federation. The Russian President's Decree No. 1324 'On the imposition of a state of emergency regime on the territory of North Ossetia and the Ingush Republic' was adopted on 2 November 1992. The operation of disengagement was performed jointly by the internal forces of the Russian Ministry of the Interior and units of the North Caucasian military district. The latter consisted of the third batallion of the 503rd motorized rifle regiment, the second batallion of the 429th motorized rifle regiment of the 19th division, the task group of the 132nd separate motorized rifle brigade, and units of the Vladikavkaz garrison. According to the Russian Ministry of Defence, 6964 military personnel, 116 tanks, 276 combat armoured vehicles and 156 artillery units were involved.

The formulated tasks included the disengagement of the sides involved, the prevention of new armed groups from roaming into the conflict zone, the guarding of military installations, and the staged disarming of the sides in Mozdoc, Pravoberezhnij and Prigorodnyi districts, as well as in Vladikavkaz city and the airport. Concurrently with operations in Ossetia, operations were also undertaken in the Nazran and Malogbek districts of the Ingush Republic. These were largely successful.

The exchange of numerous hostages continued over several months during uneasy negotiations. By the Russian President's Decree of 4 April 1994 the state of emergency regime was prolonged over the territory of certain districts of Ossetia and Ingushetia to provide stability, a ceasefire and conditions for negotiations between the respective political authorities. In late 1994 and early 1995 there was a concentration of armed forces and interior forces in the area because of the military operation in the nearby region of Chechenia. The state of emergency was thus prolonged because of the Chechen operation.

South Ossetia

Within the territory of Georgia, South Ossetian autonomy became an area of conflict in 1992 after the South Ossetian authorities expressed their intention to secede. Numerous armed volunteers from North Ossetia swelled the ranks of their 'southern compatriots'. Negotiations between the Russians and Georgians were arranged in Dagomys near Sochi and ended on 24 June 1994, with what is known as the Dagomys agreements on the Georgian–Ossetian conflict settlement.[3] Peacekeeping forces were created on a trilateral basis, including military patrol contingents from Russia, Georgia and Ossetia. Initially, the Russian forces were composed of a regiment from the 76th airborne division. At the present time, the contingent numbers 503 men, along with 37 combat armoured vehicles from the first batallion of the 129th regiment of the 45th Guards motorized rifle division.

Political representatives from the three sides met to establish a commission based in Tzhinval, the capital of South Ossetia. The trilateral military contingent is answerable to this civilian political organ, although progress in achieving a long-term settlement over the status of South Ossetia has been slow. Nevertheless, a cease-fire has been preserved (with minor violations by small armed groups and individuals). Disarmament is not within the mandate of the operation and is not taking place, in contrast to the North Ossetian case.

Abkhazia

Armed hostilities continued for three years on the territory of autonomous Abkhazia, though Russia's formal peace-keeping involvement only began with the Georgian–Abkhazian ceasefire agreement; actual disengagement was achieved on 14 May 1994.[4] The agreement stabilizes the situation between the Georgian and Abkhazian forces on a line formed along the Inguri river. The negotiated mandate for the forces includes the creation of a 12-kilometre-wide 'security zone' along the whole length of the river, and the patrolling of the Kodor Valley after the withdrawal of Georgian troops. One of the important tasks for the Russians is the provision of protection for the numerous returning refugees, especially those from Galsky district.

It is important to note that it was the Georgians and Abkhazians themselves who applied for CIS combined peace-keeping forces to be sent to Abkhazia. The legal decision by the CIS heads of states could only be processed (under the condition of political consensus) at the CIS summit. At the time of writing only Russia had preliminarily nominated a contingent (about 3000 men) for this purpose. Any practical involvement of this contingent in the operation was, however, temporarily suspended by a veto of the upper chamber of the Russian parliament. Nevertheless, about 1100 Russian soldiers have been allocated for the whole duration of hostilities. They are located in the area with the limited mission of protecting military installations and humanitatian supplies, without interfering in the conflict.

The Trilateral Operation in Moldova–Transdnestria

The roots of another conflict involving Russian forces dates back to 1992, when the Transdnestrian area of the former Soviet Republic of Moldova, populated mainly by Russians, rejected subordination to the government of the newly independent state of Moldova. A separate Transdnestrian Moldavian Republic was proclaimed in the region as a reaction to the strong policy towards the regions from the central Moldavian authorities. The stakes at this stage were especially high for the Moldavian government because the region was industrially among the most developed in Moldova and was a significant energy supplier for the whole state. It also possessed much of the most skilled manpower and housed the headquarters and garrisons of the former Soviet (now Russian) 14th Army. Tensions exploded in the summer of 1992, with mass armed violence between supporters of the Kishinev central authorities and the proponents of a separate Transdnestrian state. A chain reaction of uncontrolled mass clashes began to spread, involving many civilian casualties.

Under these circumstances, a preliminary trilateral political agreement was achieved between the Russian, Moldavian and Transdnestrian leaders, and later a basic document was signed by President Yeltsin of Russia, President Mircea Snegur of Moldova and representatives of Transdnestria.[5] This agreement became a mandate for the disengagement operation performed by Russian troops, and trilateral patrols of the area to prevent the unauthorized use of arms. It is important to stress that locally based contingents of the 14th Army were not used for the operation – batallions of the 45th motorized division of the Leningrad military district and the 106th airborne division were deployed. By mid-August, after the disengagement and ceasefire operation (started on 23 July 1992), the peace-enforcement operation changed to a peace-keeping one. Trilateral peace-keeping forces were composed of four Russian batallions (about 1800 men) plus three Moldavian and three Transdnestrian batallions.

The United Control Commission was created as the main multilateral political organ supervising the peace-support efforts, and was responsible for further diplomatic negotiations and the peaceful settlement of the crisis. Formally, all the military authorities involved in peace-keeping were under the jurisdiction of the commission. Though a political settlement has not yet been achieved, both the peace-enforcement and peace-keeping stages of the operations were more or less effective in achieving their goals; there have been no reported cases of major armed conflict in the region since 1992. The Organization for Security and Co-operation in Europe (OSCE) set up a long-term observers' mission in the region, which co-operates with the trilateral Russian–Moldavian–Transdnestrian political and military authorities. The political situation is moving slowly towards the preservation of a higher level of autonomy for the Transdnestrian region, but still within the internationally recognized state of Moldova. Though the industrial, agricultural and civil life of the region is being significantly revitalized, the conditions for the removal of peace-keeping contingents from the area have not yet been achieved.

Tajikistan: The Development of CIS Peace-keeping

Operations in Tajikistan are of a different status, mandate and structure than those previously described. The uniqueness of the Tajik operations lies in their broader multinational character and in the presence of a full CIS mandate. Operations in Tajikistan started on a full-scale basis in October 1993, after the end of the most bloody stage in the regional civil war. The war brought new leadership to power in the capital city of Dushanbe, and armed hostilities between the different clans and ethnic groupings took tens of thousands of lives over several months. Opposition forces had established connections with mujahedins from Afghanistan, who regularly entered the country across the poorly controlled mountain border (the tribal and ethnic interconnections between Afghans and Tajiks are significant). The Dushanbe government was afraid that the armed groups on the territory of Tajikistan itself would get out of control. Such groups had amorphous origins and goals, and there were endless mutual hostilities which led to bloody clashes and a terrorizing of the civilian population.

Reacting to appeals for help from the Dushanbe authorities, the heads of states from the CIS countries adopted joint statements on the situation (in October 1992 and January 1993) and an agreement on the creation of multilateral CIS peace-keeping forces for Tajikistan.[6] This agreement was concluded on 24 September 1993, after tension increased inside Tajikistan and particularly at the Tajik–Afghan border.

Initially, it was decided that military contingents from Russia, Kazakhstan, Kyrgyzstan, Uzbekistan and Tajikistan would comprise the peace-keeping forces. Several months later Tajik forces were excluded to ensure impartiality. The decisive contribution was from Russia, with around 6000 men of the 201st motorized division (situated in the region during the Soviet era).

Small contingents were provided by Kyrgyzstan and Uzbekistan, but later the parliaments of Kazakhstan and Kyrgyzstan opposed the participation of their soldiers in operations outside national borders. In early 1995, less than 10,000 troops were involved in operations (in contrast to the approved but unrealized plans to increase them to 25,000). While these forces perform peace-enforcement and disarming tasks, the separate but crucial task of sealing the border between Tajikistan and Afghanistan is performed by the Russian border guards at the request of the Tajik government.

The nature of the operations has shifted from an emphasis on a ceasefire and the disarming of armed groups to the more effective, CIS-supported efforts to seal the border, to prevent the free movement of armed mujahedin, drugs and weapons across the border: threats not only to Tajikistan but to all the nearby Central Asian CIS states and to Russia (borders are open within the CIS). The operations have been difficult and costly, and the bill has been paid almost entirely by the Russians. Though many local gangs are disarmed and certain areas are under control, intertribal hostilities continue, leading to prolonged destabilization of the region. The possible settlement in Tajikistan is not one between visible 'sides', but rather a multilateral balance of power among numerous mutually hostile, amorphous armed groups influenced by the border war.

Specific Features of Russian Peace-keeping Operations

Several main features are characteristic of the Russian peace-keeping operations. First, they exist under a 'reduced' mandate. In contrast to UN practice operating through UN Security Council resolutions, a bilateral or trilateral decision (agreement) by representatives of the conflicting sides is considered to be the mandate necessary to initiate the operation. Typically, the initial political agreement provides only a partial definition of the operational tasks, and 'adjustment' is made later within the course of the operation. Second, instead of using forces from 'impartial' third parties, peace-keeping forces involve contingents from the conflicting parties, and by Russia (which typically has its own security interests in the area). Third, representatives of international organs (such as UN or OSCE observers) operate separately from the peace-keeping forces. Fourth, there is a visible shift from peace-keeping activities to peace-enforcement operations (including establishing and maintaining cease-fires, and actively disarming groups within the conflict areas). Though different from UN practices, this type of operation in the Caucasus, Tajikistan and Moldova nevertheless retains the main technical features of peace-keeping and peace-enforcement activities carried out by the United Nations.

UN, OSCE and NATO representatives have often rejected any possibility of the international community taking responsibility for providing stability on the territory of the Former Soviet Union. Although criticizing Russia for deviations from UN practices, representatives of international organizations have nevertheless expressed an understanding that its efforts to stabilize conflict areas in regions contiguous to its borders could be the only possible option for promoting chances for peace.

Russian diplomacy and military missions are trying to proceed stage by stage, from stopping the conflict, to conflict resolution, and possibly later to conflict prevention. A considerable arsenal of measures for conflict resolution and preventive diplomacy have been elaborated and tested, and it is important to compare how they fit into the international criteria elaborated within the implementation of UN-supported operations.

Preventive Diplomacy Arsenal

The notion of 'preventive diplomacy', as it is used in the UN Secretary-General's well-known document 'Agenda for Peace', has been widely used in conflict areas. There is an elaborate arsenal of preventive diplomacy tools (for use by multilateral civilian and military personnel). An analysis and comparison of the UN experience with the Russian operations on CIS territory can be summarized in the following measures applicable for conflict prevention and resolution at different stages in the conflict.[7]

Confidence-building measures include:

- the development of contacts between multilateral contingents and political civilian authorities representing the different sides and politically influential forces;
- the development of contacts between peace-keeping personnel and local military forces and commanders;
- the use of diplomatic, civilian and civilian–military mediating missions and inspections, as well as fact-finding missions to the conflict region;
- the development of effective dialogue with mass-media representatives. (This would involve serious attention being paid to providing regular up-to-date press releases on tensions in the area and the scope of operations, organizing special press conferences involving representatives of those involved in the dispute, mediated by peace-keeping mission representatives, and providing for the safety of journalists.)

Early conflict-prevention measures include:

- the comprehensive gathering and analysis of information;
- economic sanctions;
- blockading the region;
- the prevention of the activities of armed insurgent groups and the halting of imports of armaments into the conflict region.

The deployment of military forces aimed at limiting the escalation of conflict may involve:

- a demonstration of force in support of political appeals addressed to all sides;
- the disengagement of rival sides in areas where they might start provoking or probing each other;
- the partial evacuation of the population or endangered ethnic minorities out of the area of potential conflict, if necessary;
- the provision of humanitarian, medical and food aid to the population in the area of conflict.

The creation of demilitarized zones in the conflict regions may involve:

- the establishment and support of a no-fly zone in the region to prevent bombing and other means of mass destruction;
- the control of the means of communication (including jamming) used by conflicting parties for operational and propaganda purposes;
- providing a cease-fire regime;
- the creation of 'corridors' open for the supply of humanitarian aid.

Additionally, if an armed conflict breaks out and a 'peace-enforcement' mandate is provided for the peace-keeping multilateral forces in the area, there might be specified objectives and strategies to stop the conflict, such as:

- disarming and arresting unauthorized armed groupings;
- re-establishment of infrastructure and state borders;
- protection of legally elected civilian authorities;
- provision of conditions for free elections of civilian authorities after the conflict ends (if the former power structure is distrusted or dismissed);
- protection of refugees or migrants, including the organization of refugees camps, providing medical assistance and food supplies;

- protection of ethnic minorities;
- interpositional 'screening' between the conflicting parties during negotiations;
- protection of basic human rights of the civilian population;
- gradual expansion of the demilitarized zone;
- protection of strategic objects and installations (such as mass destruction and conventional weaponry arsenals, nuclear power stations, border posts, dams, large industrial complexes) from destruction or damage;
- protection of diplomatic, mediation and negotiation missions.

Modern peace-keeping practice shows that *de facto* national military forces (as in the case of Russia) and international military contingents (such as NATO forces in the former Yugoslavia or CIS forces in Tajikistan) begin to implement not only clearly military functions but also functions of a humanitarian, diplomatic and mediatory character. They often initiate and participate in negotiations, inform the mass media about current developments, distribute humanitarian aid, work with refugees and ethnic minorities, trace human rights violations, and provide conditions for post-conflict political settlement and elections. Such activities should be performed under appropriate political and civilian control. It is also extremely important to promote the participation of wider non-governmental organizations in conflict settlement.

The world community is becoming more experienced in the elaboration, organization and implementation of peace-support, peace-enforcement, peace-keeping and peace-protecting activities. To ensure that such non-traditional peace-keeping is as legal and non-confrontational as possible has become one of the most important tasks on the modern international agenda.

Notes

1   A detailed description of these types of changes in peace-support operations can be found in J. Mackinlay and J. Chopra, *Draft Manual of Second-Generation Multinational Operations: Concept of Operations* (Thomas J. Watson Institute for International Studies, Brown University, 1994).

2   'Strengthening Russian Statehood', Address of the President of the Russian Federation to the Federal Assembly, 24 February 1994.

3   Agreement on the Principles of Settlement of the Georgian–Ossetian Conflict, signed at Sochi on 24 June 1992.

4   Recent documents regulating plans for the use of force in the Abkhazian region include: Statement on the Measures towards Political Settlement of the Georgian–Abkhazian Conflict, signed in Moscow, 4 April 1994; Statement on the Measures of the Heads of the CIS States, Documents of the CIS Summit of 15 April 1994; and Agreement on the Cease-fire and Forces Disengagement, Moscow, 14 May 1994.

5   'Agreement on the Principles of the Peaceful Settlement of the Armed Conflict in the Transdnestrian Region of Moldova', signed in Moscow on 21 July 1992.

6   The first collective CIS agreements were adopted at the CIS summits in Kiev and Tashkent. The main documents regulating the creation (still unaccomplished) of the CIS forces and their involvement in Tajikistan are the following: Agreement on the Military Observers Groups and Collective Peace-keeping Forces in the CIS, Kiev, 20 March 1992; Protocol on the Status of the Military Observers Groups and Collective Peace-keeping Forces of the Commonwealth of Independent States, 15 May 1992; Protocol on the Temporary Order of Formation and Use of the Groups of Military Observers and Collective Peace-keeping Forces in the Zones of Conflicts between the CIS States and inside the States-Members of the CIS, Tashkent, 16 July 1992; Statement of the Heads of the CIS States in Connection with the Social–Political Situation in the Republic of Tajikistan, Minsk, 22 January 1993; Agreement on the Collective Peace-keeping Forces and Joint Measures on their Logistical and Technical Maintenance, Moscow, 24 September 1993; and Decision on the Terms of Deployment, Composition and Tasks of the Collective Peace-keeping Forces in Tajikistan, Moscow, 15 April 1994.

7   The preventive diplomacy arsenal was analysed in detail at the Science Application International Corporation/US European Command Conference in Heidelberg, October 1993.

9 The Conventional Arms Treaty in the New Europe

Douglas L. Clarke

Introduction

The Treaty on Conventional Armed Forces in Europe (commonly known as the CFE Treaty) was signed in Paris on 19 November 1990 by the leaders of the 22 states possessing the bulk of the armed forces deployed in Europe.[1] This ambitious, complicated and unique agreement between the members of the North Atlantic Treaty Organization (NATO) and the states that once made up the Warsaw Treaty Organization (WTO) aimed to reduce the possibility of a conventional war in Europe between NATO and the WTO by setting European ceilings and geographic limitations on five categories of offensive conventional weaponry: tanks, armoured combat vehicles (ACVs), artillery, combat aircraft and attack helicopters. In follow-on negotiations known as CFE1A, the CFE states declared 'politically binding' limits on the number of land-based military personnel they would station in Europe. Adapting this last of the Cold War arms control agreements to the New Europe has proved to be a challenging task.

The CFE Treaty was all the more remarkable in that it grew out of the corpse of one of the most frustrating arms control negotiations ever, the 15-year unsuccessful effort to achieve Mutual and Balanced Force Reductions (MBFR) in Europe. How could CFE succeed where MBFR had failed? The new leadership of the Soviet Union was the primary factor, as well as NATO's ability to recognize the dramatic changes taking place in the ranks of its traditional enemy – the WTO – and its willingness to seize this opportunity to reduce military tensions in Europe. Important stepping stones on the road to this accord were the May 1986 North Atlantic Council call for 'bold new steps' in conventional arms control and the 11 June 1986 Budapest Appeal of the WTO suggesting negotiated mutual cuts of up to 500,000 military personnel. Informal talks on the CFE mandate began in Vienna on

17 February 1987. Soviet President Mikhail Gorbachev gave the process considerable impetus on 7 December 1988 with his address to the United Nations in which he announced unilateral cuts in the Soviet armed forces and the withdrawal of substantial numbers of men and military equipment from the Soviet forces in Eastern Europe. The CFE talks proper began on 9 March 1989 in Vienna between the 16 members of NATO and what were then the seven members of the WTO. The talks went on against the backdrop of the dramatic changes in Eastern Europe, German unification and the effective dissolution of the WTO itself. At their Malta summit meeting in December 1989, Presidents George Bush and Gorbachev pledged to seek completion of the CFE agreement by the end of 1990, the signing to be the high point of a Conference on Security and Co-operation in Europe (CSCE) summit. While much was accomplished in a relatively short span it took the November 1990 deadline of the CSCE summit meeting to spur the negotiators to find last-minute solutions to a few of the issues thought to have been intractable. The CFE Treaty was signed in Paris on 19 November at that summit by the 22 remaining original negotiators. By the time it entered into force, on 17 July 1992, both the WTO and the Soviet Union had ceased to exist. Most of the latter's successor states – with the notable exception of the Baltic republics – joined the treaty, raising to first 29 and then 30 (following the division of Czechoslovakia) the number of 'state parties' bound by it.

The treaty established numerical equality between the weapons holdings of the two opposing blocs, a radical departure from the Cold War *status quo*. By the end of 1995 each alliance could have no more than 20,000 tanks, 30,000 ACVs, 20,000 pieces of artillery, 6800 combat aircraft and 2000 attack helicopters deployed in Europe, which was defined as stretching from the Atlantic to the Ural Mountains. The ceilings, in general, were set at levels slightly lower than the NATO inventory, which meant that the bulk of the cuts would have to be made by the former WTO states. Although this numerical balance between opposing alliances was at the very core of the treaty, this fundamental premise has become increasingly irrelevant due to the dramatic political changes that have subsequently taken place in Europe. The members of each alliance (or group of state parties as they are referred to in the treaty) then decided among themselves how they would apportion their group's allowances. These national maximum levels have become far more important than the bloc limits from which they are derived. These allowed national holdings for the states of the former WTO and the successor states of the Soviet Union, plus each country's CFE1A personnel declarations, as shown in Table 1.

Not surprisingly, due to its Cold War origins, the CFE Treaty has very much of an East–West orientation, both in ideological and in geographical terms. It lays out a series of roughly concentric zones that radiate out along

Table 1: National Holdings for Former WTO States and Successor States of the Soviet Union

	Tanks	ACVs	Artillery	Aircraft	Helicopters	Personnel
Armenia	220	220	285	100	50	60,000
Azerbaijan	220	220	285	100	50	ND
Belarus	1800	2600	1615	260	80	100,000
Bulgaria	1475	2000	1750	235	67	104,000
Czech Rep.	957	1367	767	230	50	110,010
Georgia	220	220	285	100	50	40,000
Hungary	835	1700	840	180	108	100,000
Moldova	210	210	250	50	50	20,000
Poland	1730	2150	1610	460	130	234,000
Romania	1375	2100	1475	430	120	230,248
Russia	6400	11,480	6415	3450	890	1,450,000
Slovakia	478	683	383	115	25	46,667
Ukraine	4080	5050	4040	1090	330	450,000
Total	20,000	30,000	20,000	6800	2000	

Source: *Arms Control Today,* March 1993, pp. 28–9.

an East–West axis from what had long been seen as the cockpit of Europe: the Central Area, consisting of Germany, the Low Countries, Poland, Czecho-slovakia (now the Czech Republic and Slovakia) and Hungary. The treaty's various zones have been likened to the traditional Russian *matrushka* dolls, in that they are nested one inside the other. This concept allowed free movement of military equipment away from, but not towards, this Central Area. Here the various Soviet groups of forces would have been entitled to 3500 tanks, 5350 ACVs and 1400 artillery pieces. Since all these troops will have left the zone before the treaty's November 1995 deadline, these entitle-ments are meaningless.

The next larger treaty zone is what is called the Expanded Central Area. It adds Great Britain, France, Italy and Denmark on the NATO side while bringing in what were formerly four military districts (MDs) within the Soviet Union on the WTO side: the Baltic, Belorussian, Carpathian and Kiev MDs. Now, of course, these additions, comprise the independent Bal-tic Republics, Belarus and a good part of Ukraine. The only portion of the Expanded Central Area that belongs to Russia is the Kaliningrad Oblast, a 15,100-square-kilometre enclave separated from the rest of Russia by Lithuania, Poland and Belarus. The three Baltic Republics have opted out of the CFE Treaty, and while any Russian troops in the region would count against Russia's ceilings, the Russian military is entirely out of Lithuania and should be out of Estonia and Latvia before November 1995. Russia could theoretically stuff some 4200 tanks, almost 8800 ACVs and more than 3200 artillery pieces into Kaliningrad Oblast, although such a development would make little military sense and would certainly have serious negative political repercussions for Moscow. Nevertheless, as shall be discussed more fully below, the Russians have pointed to this treaty anomaly as one of the reasons they feel the treaty's flanks limits should be relaxed.

The Expanded Central Area includes two of the three Ukrainian military districts, the former Soviet Carpathian and Kiev MDs. The Odessa MD (now apparently to be known as the Ukrainian Southern Command) is outside the area, a serious complication for the Ukrainians.

The Expanded Central Area is contained within what the treaty terms the Extended Area. Spain and Portugal are brought in on the NATO side while the area extends to the east to encompass the Russian Moscow MD and what was known, in 1990, as the Volga–Ural MD. (This latter district had been formed the previous year by combining the older Volga and Ural MDs. In July 1992 this larger district was renamed simply the Volga MD and a new Ural MD was established east of the Urals – and therefore outside the CFE Treaty's area of application – largely out of territory that had belonged to the Siberian MD.) The Moscow and Volga–Urals MDs were once rear support areas for the Soviet military, containing mostly low-readiness units. The premier Soviet units were deployed in Eastern Europe with the various Soviet groups of forces, while the best divisions on Soviet soil were fanned across the arc of border military districts that are now foreign territory: the Baltic, Belorussian, Carpathian, Odessa and Kiev MDs. For Moscow, the centre of military gravity has moved far to the east. More than 80 per cent of the Russian arms covered by the treaty – the so-called TLEs (treaty limited equipment) – will have to be stationed or stored in the Moscow and Volga MDs under the terms of the treaty.

The Shrinking Flanks

The CFE Treaty's Western authors sought, through the limits on each of the nested zones described above, to cripple the Soviet Union's ability to mount what was to NATO the classic threat of a multi-echeloned WTO attack through Germany. Almost as an afterthought, and largely due to Norwegian and Turkish concerns that the Soviets might divert forces squeezed out of Central Europe to their vicinities, limits were also placed on the offensive conventional arms that could be stationed on the northern and southern flanks of Europe. Both Russia and Ukraine are dissatisfied with the restrictions placed upon them by these flanks limits.

The flank zone in the north consists of Russia's Leningrad MD, Norway and Iceland. The southern flank is made up of Greece and Turkey on the NATO side, and Romania, Bulgaria and what were once the Odessa, North Caucasus and Trans-Caucasus MDs of the Soviet Union. Despite the fact that there are two flank zones (and rather widely separated ones at that), the treaty places but one collective set of limits on the flanks. Thus, for example, the group of states making up the former WTO can deploy 4700 tanks in active units on the flanks. It is up to the states involved to decide how they should apportion this force. The first cut took place before the dissolution of the Soviet Union when the former members of the WTO divided up their 'group of state parties' allocation. Again using tanks as an example, they agreed that of the 4700 allowed on the flanks, Bulgaria would have 1475, Romania 1375 and the Soviet Union 1850.

The dissolution of the Soviet Union necessitated another cutting of the pie. This took place at Tashkent on 15 May 1992. By that time the former Soviet portion of the southern flank was made up of Georgia, Armenia and Azerbaijan in place of what had been the Trans-Caucasus MD, as well as Moldova and what was now the Ukrainian Odessa MD instead of the Soviet Odessa MD. All that remained to Russia in the south was the North Caucasus MD. Table 2 shows the flanks limits for the successor states of the former Soviet Union.

In their informal discussions regarding the need to revise the CFE Treaty the Russians cited the virulent civil unrest in the Caucasus, civil war in Georgia, an open conflict between Armenia and Azerbaijan, and the grow-

Table 2: Former Soviet Active Equipment Ceilings on the Flanks[2]

	Tanks	ACVs	Artillery	Total
Russia	700	580	1280	2560
Ukraine	280	350	390	1020
Moldova	210	210	250	670
Georgia	220	220	285	725
Armenia	220	220	285	725
Azerbaijan	220	220	285	725
Total	1850	1800	2775	6425

Source: *The Arms Control Reporter*, November 1993, p. 407.B.492.

ing threat of militant Islamic fundamentalism fomented by Iran as reasons why the earlier limits are no longer reasonable. With Russia tending to support Armenia and with both Iran and Turkey – each Moslem and sharing a common border with Moslem Azerbaijan – even more clearly championing Azerbaijan, the struggle over Nagorno-Karabakh could spill over and directly involve the three larger powers. Iranian troops have been reported in Azerbaijan, while Turkey is said to have reinforced its forces along its frontier with Armenia; and Russian border troops patrolling this frontier on the Armenian side have been fired upon from Turkish territory.[3]

On 28 September 1993 Russia formally brought the flanks issue to the Joint Consultative Group (JCG) in Vienna – a forum established by the CFE Treaty to consider, among other things, matters of dispute arising from the treaty's implementation. Vyacheslav Kulebiakin, the head of the Russian delegation, proposed that the signatories of the treaty agree to suspend Article V, the article which sets out the flanks limits. He cited the existing and potential conflicts in the Caucasus as one of the reasons justifying this step, and pointed out that the East–West orientation of the Treaty was obsolete.[4] An earlier Russian *démarche* on the flanks limits had stressed this same point, complaining that 'the preservation of flanks limitations would "freeze" the building of our forces in the east–west direction, not permitting us to reorient it in the north–south direction as a number of the NATO countries do (for example, Spain and Italy), proceeding from the new challenges to security'.[5]

The Russians also claimed that the treaty had become discriminatory since the collapse of the WTO and the Soviet Union, since it now required Russia to deploy the major portion of its forces either deep in the rear, or in such politically sensitive places as Kaliningrad Oblast or along its western borders with Belarus and Ukraine. They noted that the Leningrad and North Caucasus MDs comprised more than one-half the territory of European Russia yet was limited, under the treaty, to accommodating only 20 per cent of Russia's tanks, 12 per cent of the ACVs and 26 per cent of the artillery. Finally, Kulebiakin talked of the difficulties of finding locations to house the troops being withdrawn from Germany and the Baltic Republics. Garrisons were available on the flanks, particularly in the North Caucasus MD, to accept these troops, and the Russians would like to use these existing facilities and avoid the expense of building new bases elsewhere.

While the NATO countries recognize that the situation has changed, they argue that the CFE Treaty already provides some flexibility to Russia, particularly in combating any civil unrest along its southern borders. Article XII of the treaty allows Russia to deploy 600 armoured infantry fighting vehicles (a subset of the ACV category which includes such common Soviet/Russian equipment as the BMP and BMD series) on the flanks as long as they belonged to internal security units rather than the armed forces proper. According to one Russian commentator, there were in May 1993 three and one-half motorized rifle divisions subordinated to the Russian Internal Affairs Ministry in the North Caucasus MD.[6] This extra allowance could roughly have accommodated the ACVs in these units, but not their tanks and artillery. The treaty also permits Russia to make a 'temporary' deployment of 153 tanks, 241 ACVs and 140 pieces of artillery to the flanks – not enough equipment to outfit a motorized rifle division.

Turkey has been the strongest opponent of any move to relax Russia's flanks limits. According to the Turkish Foreign Ministry, Boris Yeltsin advised Turkish President Suleyman Demirel in mid-September 1993 that Russia would have liked to see the flanks limits lifted. The Turks reacted by forwarding Yeltsin's proposal to their NATO allies with the request that it be rejected.[7] This Turkish opposition might be called hypocritical in that the CFE Treaty excludes a significant portion of south-eastern Turkey – meaning that arms in that region of the country are not counted against Turkey's or NATO's allowances. The rationale used by the Turks during the treaty negotiations was that Turkey faced a threat from the south in Syria and Iraq, and thus her armed forces in the south-east should not figure in the East–West balance.

The Russian military's dissatisfaction with the CFE flanks limits stems from the fact that the two military districts involved – Leningrad (particularly the southern portion) and North Caucasus – have been thrust into a completely different role since the dissolution of the Soviet Union. Russian Defence Minister Pavel Grachev has announced the 'complete restructuring' of the North Caucasus MD which, in his words, has become 'the main district of the Russian Armed forces', as well as the strengthening of the Moscow and Leningrad MDs which had become, to his 'greatest vexation', border districts.[8] While the Leningrad MD has always been charged with protecting the important naval and strategic nuclear facilities on the Kola Peninsula, the main bulwark for the vital Leningrad/St Petersburg region had been in the Baltic MD. Russian troops will soon be withdrawn completely from the Baltic countries, leaving the southern Leningrad MD as the first line of defence in the Baltic – save for the isolated Kaliningrad Oblast. According to the London-based International Institute for Strategic Studies, six motorized rifle divisions, and one airborne and one artillery division have been stationed in the district, equipped with a total of 1350 tanks, 1840 ACVs and 1170 artillery pieces.[9] These figures are likely to grow, since the Russians have indicated that some of the units being withdrawn from the Baltic countries are being redeployed to the southern Leningrad MD.[10] Grachev in December 1992 told a group of Leningrad MD officers that a new army grouping would be formed in the district, one combining the best units to be withdrawn from the Baltic countries and Germany. He said that the district had now become a strategically important border district 'covering the north-west of Russia'.[11]

The transformation of the North Caucasus MD has been even more marked. During the Soviet era it had been a rear echelon district sheltered behind the Kiev, Odessa and Trans-Caucasus MDs, and with only low-readiness units. The dismemberment of the Soviet Union has thrust it into a front-line role. It encompasses Russia's only outlets to the Caspian and Black Seas as well as its border with Georgia and Azerbaijan. The district also borders on Ukraine and Kazakhstan. Grachev has pledged that a new 'combat' district would be formed in place of the old, and its task would be 'to contain possible combat operations in the southern sector'.[12] To this end, he revealed that two airborne and two motorized brigades had already been formed in the district with a third motorized brigade on the way, while an airborne division was being moved there along with military transport and army aviation units. A later reference indicated that a second airborne division had been transferred to the district.[13]

These units are the first components of the new mobile forces that are the wave of the future for the Russian military. One Russian military analyst has described them as being 'distinguished by smallness of size and … high efficiency, equipped with state-of-the-art weapons and combat hardware'.[14] While ultimately the core of the rapid-reaction mobile forces would be centralized in the Ural and Volga MDs, the vital first echelon is to be based in the North Caucasus MD.[15] In line with the new trend in Russian military thinking, the ground forces are transitioning from division structures to a more flexible organization built on corps and brigades. Grachev has indicated that in the longer term the very concept of military districts might be abandoned in Russia, to be replaced by four to six 'strategic commands' with geographical designations. One of these would be the North Caucasus command.[16]

Prior to the current reorganization Russia reportedly had 550 tanks, 180 ACVs and 530 artillery pieces in the North Caucasus MD.[17] Until more details are made public regarding the size and equipment of the new brigades it is impossible to determine how far these weapons would go in meeting the projected requirements of the region. Clearly they will not be enough. And certainly the total of 700 tanks, 580 ACVs and 1280 artillery pieces allotted to Russia for the combined inventories of the Leningrad and North Caucasus MDs will fall far short of the General Staff's needs, bearing in mind that the estimates of the recent combined totals are roughly 2000 in each category, and these in districts that are to be *strengthened*.

Grachev had indicated that, at a minimum, Russia would like to be able to locate weapons anywhere on its territory without regard to regional sublimits. At a March 1993 press conference he said that, 'owing to changes in the situation ... weapons will have to be moved from one [military] district to another while keeping the agreed general ceiling intact'.[18] Such flexibility would be available should Article V be suspended as the Russians have proposed. Of the 30 states party to the treaty, only Russia and Ukraine have restrictions on where weapons could be stationed on their own territories[19] and, indeed, the Ukrainians co-sponsored the Russian JCG initiative of 28 September 1993. Ukraine lies astride the boundary separating the Southern Flank from the Expanded Area. The treaty limits them to stationing just under 10 per cent of their equipment in active units in the former Odessa Military District – which comprises 23 per cent of Ukraine's territory. This 'singularity' argument seems to be the only one that has elicited any sympathy for the Russian/Ukrainian efforts to garner support for amending the treaty.[20] Virtually all the other signatories (the exceptions being Belarus and Armenia) are against the Russian suggestions either on philosophical or security grounds, despite the obvious irrelevance in post-Cold War Europe of lumping together weapons in the far north and far south of the country. After all, Pechanga, in the Leningrad MD along the border with Norway on the Kola Peninsula, is more than 3300 kilometres from Derbent, on the Caspian Sea coast in the North Caucasus MD – a distance greater than that from Moscow to London.

Should the treaty parties not wish to suspend the flanks limitations, Russian First Deputy Chief of Staff General Vladimir Zhurbenko has suggested another solution – that of recategorizing the North Caucasus MD as a rear district rather than one on the flanks.[21] This approach would not alleviate Ukraine's problem, and would certainly disturb Russia's northern neighbours as it implies a large build-up in the Leningrad MD.

Russian efforts to change the treaty have been persistent. The generals have never been particularly enamoured with it. They blame their present predicament on overzealous diplomats in the Foreign Ministry more eager to accommodate the West than to protect Soviet/Russian vital interests. The dissolution of the Soviet empire has been a traumatic experience for the military. As its leaders seek to develop both a new military doctrine and a new force structure to meet the many challenges they perceive in this new world, they will place far more stock on their professional judgement than the legal obligations of an unpopular treaty. The Russians have already warned that they might be forced to go their own way on this issue. In the *démarche* of September 1983, they cautioned that 'the lack of a solution of the flanks limitations problem ... could force Russia to consider the possibility of taking adequate unilateral measures in order to ensure its security', including those that would not 'respond fully to the spirit of the treaty'.[22] There is a very real danger that a Western failure to reach some sort of amicable accommodation on the flanks limits will nurture a 'Versailles' mentality among the Russian military leadership – resentment of an unjust treaty forced upon a weakened opponent. Many senior officers remain suspicious of Western motives and intentions. The conservatives in the Russian military establishment are likely to use this issue as the litmus test in judging whether or not their new security 'colleagues' in the West are truly interested in promoting the equal security of all the treaty's signatories, or wish to gain a unilateral military advantage over Russia.

Uneven Burdens

While the treaty has been lauded as curbing an arms race in Europe, particularly among the newly independent states of the former Soviet Union, there are expenses involved in its implementation. Each state must either destroy or convert any excess TLEs it might have in order to reach its authorized ceilings. In treaty terms, this obligation is known as a state's 'reduction liability', and it was determined by subtracting the state's authorized national holdings – reached by negotiations within each group of states – from the inventory of tanks, combat aircraft and other treaty-limited offensive equipment that state possessed when the treaty was signed. Over the 40 months allowed to reach the treaty ceilings a grand total of more than 42,000 offensive weapons, combat aircraft and attack helicopters will be taken out of service throughout Europe. Twenty-five per cent of these excess arms had to be either destroyed or converted by 16 November 1993, the end of the first reduction phase. By all accounts this goal was met. The Acting Director of the United States Arms Control and Disarmament Agency, Thomas Graham, reported to the UN General Assembly in October 1993 that over 13,900 military items had been destroyed or converted by the 30 states party to the treaty.[23] The next due date was set at 16 November 1994, by which time 60 per cent of the reduction liability had to be met. The final limits had to be reached no later than 16 November 1995, 40 months after the treaty came into force.

Since the former WTO had more weapons than NATO it is not surprising that the countries that once were part of the WTO generally have higher reduction liabilities than their NATO counterparts. Indeed, except for the special case of Germany – which inherited the former East German armaments – the NATO countries' liabilities can be measured in the hundreds. (Germany must destroy or convert 9457 TLEs, more than any other signatory.) Russia must eliminate more equipment (8206 TLEs) than any other former member of the WTO, but most of the Soviet Union's former allies or successor states have significant obligations: impoverished Romania must destroy more than 5000 TLEs, Ukraine more than 4000, Belarus more than 3100, the Czech Republic nearly 2700, Poland more than 2000, Slovakia 1345 and Bulgaria just over 1400. (In nationalizing the Soviet forces on their territories, Belarus and Ukraine inherited the cream of the Soviet armoured forces, which had traditionally been deployed in the forward military districts. As a consequence, Belarus must destroy 1657 tanks and Ukraine 1972 – numbers greater than Russia's tank reduction liability of 1593.) The reduction process is not a cheap one (the Germans have reported that it costs them DM11,000 to destroy one tank), and the treaty obligations represent a significant financial burden for the countries of Eastern Europe and the former Soviet Union.

The break-up of the WTO has also effectively denied the poorer states once in that alliance one of the benefits available to their NATO counterparts: receiving modern equipment cast off by their more affluent partners. In a process known as 'cascading', the United States and Germany have transferred large numbers of tanks, armoured personnel carriers and artillery pieces to Turkey, Greece, Spain, Portugal, Norway and Denmark. The recipients, in turn, are obliged to destroy some of their older equipment should the transfers bring them over their CFE allowances, but the process raises the qualitative level of NATO arms across the board. Most of the countries of Eastern Europe could have profited from a similar programme. Poland, for example, will be left with a large number of outdated T-55 tanks even after it has destroyed more than 1000 tanks required by the treaty. Belarus and Ukraine, on the other hand, will be destroying some more modern tanks like the T-62 and T-64 and perhaps even some T-72s. Were the Eastern CFE countries still thinking in alliance terms, this more modern equipment could have been 'cascaded' to Poland, allowing that country to destroy more T-55s while improving the overall quality of its tank park. But, of course, the political and security cohesion of the Eastern group of states within CFE was lost long ago, and well before the treaty negotiations had ended. The perpetuation of this figment is one of the most obvious anomalies in the treaty, and has some troublesome practical implications.

One relatively minor anomaly concerns stored equipment. The treaty largely regulates the offensive military equipment that is deployed with active military units, but it also has some provisions for stored equipment. Such equipment must be in special permanent storage sites that are subject to verification. There are aggregate group limits for the numbers of tanks, ACVs, or artillery pieces that can be removed from storage. This means, for example, that Poland would have to co-ordinate with all the other countries in its 'group of states' before removing some of its tanks from storage, and might be unable legally to do so should, let us say, Russia and Ukraine have already activated the 550 tanks allowed by the treaty.

The pressure for NATO to accept some of the countries of Eastern Europe for membership (particularly the Visegrad grouping of Poland, the Czech Republic, Slovakia and Hungary) is growing steadily. How would the CFE Treaty be adapted to such an expansion? The Russians have hinted that they would insist on retaining the treaty's bloc limits. This would mean that the two pies would have to divide once again, with each NATO member becoming entitled to fewer arms while those countries still in the Eastern group of states would have higher ceilings. Such a prospect could have a tempering effect on any push to expand NATO if such a move were to force the NATO countries to make uncomfortable further cuts in their armed forces. On the other hand, such a 're-balancing' of offensive arms might tend to ease Russian fears about a security threat from an expanded NATO. Were the Visegrad countries to join NATO, their 4000 tanks, for example, would count against the NATO rather than the former WTO limits. This would require each state belonging to this expanded NATO to reduce its tank inventory by nearly 14 per cent. The states remaining in the Eastern group of states, on the other hand, would each be entitled to 25 per cent more tanks to bring their group's aggregate holdings back up to 20,000. Russia could be entitled to 8000 tanks rather than its present authorization of 6400. A re-alignment in NATO's favour might allow the treaty's 'Sufficiency Rule' to come into effect once more. This provision mandates that no single country could possess more than roughly one-third of the European totals – for example, 13,300 tanks of the 40,000 authorized by the Treaty. The Soviet Union would have been the only state party affected by this rule, but its entitlements were divided among the six European successor states still party to the treaty.

'Trust, but Verify'

The CFE Treaty has placed legal – and reasonable – limits on five categories of conventional arms in at least a major portion of Europe. It is not without its faults and shortcomings, but it has brought about an unprecedented openness and transparency as to the military forces and deployments of 30 European states. In an era when financial and political realities make it unlikely that many of the treaty's participants will be able to afford to maintain their authorized forces, the treaty's information exchange and confidence-building measures could well be its greatest achievement.

The treaty states have exchanged an enormous amount of data on military equipment and units. Each is required to tell all the other state parties the command organization of both its land forces and its air and air defence forces, down to the level of brigade/regiment, and even down to the battalion/squadron level in the case of independent units. All other states parties must be notified at least 42 days before any permanent changes are made in the command organization, and within five days after a unit's inventory of any one of the TLEs has changed by more than 10 per cent. The location of all the treaty-limited equipment held by these units – tanks, ACVs, artillery pieces, combat aircraft and attack helicopters – must also be revealed. Other disclosures are required, on such topics as permanent storage sites, TLEs not in service with the conventional armed forces, and the sites where TLEs will be destroyed, while detailed information must be exchanged regarding each state's Objects of Verification (OOVs). These are the units, permanent storage or reduction sites where the state's TLEs are located. The treaty states declared more than 2800 OOVs at the first data exchange after the treaty came into force – that of 16 December 1992.[24] All this information must be updated yearly.

Under the terms of the treaty, there are a wide range of on-site inspections allowed to verify the information exchanged. The inspections began even before the treaty came into force, with teams conducting some 300 'trial' inspections on a bilateral and multilateral basis during 1991 and the first half of 1992. The treaty-mandated inspections proper began when the treaty came into force. First came a 120-day 'baseline validation period' during which inspectors were to confirm that the data exchanged was indeed correct. Each state party was obliged to accept inspectors at one-fifth of its declared OOVs. Roughly 70 per cent of these possible inspections seem to have been carried out, as a total of 383 baseline inspections were conducted.[25] These included 17 inspections by former WTO states within their own group – something the treaty allows but NATO has discouraged. It hopes to alleviate this problem in the future by inviting Eastern inspectors to participate in some of the NATO inspections.

When the baseline inspection phase was over, a three-year reduction period began. During this phase, each party must accept so-called 'declared site' inspections at 10 per cent of its OOVs each year, as well as an unlimited number of inspections at its removal sites so that the other parties can verify the destruction or conversion of TLEs required by the treaty. When the destruction phase is over, there will be another 120-day validation period, during which a state party must accept inspections at one-fifth of its OOVs. Thereafter, each party is liable to 'declared site' inspections at 15 per cent of its OOVs each year.

Should one party have some evidence or suspicion that TLEs are being kept illegally at undeclared locations it can request a challenge inspection. The would-be inspecting party must specify an area no larger than 65 square kilometres nor wider than 16 kilometres for its inspection. The other party can refuse to allow the inspection, in which case it must provide 'all reasonable assurance' that the area does not contain TLEs. Should it allow the inspection, it must get the inspectors to the area within nine hours.

Neither all of Russia or Europe

If the CFE Treaty is to have a lasting impact on European security it would seem that two of its exclusions must be addressed. The treaty applies to neither all of Europe, nor to all the territory of the largest European military power – Russia. Certainly, it would have been impossible at the time to draft a conventional arms agreement encompassing China as well as Europe. However, the Soviet Union blatantly abused the arbitrary eastern boundary of a Europe extending from 'the Atlantic to the Urals' when it hastily moved vast quantities of TLEs to the east of the Urals while the treaty was being negotiated. Following the break-up of the Soviet Union, Russia's military centre of gravity has shifted eastwards. The newly formed Ural MD (which lies outside the treaty's area of application) seems positioned far more for a European than an Asian role.

Since a number of European countries were neither members of NATO nor the WTO, it is not surprising that the treaty does not apply to all of Europe, even that part between 'the Atlantic and the Urals'. Surely all the countries bordering on Russia – including non-CFE states Finland, Estonia, Latvia and Lithuania – could benefit from the confidence-building measures of the treaty. With the end of the Cold War, the traditional neutrality of Sweden, Austria and Switzerland makes less sense than in the past, and they might welcome a role in European conventional arms control for political if not for security reasons. The most significant area overlooked by the treaty, however, is the former Yugoslavia. Of course, it would not be possible to bring the countries of the former Yugoslavia into the fold until the guns are silent. At the time of writing (1994) the feeble efforts of the European Union, the Organization for Security and Co-operation in Europe (formerly the CSCE), the United Nations, the Western European Union and NATO to stop the violence have been unsuccessful. But once that region is again relatively stable, it would seem prudent to incorporate the former Yugoslav republics and Albania into a conventional arms accord. Barring that, a militant and unrestrained Serbia (for example) could put considerable pressure on its neighbours, many of whom are party to the CFE Treaty.

Notes

1 Portions of this chapter first appeared in Douglas L. Clarke, 'The Russian Military and the CFE Treaty', *RFE/RL Research Report*, 22 October 1993, pp. 38–43.

2 The figures for Russia apply only to the two military districts within the flanks zone, the Leningrad and North Caucasus MDs. In addition to equipment in active units, Russia can store 600 tanks, 800 ACVs and 400 artillery pieces in the flanks. The figures for Ukraine apply only to the Ukrainian Southern Command, part of the former Soviet Odessa MD. Ukraine can store an additional 400 tanks and 500 artillery pieces in this zone. Moldova and the three countries of the Caucasus have no storage allowance.

3 RFE/RL Research Institute *Daily Report*, no. 169, 3 September 1993; no. 170, 6 September 1993; and no. 172, 8 September 1993.

4 *The Arms Control Reporter*, November 1993, p. 407.B.494/495.

5 Ibid., p. 407.D.85.

6 Pavel Felgengauer, in *Segodnya*, 7 May 1993. Translated in *Foreign Broadcast Information Service* [hereafter FBIS] *Daily Report: Central Eurasia*, no. 88, 10 May 1993 [FBIS-SOV-93-088], p. 14.

7 Reuter (Ankara), 27 September 1993.

8 From an interview broadcast on *Ostankino* Television First Channel, 9 March 1993.

9 See International Institute for Strategic Studies, *The Military Balance 1992–93* (London, 1992), p. 100.

10 During a visit to Finland, Colonel General Sergei Seleznev, the commander of the Leningrad Military District, reassured his hosts that redeployed units would not be stationed near the Finnish border. He was quoted as saying that the troops returning from Estonia, Latvia and Lithuania were being stationed south of St Petersburg (Baltic News Service, 25 August 1993).

11 Quoted by Baltic News Service, 27 December 1992.

12 From an interview published in *Rossiyskiye vesti*, 6 March 1993.

13 *Krasnaya Zvezda*, 7 May 1993.

14 Vadim Solovyev in *Nezavisimaya Gazeta*, 7 May 1993.

15 Grachev, in *Rossiyskiye Vesti*, 2 December 1992.

16 *Rossiyskiye vesti*, 4 January 1993. The others he mentioned were the West, Central, Volga–Urals, Siberian and Far East strategic commands. The formation of the first such command, in the Far East, was announced by Grachev in April 1993 (*Krasnaya Zvezda*, 21 April 1993).

17 International Institute for Strategic Studies, *The Military Balance 1992–93*, p. 100.

18 Quoted in *Segodnya*, 7 May 1993, as cited in FBIS-SOV-93-088, 10 May 1993, p. 14.

19 Kazakhstan could be considered a third example, but it is really marginal to the treaty, with only a small western sliver of the country falling within the treaty area.

20 See *The Arms Control Reporter*, July 1993, p. 407.B.490.

21 *Krasnaya Zvezda*, 21 October 1993.

22 *The Arms Control Reporter,* November 1993, p. 407.D.86.

23 Ibid., p. 407.B.497.

24 Ibid., February 1993, p. 407.B.483.

25 Ibid.

10 At the Border of European Security: The Case of Ukraine

Gerard Snel

Introduction

Ukraine literally means 'at the border', and that exactly characterizes the security situation faced by Ukraine in its first years of independence.[1] For on the one hand, Ukraine is at the border of Central Europe and yet does not belong to it for historical and geographical reasons; in addition its own policies have alienated it from the West. On the other hand, Ukraine is at the border of Russia and the Commonwealth of Independent States (CIS) from whose political control it desperately seeks to escape. Ideally, Ukraine could be the centre of Eurasia, linking Western and Central Europe to Russia and the CIS. In practice, it might develop into a buffer between the two.

This chapter focuses first upon the main problem concerning Ukraine's security: its relationship with Russia. It argues that this problem stems from different concepts of Ukrainian state-building and great-Russian nation-building. This argument is illustrated by describing the three main contentious issues in Ukrainian–Russian relations: first, the status of the Commonwealth of Independent States (CIS); second, the dismantling of Soviet nuclear weapons on Ukrainian territory; and third, the status of the Crimean Peninsula and the Black Sea Fleet. In the first two years of independence Ukrainian policy on these issues led the country into international isolation. Thereafter it has gradually backtracked from this policy in an effort to relieve this isolation.

The next section analyses the domestic constraints that influenced Ukrainian security policy: the asymmetrical economic interdependence with Russia and the political positions taken in the parliament. It will be argued that, following the elections of spring 1994, a temporary domestic window of opportunity for Ukrainian economic and security reforms has been opened.

The final section will assess Ukraine's current security position. This position is characterized by a temporary opportunity to settle some contentious issues with Russia. Considering the coincidence of domestic and foreign opportunities, the West should now help Ukraine to make the best use of this situation. In particular, it should resist the temptation rapidly to expand the North Atlantic Treaty Organization (NATO) eastwards, and it should support Ukrainian efforts to restructure its economy, armed forces and military industry.

Independence or Commonwealth?

On 24 August 1991, after the attempted *coup* against Soviet President Mikhail Gorbachev, the Ukrainian Supreme Soviet declared the independence of Ukraine, with the proviso that the Ukrainian people would approve this decision in a referendum. This referendum, held on 1 December, showed that an overwhelming majority, 90 per cent, was in favour. Not only the strongly nationalist western part of the country, but also the more pro-Russian eastern part and the Crimea had voted for independence. After centuries of foreign invasions by Tatars, Poles, Austrians, Germans and Russians, Ukraine had to establish its statehood within borders in which it had never existed before.

Despite its broad popular support in the referendum, Ukraine's political independence was not based upon a strong and broadly shared Ukrainian ethnicity. Around one-fifth of Ukrainian citizens, mostly living in the eastern and south-eastern part of the country and on the Crimean peninsula, are ethnic Russians. Moreover, of those denoted as ethnic Ukrainians many regard Russian to be their first language. It is only in the western parts that Ukrainian nationalism is very strong. Ukrainian independence was therefore more a matter of state-building than of nation-building. It was not based on the positive feature of a distinct Ukrainian identity but on the negative feature of not being under Russian control, whether directly or under the guise of the CIS.[2]

However, Ukraine's history and culture are strongly intertwined with those of Russia, exemplified by the fact that Kiev is the cradle of Russian statehood. For many Russians Ukraine is a natural part of their concept of Russian nationhood. According to a 1994 opinion poll, 'nearly three-quarters of all ethnic Russians in Russia do not think Ukrainians are a separate nationality or that Ukraine should be an independent state'.[3] Without directly questioning the political independence of Ukraine, the Russian government and parliament have tried to re-establish some measure of Russian control over Ukraine, and thus the different concepts of Ukrainian state-building and great-Russian nation-building have led to recurrent Ukrainian–Russian disputes.

Strained relations between the two countries began with the first official reaction from the Russian government to the independence declaration by the Ukrainian Supreme Soviet. The presidential press secretary said that Russia reserved the right to redraw her borders with those republics that declared their independence. This statement directly contradicted the Ukrainian–Russian agreement of November 1990 in which both states had recognized their mutual borders.[4] The statement not only questioned that agreement and the borders of Ukraine, but also reflected a more deep-seated Russian unease with the whole idea of Ukrainian statehood.

Early in December 1991, Russian President Boris Yeltsin and Belarussian President Stanislau Shushkevich tried to persuade their Ukrainian colleague Leonid Kravchuk to accept a more centralized Union, but the latter refused to go any further than a loose form of co-operation. At the Alma Ata summit meeting later that month, the other republics of the Soviet Union formed the CIS and dealt the death-blow to the Soviet Union. For Ukrainian politicians it was also fatal to any federal structure. They repeatedly asserted that the CIS did not have a leader, that Russia did not have a special position in the CIS and that the CIS was no state. In February 1992 Ivan Plyushch, then speaker of the Ukrainian parliament, said that the CIS was 'a way of helping the states of the former USSR go through a divorce process'.[5] When in January 1993 the CIS states signed the Commonwealth Charter Ukraine abstained. Kravchuk sharply criticized the charter's tendency towards developing centralized structures and argued that CIS co-operation should be limited to regulating common economic problems.[6]

There can be no doubt that Ukraine's first foreign and security priority was to establish and assert its independence and territorial integrity – essentially, escaping as much as possible from Russian control. Russia's ambiguity about these questions encouraged an obsessive Ukrainian craving to assert and reassert its independence, though this policy led to the break-up of Ukraine's economic relations with the other former Soviet republics. As the Soviet economy had been characterized by a far-reaching regional division of labour, the break-up of economic ties caused serious economic difficulties, and the economic crisis that followed actually made Ukraine more dependent on Russia.

Nuclear Weapons

In one respect Ukraine had to accept a compromise concerning its independence: it could not fully control the nuclear weapons based on its territory. When the Soviet Union fell apart, Russia, Ukraine, Belarus and Kazakhstan inherited its nuclear arsenal. Ironically, in all the republics but Russia there are strong anti-nuclear sentiments in the population, largely because of the results of Soviet nuclear experiments: the nuclear weapon tests in Semipalatinsk (Kazakhstan) and the catastrophic nuclear energy accident in Chernobyl (affecting especially Ukraine and Belarus). As early as July 1990 the Ukrainian parliament had stated in its sovereignty declaration its intention of becoming a nuclear-weapon-free state. And at the Alma Ata summit both Ukraine and Belarus declared that they would become parties to the Non-proliferation Treaty (NPT), implying that they would become non-nuclear-weapon states.[7]

In the last days of 1991 Russia, Ukraine, Belarus and Kazakhstan signed the Agreement of Minsk in which they established a common command for the strategic forces and united control over nuclear weapons. Ukraine also agreed that before July 1992 all the tactical nuclear weapons on its territory would be transferred to Russia for their destruction. A neat and peaceful nuclear transition from the Soviet nuclear heritage seemed assured. In March 1992, however, Ukraine stopped the transfer of tactical nuclear weapons, declaring that it had strong doubts over the Russian commitment to the immediate destruction of these weapons.[8] This quarrel was quickly resolved, but it was only the beginning of much more serious trouble in the strategic nuclear field. The quarrel had fuelled the mutual distrust between Russia and Ukraine and, more importantly, had shown the Ukrainian government that nuclear weapons could be an effective means of political pressure. The first doubts about Ukraine's non-nuclear status had arisen.

These doubts influenced Ukraine's strategic nuclear policy. Ukraine had inherited from the Soviet Union a formidable nuclear arsenal of 1768 strategic nuclear warheads (1240 on ICBMs and 528 on strategic bombers), making it the third-largest nuclear-weapon power in the world. The strategic nuclear field is strongly regulated by international treaties and, although Ukraine was not party to these treaties, it could not ignore their consequences. The most important was the NPT, negotiated to prevent the spread of nuclear weapons to non-nuclear-weapon states. Western countries, in particular the United States, recognized Russia as the only inheritor of Soviet nuclear weaponry in order to prevent an increase in the number of nuclear-weapon states. The pressure to confirm this to protect the already shaky edifice of the international non-proliferation regime increased as the 1995 NPT Review and Extension Conference approached.[9] Another important agreement in the strategic nuclear field was the first treaty arising from the Strategic Arms Reduction Talks (START I) that was signed by the United States and the Soviet Union in July 1991. The signatories had agreed to reduce their strategic nuclear arsenals by one-third, and believed that the nuclear arsenals of the other three nuclear-weapon states of the former Soviet Union were naturally to be included in the calculations.

Previous Ukrainian declarations and international pressure notwithstanding, the Ukrainian president refused to give up dual Ukrainian–Russian control over the strategic nuclear forces on Ukrainian territory. He could not, however, completely ignore international pressure, coming mainly from Russia and the United States. For example, in May 1992 Kravchuk signed the Lisbon Protocol by which Ukraine promised 'in the shortest possible time' to become party to the NPT and to undertake the required steps.[10] However, in October 1992 the Ukrainian government declared that it had taken control over the launch systems (missiles and bombers) and fissionable material of the nuclear weapons on its territory. The CIS strategic command maintained operational control, that is, the capacity to use the weapons.

At the beginning of 1993 the United States and Russia signed START II. Ukraine was excluded from the negotiations, and not consulted on its provisions. Not surprisingly, the Ukrainian leadership immediately declared that it was not bound by the provisions of this treaty. When in April 1993 Ukraine assumed control over a nuclear missile unit and a nuclear bomber unit, Kravchuk gave a strong signal that further neglect of Ukrainian interests would have very unpleasant consequences for both Russia and the West.

In practice, however, Ukraine never did have full nuclear-weapon status. Even its administrative control over nuclear weapons was weak, as the commanders of most of the nuclear sites were still loyal to the strategic command of the CIS or to the Russian army. Moreover, the Ukrainian government did not possess the codes that would have enabled it to launch the missiles or to release the nuclear charges from the strategic bombers. Finally, Ukraine was not able to change the targeting software of the strategic missiles. Ukraine lacked the financial and certain crucial technical resources to transform its nuclear assets into a credible *force de frappe*. By mid-1993 Ukraine had become a very peculiar phenomenon: a state administratively possessing nuclear weapons but not able to use them.

The question arises why the Ukrainian government, despite the once-strong anti-nuclear sentiments of the populace and in political circles, had become mesmerized with its ambiguous nuclear status. The first answer lies in its strained relationship with Russia. Ukrainian politicians reasoned that the possession of nuclear weapons could give Ukraine a security guarantee against imperialist or expansionist tendencies in Russian policy. However, the existing arsenal, as will be seen, could not and has not deterred Russia from assertive behaviour over disputes concerning borders or economic issues.[11] Secondly, the Ukrainian authorities used their nuclear status as a source of legitimacy, as they lacked more traditional sources. The political system was dominated by the former Communist leaders, economic performance was disastrous, and a strong ethnic basis was absent. Thirdly, Ukraine tried to exploit the nuisance value of its nuclear status to irritate other countries, to attract their attention and demand security and financial guarantees in return for better behaviour.[12] Their practical experience with the transfer of tactical nuclear weapons gave the Ukrainian leaders a strong belief in the nuisance value of nuclear weapons.

Ukraine demanded from other nuclear-weapon powers guarantees against threats to its security and territorial integrity, but the only state willing to give such a guarantee was Russia! Ukraine also wanted to be compensated for the destruction of the launching systems and of the fissionable material in the warheads that it had to hand over to Russia for dismantling. In total it asked for $2.8 billion, whereas the United States had promised $175 million.[13] The Ukrainian attitude in the first half of 1993 caused great annoyance in the West, to an extent that was counter-productive; it led to an estrangement from both Russia and the West, leaving Ukraine isolated.

Around mid-1993 the Ukrainian government reassessed its position.[14] The first reason was that Ukraine's semi-nuclear status was withering away. The condition of the warheads and missiles rapidly deteriorated because of lack of maintenance work (although for tactical reasons the Ukrainian leaders did not openly admit this). Secondly, the government realized that it could not obtain security by deterring Russia with its semi-nuclear status, the more so as the West was not willing to commit itself to assuring Ukrainian security against Russia. Thirdly, and most importantly, the Ukrainian economy had been much more dependent upon Russia than Ukrainian politicians had been willing to admit. Due to the serious decline of the economy the Ukrainian authorities could no longer pay their energy debts to Russia, which gave Russia a lever over Ukraine.

In the autumn of 1993 Ukraine's economic situation was so catastrophic that it had to seek a rescheduling of its debts with Russia. When in September the Ukrainian and Russian presidents met in Massandra in the Crimea they seemed to have struck a deal: all nuclear warheads on Ukrainian territory would be transferred to Russia for dismantling, while Ukraine would receive fissionable resources in return.[15] However, when Kravchuk and his foreign minister, Anatoly Zlenko, were sharply criticized for having sold the Ukrainian national interests to Russia, they claimed that they had only agreed to study these proposals.[16] These remarks only partially reassured the Ukrainian parliamentarians. After a year of procrastination, they finally voted on the ratification of START I. They made their approval dependent upon several conditions, however, including reliable security guarantees from other nuclear-weapon states, economic support and control over the destruction of nuclear warheads. Although these conditions had been repeated at various times, two other features were new: START I would only relate to a part of the Ukrainian nuclear arsenal, and Ukraine no longer felt itself bound by the Lisbon Protocol that promised a rapid entry into the NPT regime.[17]

The United States had reassessed its relations with Ukraine in the summer of 1993, which until then had supported the Russian standpoint. It came to realize that Ukraine was an independent entity that had its own legitimate security interests. The emphasis in US policy gradually shifted from the stick, threatening Ukraine with sanctions, to the carrot, promising Ukraine assistance. But the move of the Ukrainian parliament turned back the clock, and led the Americans to threaten to renounce its economic assistance and to veto Ukrainian participation in NATO's 'Partnership for Peace' programme.[18] It seemed that Ukrainian isolation was complete, but this episode actually accelerated a Ukrainian rapprochement with Russia and the West. Kravchuk appreciated Ukraine's strong economic dependence upon Russia and the West and realized that it could no longer afford isolation. He undertook various measures to reassure the West and Russia, such as the deactivation of 17 ICBMs on Ukrainian territory.

The diplomatic stalemate between Ukraine, Russia and the United States was partly broken by the Trilateral Agreement signed in January 1994. The three countries emphasized their 'respect for the independence, sovereignty and territorial integrity of each nation', while Kravchuk made a personal commitment to ensure Ukraine's joining the NPT regime 'in the shortest possible time'. The Ukrainian government repeated its intention to eliminate all its nuclear weapons in the seven-year period of START I and promised to transport within ten months 200 nuclear warheads to Russia. Ukraine would be compensated for its nuclear warheads with enriched uranium to the value of $1 billion. Although the Trilateral Agreement contained many technical ambiguities and loopholes, its political significance was high. The Ukrainian government clearly distanced itself from the growing sentiment in the country for maintaining its nuclear weapon status; Russia restated its respect for the territorial integrity of Ukraine; and the United States committed itself to an intermediary role between Ukraine and Russia.[19] Moreover, the United States began to support Ukrainian requests for membership to the 'Partnership for Peace' programme and for financial support from the International Monetary Fund and the World Bank. Apart from the $175 million for the dismantling of missile launchers, the United States also promised $155 million to promote economic reforms.

Kravchuk and his colleagues initiated a campaign to explain their new policy to parliament and the people. Their first argument was that Ukrainian nuclear weapons could provide no deterrence as only Russia could launch them. Their second argument was that the condition of the missiles was rapidly deteriorating through lack of maintenance, making them an internal danger rather than an external threat.[20] Although not openly acknowledged by the Ukrainian authorities, the rate of deterioration of the missiles militated against obtaining full operational control over the nuclear weapons by Ukraine in time.[21] Lastly, even if it were technically possible, acquiring a reliable deterrent was too costly for Ukraine.[22]

The campaign was successful, for early in February 1994 parliament ratified START I and the Lisbon Protocol. Apparently parliament was satisfied with the financial and security guarantees of the Trilateral Agreement. However, when it came to voting on signing the NPT so many members of parliament abstained that the necessary quorum was not reached. Nevertheless, the US government decided to reward the positive Ukrainian steps by increasing its economic aid to $700 million. In March 1994 the first 60 warheads arrived in Russia. Although further transfers were accompanied by Ukrainian–Russian bickering about time schedules and financial compensation, the dismantling progressed steadily. Despite a threat by Yeltsin of a 'Cold Peace' in Russian–Western relations, the heads of state of the United States, Russia, Belarus, Ukraine and Kazakhstan exchanged the START I ratification documents at the Organization for Security and Co-operation in Europe (OSCE) in December 1994. Thus, the last obstacle to the implementation of the treaty was overcome and the door to the ratification of START II was opened. Moreover, Ukraine signed the NPT; in return it received (together with Belarus and Kazakhstan) security guarantees from the other nuclear powers in the OSCE. Thus, the major obstacle in Ukrainian–Western relations was removed. But other problems continued to strain Russian–Ukrainian relations, in particular the position of the Crimea and the Black Sea Fleet.

Crimea and the Black Sea Fleet

The Crimea is a Russian peninsula given to Ukraine in 1954 by the First Secretary of the Communist Party of the Soviet Union, Nikita Khrushchev, to commemorate 300 years of Ukrainian–Russian friendship. In January 1992 the Russian parliament called this decision in question by charging two parliamentary commissions to study the legal status of Khrushchev's move. Two arguments were advanced by Russian parliamentarians: the majority of the Crimean population was Russian, and the Black Sea Fleet was predominantly staffed by Russians. Indeed, the Crimean population consisted of 61.6 per cent Russians, 23.6 per cent Ukrainians and 9.6 per cent Tartars, and only 19–30 per cent of the officers and 30–60 per cent of ordinary seamen in the Black Sea Fleet were Ukrainian (1991 estimates).[23] These statistics, however, do not justify the unilateral Russian move.

Although he distanced himself from the implicit parliamentary claim on the Crimea, Yeltsin refused to accept Ukrainian authority over the Black Sea Fleet. He initially claimed that the fleet was strategic and thus belonged to the CIS strategic command. Later he demanded for Russia a share of the fleet and partial jurisdiction over its home base, Sevastopol. In the spring of 1992 a war of decrees emerged between Kravchuk and Yeltsin who asserted their respective commands over the fleet and its crew. At their August 1992 and June 1993 summit meetings in Yalta and Moscow the two presidents agreed on the principle of the fleet's division, though many financial and legal details remained unresolved and different interpretations were given of the agreements.

In July 1993 the Russian parliament unilaterally declared the Sevastopol marine base to be Russian territory. Ukraine immediately took the issue to the United Nations, and the Russian decree was declared 'null and void'.[24] Yeltsin distanced himself from parliament's declaration; he sought and apparently obtained success at the Massandra summit in September 1993. Yeltsin claimed that Ukraine had consented to sell the Black Sea Fleet and to lease Sevastopol to Russia in return for the cancellation of Ukrainian debts. As mentioned above, upon returning to Kiev Kravchuk denied that any such deal had been made.

At first sight, important military stocks seem to be at stake: nearly 300 vessels, 28 submarines and approximately 60,000 navy personnel. In practice, however, most of the vessels are outdated and rusting, while the personnel is divided between a large Russia-oriented and a much smaller Ukraine-oriented part. The importance of the Black Sea Fleet does not lie in its material components, but rather in its control over the southern coast of Ukraine and the Crimea. The Ukrainian government fears, in short, that a Russian marine base in the Crimea would create a basis for Russian imperialism and Crimean separatism.[25]

The existence of a Crimean government and parliament with important rights autonomous of Kiev was a further complicating factor. In May 1992 the Crimean parliament voted for a new constitution establishing Crimean sovereignty, but subsequently it partially backtracked for fear of Ukrainian countermeasures.[26] However, the unexpected support for Vladimir Zhirinovsky in the Russian elections of December 1993 again stimulated the Russians in the Crimea to become more self-assured. In the January 1994 elections for Crimean president, Yury Meshkov, the candidate of the strong pro-Russia Party Bloc *Rossiya*, received nearly three-quarters of the votes. Then, in the Crimean parliamentary elections in March 1994, Meshkov's party obtained an absolute majority of seats. Meshkov had campaigned for more autonomy for the Crimea from Ukraine and, in the longer term, a 'reunification' with Russia. The Crimean voters had also supported his main demands in a referendum that was held alongside the March elections: nearly 80 per cent voted for more Crimean autonomy and more than 80 per cent for the possibility of dual Ukrainian–Russian citizenship.[27] In March Meshkov demanded the withdrawal of Ukrainian forces from the Crimea. Thus, the issues of the Black Sea Fleet and the status of the Crimea were directly linked.

In April 1994 there were skirmishes between Russian and Ukrainian naval units in the Crimea, which threatened to escalate. However, at the CIS summit in Moscow Yeltsin and Kravchuk agreed on a new division of the Fleet: Ukraine would receive one-fifth of the vessels and would sell the rest of its share to Russia. However, when subsequently the defence ministers convened to settle the details of a dispute on the status of Sevastopol prevented a final agreement.[28] Ukrainian apprehensions deepened when the Crimean parliament, on 20 May 1994, re-established its constitution of 1992 declaring Crimean sovereignty and providing the legal basis for raising a national guard.

Ironically, this act undermined the Crimean position *vis-à-vis* Ukraine. The constitution of 1992 gave strong powers to the president. Although Meshkov had initially promised not to use these powers, after the summer vacation of 1994 he conveniently forgot his commitment. On 11 September Meshkov had the parliament building occupied, declared that the parliamentary activities were illegal, and assumed all the powers of the parliament. Parliament then convened in a building close by and voted for the removal of Meshkov from office.[29] There was a stalemate between the pro-Russian parliament and the less than pro-Russian but politically weakened Meshkov. This stalemate provided the Ukrainian government with considerable leverage. In November 1994 the Ukrainian parliament decided to abolish all Crimean laws, including the Crimean constitution, that contradicted the Ukrainian constitution. Moreover, it threatened to suspend budgetary aid for the Crimean militia, security services and television if these organizations did not observe the Ukrainian laws.[30]

The issue of the Black Sea Fleet was again addressed during the CIS summit meeting of October 1994 and bilateral talks in December 1994. The agreement on dividing the fleet (50-50, with Ukraine handing over 30 per cent to Russia to reduce its debt) was confirmed. But Ukraine refused to submit to Russia's demand that this division included the infrastructure of the fleet. The status of Sevastopol remained a point of contention; Ukraine was willing to lease the base for four to five years to Russia, but Russia demanded a 99-year period.[31] In recent years, then, economic dependence on Russia has forced the Ukrainian leaders to acquiesce in some Russian military presence in the Crimea and to give or sell to the Russians the largest share of the fleet. However, their apprehensions about Russian encroachment upon Ukrainian independence have led them strongly to resist Russian jurisdiction over Sevastopol. It seems, therefore, that the problems over the status of the Crimea and the Black Sea Fleet will linger on until Russia and Ukraine have normalized their relations.

Domestic Constraints

Three domestic constraints on Ukrainian policy stand out: fluctuating sentiments in the parliament and among the public concerning nuclear weapons; the economic situation; and pro-Russian sentiments among a part of the population. The Ukrainian parliament that in August 1991 had declared Ukrainian independence was strongly dominated by nationalist Ukrainian sentiments. Kravchuk relied upon broad parliamentary support for establishing and confirming Ukrainian independence. His government refused to get entangled in CIS structures and tried to orient Ukraine towards the West. At the same time, the Ukrainian government wanted to use its temporary nuclear-weapon status to combat perceived Russian neo-imperialism. But these two objectives could not be pursued simultaneously, as the West rejected Ukraine's nuclear-weapon policy. Hence in the course of 1993 the Ukrainian government realized that the pursuit of nuclear autonomy had isolated the country internationally, while its dependence upon Russia had grown. When the government sought to redress the situation, however, it was confronted with a defiant parliament.

In the course of 1993 the original anti-nuclear sentiments among the Ukrainian public and parliamentarians had given away to an attachment to Ukraine's semi-nuclear status.[32] Many parliamentarians wanted to draw out the process of denuclearization in order to prolong its deterrent against Russia and to obtain security guarantees and financial compensation from the West and Russia. In strongly nationalist circles there were some who believed that Ukraine should not completely renounce its nuclear status.[33] Even inside the government resistance against co-operation with the West and Russia grew. After the Massandra summit, Kravchuk and Foreign Minister Zlenko were sharply criticized by Defence Minister Konstyantyn Morozov, who subsequently resigned in October 1993, and the Minister for the Environment, Yury Kostenko, both of whom defended Ukraine's nuclear weapon status. In the first months of 1994, however, Kravchuk and Zlenko succeeded in convincing parliament that Ukraine's nuclear weapon status was in reality very limited and rapidly deteriorating because of the condition of the warheads. Parliament accordingly endorsed the Trilateral Agreement and ratified START I.

An even more important domestic constraint on security policy was the economic situation. Ukraine had strongly resisted Russian pressure to reintegrate the economies of the former Soviet states within the context of the CIS. Ukraine feared Russian dominance of these structures and thus an encroachment upon its much-cherished national independence. But the Ukrainian government under President Kravchuk did not inaugurate any significant economic reforms. Such reforms were resisted by the old political and economic *nomenklatura* which feared the loss of its position and the social consequences of mass unemployment. The breaking of economic ties with CIS countries had led to a crumbling of the old economic mechanisms, but there was no economic reform and the old mechanisms were not being replaced by new ones. As a result, there was a dramatic decline in production, consumption and investment, and an explosion of inflation and state deficit. The most important economic issue that most directly influenced relations between Ukraine and Russia concerned Ukrainian energy imports. There was a strong reliance upon gas and oil from Russia and Turkmenistan, two countries that now charged world market prices. Ukraine could no longer pay its bills, while the increased prices of Ukraine's energy-intensive products led to reduced demand and export. As a result, at the end of 1993 Ukraine had a foreign debt to Russia of $3 billion and to Turkmenistan of $1 billion. Turkmenistan stopped its deliveries and Russia cut them in half.[34] Russia did not shy from using Ukraine's dependence upon Russian energy deliveries to pressurize its neighbour, and the change in Ukraine's security policy in mid-1993 can thus partly be explained by Russia's use of its energy weapon. There were limits, however, to the use of the weapon, as the Ukrainian–Russian energy relationship was and is an interdependent one. First, Russia's gas exports to Western Europe are transported over Ukrainian territory, which hosts 8600 kilometres of pipelines and twelve reservoir stations with a capacity sufficient for three months' Ukrainian domestic consumption. Whenever Russia reduced its deliveries, Ukraine simply took gas from the reservoirs![35] Secondly, Ukraine's energy-intensive heavy industry and military–industrial complex are concentrated in the eastern and south-eastern part of the country where most of its Russian population lives. Therefore, if Russia were to be too enthusiastic in shutting off energy supplies, the most immediate repercussions would be experienced by ethnic Russians. Hence, unless Russia makes the desperate choice of seeking decisively to destabilize the Ukrainian state, it cannot ignore this interdependence. Of course, Ukrainian–Russian energy interdependence is asymmetrical, for it is Ukraine that has strongly undermined its economic position by not initiating serious reforms and thus increasing its dependence on Russia. The growing discrepancy between, on the one side, economic dependence on Russia, and, on the other, the policy of symbolic political independence from Russia could not but force Kravchuk's government to make a U-turn. It should incidentally be noted that the Ukrainian population voted so massively for this independence because of expectations that its economic fortunes would be better than those of Russia. The result of a disastrous economic policy was therefore not only an increased dependence upon Russia, but also an undermining of support for Ukrainian independence among its more pro-Russian population.

The 1994 elections vividly demonstrated widespread dissatisfaction with the government's performance and the growing geographical division of the Ukrainian electorate. Parties and independent candidates that opted for pro-Russian and pro-CIS policies received wide support in the eastern and south-eastern parts of the country and the Crimea. The more Ukrainian nationalist and pro-Western parties and independent candidates received their support in the western part of the country.[36] As a result, parliament is split into two parts that have very different views of Ukraine's future. At the same time, the large number of parties and independent candidates has made voting behaviour in parliament far from predictable. In June 1994 the electorate again had to cast their votes, this time for a president. In the second round sitting president Kravchuk, who emphasized Ukrainian independence and an orientation to the West, was defeated by Leonid Kuchma, who emphasized the need for a reorientation to Russia and the CIS countries.[37]

Kuchma was confronted with enormous economic and political problems. In October 1994 he announced a programme of economic reform, which he defended by saying that Ukraine could establish itself as a really independent state solely on the basis of a powerful economic and social policy.[38] By the beginning of 1995 the general outlines of the programme still had to be transformed into concrete laws and actions. Kuchma's reform programme was, however, an important step forward, looking to attract badly needed Western financial support and foreign investment, along with a re-establishment of former economic ties. At the same time, this programme faced serious difficulties. First, the government bureaucracy was still infested with the old industrial and financial oligarchy. Second, parliament still had to be convinced of the necessity to develop and support laws that would dismantle the old structures and create the conditions for a market economy. For example, although parliament approved by a majority vote Kuchma's programme of reform, the next day it voted for continuing subsidies for the unprofitable agricultural production sector. Third, a serious reform effort creates major political problems for the president. Kuchma's major support came from the south-eastern part of the country where the obsolete coal mines, the outdated steel industry, the environmentally disastrous chemical industry and the largely superfluous military industry are located. Economic reform would undoubtedly lead to mass unemployment in these sectors and thus undermine Kuchma's political base.[39]

Kuchma's domestic constraints may nevertheless be less severe than those of his predecessor. Unlike Kravchuk, Kuchma could probably gain the support of the Russians from the eastern and south-eastern parts of the country for remaining within the Ukrainian state. They might also be attracted by his policy of reorientation to the CIS and Russia. At the same time, economic reforms might attract Western finance and thus give him support from reform-minded Ukrainians. This potentially expedient situation has thus created a window of opportunity for an improvement in Ukraine's internal economic and external security situation.

Ukraine's Security: A Reassessment

Ukraine's foreign and security policy has been dominated by Ukrainian–Russian relations. These relations can be characterized as what has been called a 'security trap': the unilateral pursuit of the security goals by each side makes impossible the achievement of their mutual security goals and thus in fact reduces their security. If Ukraine tries to strengthen its nationhood at the cost of the Russian minority, this would support those forces in Russia that are inclined to reimpose a degree of political control over at least a part of Ukraine. If, however, Russia initiates a policy along the latter line, this would strongly increase the activity of Ukrainian radical nationalists.[40] In short, the security of Ukraine and Russia is interdependent, and Ukrainian–Russian relations can only be harmonious when both sides recognize the security interests of the other.

While emphasizing such a security interdependence, it is easy to overlook an important point: the security interests of these countries are not only interdependent but also asymmetrical. For Ukraine the recognition of its political independence by Russia is a vital security concern. By contrast, for Russia a Ukrainian recognition of Russian minority rights and economic integration are important but not vital interests. Thus the stakes are much higher for Ukraine. Also of consequence is the multifaceted nature of their security interdependence; not only military, but also political, economic, ecological and minority issues are at stake and are interwoven. The fact that Ukraine ignored the importance of economic security (its energy debts) and its ecological security (the deterioration of its missiles) fundamentally undermined the strength of its position *vis-à-vis* Russia. A further important aspect is the influence of third countries, notably the United States. Whereas Ukrainian missile policy might have been temporarily useful in its bilateral relationship with Russia, Ukrainian disregard of Western demands and interests led to its isolation. Its concept of political independence was naïve, as it ignored the complexity of security interdependence in the modern age.

The new leadership has set out to reorient Ukraine's foreign and security policy. According to the new foreign minister, Gennady Udovenko, Ukraine has opted to 'stabilize' its relations with Russia, 'restore ties' with the CIS countries and not detract from its co-operation with the West.[41] Apparently, Ukrainian politicians have overcome their self-inflicted isolation by ratifying START I and signing the NPT. Western governments are more forthcoming towards Ukraine with financial and technical aid, and the announced reform programme has interested the International Monetary Fund, the European Bank of Reconstruction and Development and the World Bank in supporting Ukraine's economy. Moreover, the Ukrainian leadership has understood that it cannot obtain security at the cost of Russia. Thus, the new leadership is willing to make use of its domestic opportunities to reorient its security policy.

Unfortunately, this new policy has emerged at a moment when the Russian leadership is less inclined to benign and equal co-operation with its neighbours. The December 1993 elections for the Russian parliament have led to a growing great-Russian nationalism, first in the parliament and subsequently also in the government. This is illustrated by the Russian manipulation of the Georgian–Abkhazian war, which resulted in Georgia's forced entry into the CIS military alliance. The shift in Russian international diplomatic policy from a Russian–Western partnership towards a Russian Cold Peace policy is evident from its approach to the war in Bosnia-Hercegovina. Thus, while Ukraine's domestic window of opportunity has opened, its foreign window of opportunity is closing.

At first sight the Russian military intervention in Chechenia seems to have closed the window altogether. Russia has chosen to impose its will by brutal military force upon an administration that defies its wishes, although in this case the object is not the 'near abroad' but the 'distant home'. However, at second sight the opposite might be the case. The intervention has seriously undermined the moral, political and military prestige of the Russian leadership both at home and abroad. Moreover, it has further divided the army and decreased its self-confidence. The Russian leadership is licking its wounds and therefore might be more inclined to act cautiously with respect to other issues. In the longer term, the consequences of the war in Chechenia might be that Russian politics will become increasingly authoritarian and chauvinist, which will be very disturbing to the countries of the 'near abroad'. In the short term, however, the opposite might be the case.

Ukraine may, then, have an opportunity to escape from its former isolated position, which was to a large extent self-inflicted. Ukraine's asymmetrical security interdependence forced the country to accept unequal terms in its dealings with Russia, and Ukrainian politicians must thus accept that the Crimea cannot be restored to full Ukrainian control. Their political basis in the Crimea is very limited; despite the fact that nearly a quarter of the population consists of ethnic Ukrainians, in the elections the pro-Ukrainian parties received only a very small percentage of the votes.[42] The predominant sentiments are and will be pro-Russian. On the other hand, Ukraine is able to limit the demands it can accept from Russia: no full Russian control over the Crimea and no subordination of Ukraine to supranational CIS military and political structures. The West should make clear that it will not accept Russian pressure on Ukraine to submit to such demands, for increased Russian control over parts of Ukraine will arouse tensions between Ukrainian nationalists and pro-Russian forces that might easily escalate into a disastrous civil war. The West should demonstrate that it does not perceive Ukraine as a derivative of Russia nor as a residue of Western and Central European security. Ukraine's asymmetrical security interdependence should induce the West to engage in some counterbalancing without directly violating Russian interests. This will not be an easy task, and sometimes it will perhaps be impossible; that is a reflection of the complexity of security interdependence.

The worst signal the West could give to Ukraine and to Russia would be to extend NATO to Ukraine's borders and no further. Its implicit message would be that Ukraine belongs to the other sphere of influence – Greater Russia under the guise of the CIS – and not to a broader European defence community. Central European countries will undoubtedly demand that, considering Russia's military misbehaviour on its southern flank, they should be rapidly included in NATO. The 'Partnership for Peace' programme only temporarily tempered their demands in this respect; by 1994 they were renewing their campaign for full membership, referring to Russia's Cold Peace policy. However, expansionist tendencies in Russian foreign policy are directed against the 'near abroad', the former republics of the Soviet Union, and not against Central Europe. It would therefore be better to create a large grey zone to the east of NATO than to extend NATO and isolate a small buffer between it and greater Russia. Security and defence co-operation could be gradually deepened and extended in the 'Partnership for Peace' programme and in bilateral programmes for all Central and East European countries. Moreover, this would not fully confront Russia at a moment when its policy in the coming decade has yet to be decided.

There are various forms of help for Ukraine that the West could provide, especially expertise and financial support. First, it could help in the restructuring of the armed forces. In particular, there is a requirement under the Conventional Forces in Europe Treaty for the 700,000–800,000 Soviet armed forces on Ukrainian territory to be reduced to 200,000–220,000, and for the offensively pitched forces located in the west to be redeployed as more defensively oriented forces in the east and south.[43] Second, the West could help in the conversion of Ukraine's large military industry that makes up nearly 40 per cent of its industrial capacity; successful conversion is a precondition for successful economic reform and for preventing mass unemployment and unrest among Ukraine's Russian minority. Third, Ukraine needs help in closing down its Chernobyl nuclear reactors without incurring increased energy dependence. By making such a closure a precondition for economic support, the European Union increases Ukraine's energy dependence. Instead, the West should seriously support Ukraine in developing alternative energy sources.

In the first two years of its independence Ukraine had manoeuvred itself to the margins of European security, and it spent another year extricating itself from this situation. Now its neighbours threaten to push Ukraine back to those margins once again. For political and security reasons the West should neither further this development nor acquiesce in it. Ukraine is not located on the margins but in the centre of the grey zone of European security, and hence instability in Ukraine would mean instability for Europe.

Notes

1   This chapter is an adapted and enlarged version of Gerard Snel, 'Oekraïne op zoek naar veiligheid: De precaire positie van een niet-nucleaire kernwapenstaat' [Ukraine Looking for Security: The Precarious Position of a Non-nuclear/Nuclear-weapon State], in René Does and Harm Ramkema (eds), *Demonen aan de Dnipr: De moeizame staatsvorming van Oekraïne* [Demons at the Dnipr: The Laborious State-building of Ukraine] (Amsterdam, 1994), pp. 89–101.
2   See Paul A. Goble, 'The Ukrainian Security Trap', *The Ukrainian Quarterly*, vol. 50, no. 3, Fall 1994, p. 230; and Roman Szporluk, 'Reflections on Ukraine after 1994: The Dilemma of Nationhood', *The Harriman Review*, vol. 7, nos. 7–9, March–May 1994, p. 1.
3   Cited in Goble, 'The Ukrainian Security Trap', p. 230. See also Szporluk, 'Reflections on Ukraine after 1994', p. 3.
4   See Roman Solchanyk, 'Ukraine', *RFE/RL Research Report*, vol. 1, no. 7, February 1992, pp. 1–5.
5   Roman Solchanyk, 'Kravchuk Defines Ukrainian–CIS Relations', *RFE/RL Research Report*, vol. 1, no. 14, March 1992, p. 9.
6   Roman Solchanyk, 'Ukraine and the CIS: A Troubled Relationship', *RFE/RL Research Report*, vol. 2, no. 7, February 1993, p. 25.
7   Peter van Ham, 'Ukraine, Russia and European Security: Implications for Western Policy', (Chaillot Paper no. 13, Institute for Security Studies–West European Union, Paris, February 1994), p. 14.
8   Ibid., p. 15.
9   See Michael E. Brown, 'Will START Stall?', *UNIDIR Newsletter*, nos. 22–23, June/September 1993, p. 29.
10 van Ham, 'Ukraine, Russia and European Security', p. 15.
11 Ibid., p. 24.

12   Ibid., pp. 24–5. Another example of a country exploiting its nuisance value is North Korea.

13   For the guarantees, see Anatoly Shevtsov and Mikhail Budnik, 'The START I Treaty and its Future: A Ukrainian Perspective', *UNIDIR Newsletter,* nos. 22–23, June/September 1993, pp. 19–20.

14   For the American shift, see Brown, 'Will START Stall?', p. 28; for Ukraine, see, for example, Anatoly Zlenko, Ukrainian Foreign Minister, 'Ukrainian Security and the Nuclear Dilemma', *NATO Review,* vol. 41, no. 4, August 1993, pp. 11–14.

15   At the press conference after the summit Kravchuk remained silent during Yeltsin's explanation of the deal, which strongly suggested that the former agreed.

16   Bogdan Nahaylo, 'The Massandra Summit and Ukraine', *RFE/RL Research Report*, vol. 2, no. 37, September 1993, pp. 1–6.

17   See John W.R. Lepingwell, 'Negotiations over Nuclear Weapons: The Past as Prologue?', *RFE/RL Research Report,* vol. 3, no. 4, January 1994, pp. 8–10.

18   See John W.R. Lepingwell, 'The Trilateral Agreement on Nuclear Weapons', *RFE/RL Research Report,* vol. 3, no. 4, January 1994, p. 12.

19   See ibid., pp. 19–20.

20   See ibid., pp. 18–19.

21   According to Bruce Blair, a nuclear command and control expert at the Brookings Institution, the obtaining of full operational control by the Ukraine was a matter of time. Conversation with the author, Washington, 17 June 1994.

22   Serhiy Tolstov, 'International Factors of Nuclear Disarmament of Ukraine', *The Ukrainian Review*, vol. 41, no. 1, Spring 1994, p. 14.

23   On the population figures, see Andrew Wilson, 'The Elections in Crimea', *RFE/RL Research Report*, vol. 3, no. 25, June 1994, p. 8. On the fleet, see John F. Dunn, 'Ukraine's Continuing Security Dilemmas: A Summary Update', in *Programme Book Colloquium: 'Oekraine en de Europese Stabiliteit'* (KHID/KIIB, Brussels, 7 December 1994), p. 35.

24   van Ham, 'Ukraine, Russia and European Security', p. 27.

25   See Dunn, 'Ukraine's Continuing Security Dilemmas', pp. 35–7.

26   Roman Solchanyk, 'The Crimean Imbroglio: Kiev and Simferopol', *RFE/RL Research Report,* vol. 1, no. 33, August 1992, pp. 13–16.

27   See Wilson, 'The Elections in Crimea', p. 18.

28   Ustina Markus, 'The Ukrainian Navy and the Black Sea Fleet', *RFE/RL Research Report,* vol. 3, no. 18, May 1994, pp. 32–40.

29   Sergei Tikhy, 'Krym: osen' prezidenta', *Moskovskie Novosti,* no. 38, September 1994, pp. 1, 4.

30   Sergei Tikhy, 'Crimea Experiences a New Wave of Confrontation', *Moscow News,* no. 47, November 1994, p. 5.

31   Ukrainian Information Center Amsterdam, *UNIAN Weekly Analysis,* no. 43 (1994).

32   According to an opinion poll in Kiev the support among the public for retaining nuclear status had grown from 18 per cent in May 1992 to 36 per cent in March 1993. See Roman Solchanyk, 'Ukraine's Search for Security', *RFE/RL Research Report*, vol. 2, no. 21, May 1993, p. 1.

33   See Brown, 'Will START Stall?', pp. 24–5.

34   See René Does, 'Een valse start: De economie van de onafhankelijke Oekraïne' [A False Start: The Economy of Independent Ukraine], in Does and Ramkema (eds), *Demonen aan de Dnipr,* p. 65.

35   Ibid., p. 66.

36   Dominique Arel and Andrew Wilson, 'The Ukrainian Parliamentary Elections', *RFE/*

RL Research Report, vol. 3, no. 26, July 1994, pp. 6–17; and Szporluk, 'Reflections on Ukraine after 1994', pp. 1–2. The split was not so much an ethnic as a linguistic one: the first-preference Russophones (including ethnic Ukrainians) voted for the former parties and candidates, the first-preference Ukrainophones for the latter.

37 David R. Marples, 'Ukraine after the Presidential Elections', *RFE/RL Research Report*, vol. 3, no. 31, August 1994, pp. 7–10.

38 Kuchma to the Parliament, as cited in Ukrainian Information Center Amsterdam, *Press Digest*, October 1994, p. 2.

39 Marples, 'Ukraine after the Presidential Elections', p. 10.

40 Goble, 'The Ukrainian Security Trap', pp. 230–1.

41 Dmitry Yakushkin, 'Gennadi Udovenko: "Treaty with Russia Should Not Be Delayed"', *Moscow News*, no. 47, 13–20 November 1994, p. 5.

42 Wilson, 'The Elections in Crimea', pp. 7–19.

43 See Vyacheslav Pikhovshek and Christopher Pett, 'Transformation of the Ukrainian Armed Forces', *NATO Review*, vol. 42, no. 5, October 1994, pp. 21–5.

11 Turkey and the Independent States of Central Asia

Ciro E. Zoppo

Introduction

The emerging foreign policy of Turkey towards the newly independent states of Central Asia cannot be understood without examining the magnitude of the changes that have occurred since 1991 in the geopolitical dynamics of the region. The historic context that preceded the sudden independence from the Soviet Union and Russia of the Turkic republics of Azerbaijan, Kazakhstan, Kyrgyzstan, Turkmenistan and Uzbekistan cannot be ignored in terms of Russian as well as Soviet antecedents.

There are several reasons for including historical aspects in the discussion of the relations that are developing between these states and Turkey. Without making explicit the historical cultural kinship between the Turks of Turkey and those of Central Asia, a unique psychological dimension of their budding diplomatic relationships will be absent from the analysis. This psychological aspect is subtle but evident in the mutual perceptions of the leaders of the Turkic states and of Turkey. The sense of a shared ancestry and linguistic culture may not guarantee the success of Turkey's policies: it will, however, give a ready access to Turkey's diplomacy.

Another reason for including historical background involves the definition and construction of the state and the nation in these countries. If Turkey is to offer a model of the secular state, with political democracy and a free market economy, the ideological guidelines and the historic development of the Turkish state will necessarily be important aspects of its promotion in Turkey's foreign policy. The model of the Turkish secular state is not only in competition with Iran's Islamic state, but also with vestigial elements of the former Soviet state.

The impact of Turkish Central Asian policies on relations between Turkey and Russia is also a significant aspect of the international dynamic of the area. The interactions between Moscow and Ankara may define, at times crucially, regional security, economic development and regional nationalist politics. Turkey's foreign policy towards Central Asia is incipient and evolving, and the geopolitics of the region are dynamic and in transition.

The Geopolitics of Central Asia After the Dissolution of the Soviet Union

By any measure of classical geopolitics, Russia must now significantly alter its geopolitical orientation for the first time in well over two centuries. The advent of the nuclear age had already forced the Soviet Union to modify its geostrategic ambitions in order to accommodate the impact of the space weapons of mass destruction and revolutionary communications technology. However, because *inter alia* nuclear deterrence did not prove to be a useful instrument for conquest, the geopolitical *status quo* prevailed.[1] Until internal political factors brought about the collapse of the Soviet Union, the Russian empire survived.

The disintegration of the Soviet Union has eliminated the last European empire in modern history. The Eurasian continent was a crucible of modern empires, where the imperial ambitions of Russia, Austria, Ottoman Turkey and Great Britain clashed in the eighteenth and nineteenth centuries. As modern nationalism took root in the Balkans and eroded Ottoman imperial power in the nineteenth century, Russia expanded its domains by annexing nearly all of Central and East Asia to forge the Russian empire that the Soviet Union inherited and consolidated in this century.

Most of Central Asia was conquered by tsarist Russia about the same time that Great Britain and France were building their empires in the Middle East and the Maghreb, Africa and Asia. After 1870, a wave of empire-building began. In less than two generations, the major European powers, later joined by the United States and Japan, partitioned virtually all of the Eastern Hemisphere among themselves. Russian imperialist expansion was also completed during this period. After the death of Tsar Peter the Great, Russian expansion concentrated, in the nineteenth century, on the regions inhabited by the Kazakhs. By 1822, Russian sovereignty over the area ceased to be nominal and became a reality.[2] The battle of Geok Tepe in 1881 marked the completion of the conquest of Central Asia and of the Transcaspian region by tsarist Russia. The khanates of Bukhara, Khiva and Kokand had been gradually overrun and ceased to exist as independent political domains.[3]

Another historical factor of relevance to the present situation in the Caucasus and in the south-west of Central Asia is the Ottoman Empire. The

Turks of the Ottoman empire shared ancestral origins with those in Central Asia. However, although Bukhara and the Crimea khanates had maintained a slack vassalage with the Sublime Porte in Istanbul, Central Asia never came to represent the imperial ambitions of the Ottoman empire. In 1774, the Ottoman protectorate over the Crimea came to an end and was replaced by a Russian one. The unsuccessful Pan-Turkism of Enver Pasha did not appear until the last gasp of the Ottoman empire, before and during the First World War. The several wars between Russia and Ottoman Turkey, during the eighteenth and nineteenth centuries, were concerned primarily with the control of the Black Sea region and the Straits.[4]

Nevertheless, the collapse of the Ottoman empire at the end of the First World War, followed a few years later by the abolition of the caliphate, had a strongly negative effect on the Turkic peoples of Central Asia. The majority, Muslims and Turkic, had regarded Ottoman Turkey as their spiritual and cultural mentor. Total segregation did not take place, however, until the consolidation of the Soviet regime in 1927.[5]

Today, and for the decades immediately ahead, the 'tiger is at the gates'. An arc of potential ethnic and nationalist conflicts surrounds Russia with no territorial spaces to buffer the impact at its frontiers. In Central Asia the combination of the systemic changes in international politics and the awakening of nationalism with uncertain blueprints for internal politics – polarized by democratic and Islamic ideologies – is likely to perpetuate regional instability for years to come, and to threaten Russian economic and political interests, as well as its security in its Asiatic borderlands.

The regime in Uzbekistan, faced with nascent democratic and Islamic political oppositions, is one example. The civil war in Tajikistan is another. So is the war between Armenia and Azerbaijan, and the separatist civil war in Georgia. Except for Armenia and Georgia, beyond Russia's new frontiers in the contiguous territories of Central Asia are peoples without historically established autonomous nations, in search of viable definitions of the modern state.

Cultural, social, political and economic grievances against the Soviets for decades have surfaced in the context of emergent nationalisms fuelled by local self-assertion. Under conditions of domestic political instability, caused by the weakness of existing regimes and the unavoidable transition from the Soviet economic model to market economies, there is the potential not only for disputes among the new states of Central Asia but between national élites and emerging transnational political movements. The most disruptive of these transnational movements in regard to the development of modern states is Islamic fundamentalism, patterned on that of Iran.

Although the national leaders of Central Asian states are secularist and the product of 70 years of Soviet education, ideology and administrative experience, the history of an independent Central Asia is too short, popular legitimacy for the regimes too untested, to exclude the growth of Islamic fundamentalism. Islamic fundamentalism in Central Asia raises Russian concerns that extend beyond that region. One possible effect of the growth of fundamentalism would be its impact on the Russian Federation's own Muslim peoples. Potentially, such a development could undermine the territorial integrity of Russia itself. A similar potential threat also exists for China. In the Xinjiang autonomous region, some 60 per cent of the 15 million inhabitants are Turkic Muslims, among them six million Uygurs, one million Kazakhs and 140,000 Kirghiz. Since 1993, a movement for an independent Eastern Turkestan has led to political turmoil in Xinjiang, and in its major cities Chinese police and paramilitary forces have been reinforced.[6]

Central Asia may not be as populated as the surrounding regions, but its birth rate is on the rise and its territory and natural resources loom large in the future geopolitics of Eurasia. Kazakhstan, Kyrgyzstan, Tajikistan, Turkmenistan and Uzbekistan contain 50 million people living over a vast territorial expanse. Kazakhstan alone is larger than the whole of Western Europe. In addition to petroleum and natural gas, the region has uranium and a uranium-processing complex, manganese, lead and zinc, iron ore, bauxite, gold and copper, some coal, hydrocarbons, and weapons production mostly in Kazakhstan.[7]

Complicating the geopolitics of the region further is the existence in the newly independent states of Central Asia of sizable percentages of Russians in the populations. The 1989 census revealed that the Russian inhabitants of Uzbekistan constituted 12.5 per cent of the population. In Kazakhstan, they were 43 per cent. In Azerbaijan, they amounted to 10 per cent. In Tajikistan, they were 12 per cent. In Kirghizia, Russians accounted for 30 per cent, and in Turkmenistan for 15 per cent.[8] The potential for ethnic conflict has led President Boris Yeltsin to appeal to the West to support the policy that Russia be allowed a special role in policing former Soviet areas, especially to protect Russian-speaking citizens.

Decolonization in other areas of the world suggests that nation-building, even when successful, is attended by often violent and lingering conflict, or at the very least political turmoil. The violence in Georgia and the conflict between Armenia and Azerbaijan provide a clear example of this. The Armenian–Azerbaijani conflict also illustrates the fact that national boundaries drawn by imperial powers for their own designs of governance will spawn future conflict. Most boundaries in Central Asia were drawn by imperial Russia with little regard for tribal and ethnic history. The approach was continued by the Soviets.[9]

The reshaped geopolitics of the region are made more problematic not only by ethnic and political factors but also by economic ones. No independent national economies, in the true sense of the word, exist in the Central Asian states. The vanishing command economy of Russia was directed and controlled from Moscow but, although Russia controlled from the centre, it was also dependent on the periphery for raw materials and certain products. The efforts made through the Commonwealth of Independent States (CIS) to establish a common market based on trade may eventually establish a new *modus operandi* not based on Russian control, replacing the current ascendancy of Russian economic interests.[10]

Meanwhile, none of the Central Asian independent states have complete control of their economies. After the *coup*, Yeltsin was quick to take control of the Soviet Union's foreign holdings and to use economic blackmail to press republics to accept Russia as the centre of a single financial system and currency zone. However, there will be opportunities for trade, outside the CIS, particularly in essential materials like petroleum. Already under way is a Turkish initiative to engage Azerbaijan in an effort to channel oil to Turkish ports for shipment to Turkey and the Mediterranean, using in part the existing Iraq pipeline.[11] The national leaders of Central Asia are increasingly seeking foreign partners to help develop their economies in ways that are useful to their own economies, not Russia's.

Russia remains the geopolitical 'heartland' of Eurasia, but its dominance in the region, including Central Asia, can no longer be assumed. In the international strategic space of the area, in political and economic terms a dynamic situation is developing to give scope for action to other regional actors, particularly Iran and Turkey, but also China, Pakistan and India. The geopolitical factors are changing into a dynamic that may be hard to control by Russia, the dominant military power in the region. With Russia's historic hegemony at an end, a power vacuum has emerged in Central Asia to create a geopolitical space for internal strife and external rivalry and intervention.

Consequently, Turkey's role in Central Asia is being defined and must operate in this developing geopolitical environment. The characteristics of the newly-independent states of the region, the assertion of Russian interests and those of other regional actors, and Turkey's own political, economic and military resources available for the task at hand provide the limits and opportunities for Turkish policies toward the region.

One unique factor that could advance Turkey's foreign policy objectives in Central Asia is the perceived cultural kinship between the people of Turkey and those of the states of Central Asia. Another is the example of the successful construction of a modern Turkish secular state from the ruins of the Ottoman empire. While Turkic kinship by its very nature facilitates diplomatic dialogue between the political leaders of Central Asian states and the leaders of Turkey, the Turkish model of the secular state is not amenable to straightforward and appreciable transfer from Turkey to Central Asia. Intrinsic factors arise from the historical antecedents regarding nationalist identity of the newly-independent states of Central Asia, and the nature of the institutions created by the Soviets that constitute the state in them. Both the nation and the state are inchoate in Central Asia and derivative of Russian conquest and Soviet ideological and administrative control. Asian Turks have yet to define conclusively and independently either the state or the nation. To the degree that Turkey's diplomacy contributes to their definition, to that degree will Turkish policy influence the political values and the institutional structure of the newly-independent states. The outcome will have crucial consequences for Turkey's policies in the region.

Asian Turks in Search of the Nation and the State

The first requirement for Turkey's policies toward Central Asia is to understand the basic characteristics that define the newly-independent states of the region, particularly those of Turkic culture. That culture is the psychological bridge between Turkey and the Turkic independent states of Central Asia, providing a unique political factor available to Turkish foreign policy. Of course common ethnic origins, linguistic traits and a shared religion (most of the citizens of Turkey and of the newly-independent states are Sunni Muslims) neither guarantee success for Turkish efforts nor do they close the door to the diplomatic and economic efforts of other non-Turkic regional and international actors. Yet they do provide a ready audience for Turkish diplomacy, based on a mutually recognized kinship.

The 'Turkishness' of the peoples of Central Asia is the most psychological diplomatic asset available to Turkey. Before the founding of the Turkish Republic the Central Asian origins of the Turks who migrated to Anatolia and the Middle East was the subject of politicized scholarly and literary concern. The legendary Turkic epic *Kitab-i Dede Qorqut* (The Book (of Tales) of Old Man Korkut) is focused on the Oguz Turks. The Oguz in the eighth century AD inhabited Central and Eastern Asia, in the region of Lake Baikal and the Altai mountains.[12]

After embracing Islam, the Oguz constituted the bulk of the armies of the Seljuks, themselves Oguz, who conquered Iran and most of Anatolia during the eleventh and twelfth centuries. The Ottomans, who later took over the Seljuk empire in Anatolia to create the Ottoman empire by also annexing the Balkans and eventually destroying the Byzantine empire, also boasted their descent from the Oguz. Whether they were Oguz has been a matter for scholarly debate. In terms of political legitimacy under the Ottomans and the potential political utility of this belief about historical kinship, however, there is no debate about the mutual ancestral origins of Turks in Turkey and in Central Asia. The memory of the Oguz and their legends disappeared in the ethnic cauldron of the late Ottoman empire. Then and now, however, the legends of *Dede Qorqut* and other evocative works remain in the memory of poets and scholars in Turkey.

There are two qualifications to the thrust of this analysis relevant to the discussion of Turkey's emerging policies toward Central Asia. Ziya Gokalp, the literary precursor of modern Turkish nationalism and a mentor of Kemalism, who died in 1924 just as the Turkish Republic was being born, redefined the Turkish cultural ethos on the basis of a presumed affiliation with Western civilization.[13] His ideological premisses combined a form of democratic populism with the concept of a Turkish national identity. Institutional Islam was to be separated from government, or depoliticized. This laid the foundation for the Kemalist approach to Islam, and provided the guidelines for detaching the state from the Islamic institutional framework of the Ottoman government. Gokalp thus anticipated a liberal democratic Turkish republic.[14]

The other qualification deals with the lack of shared, or even similar, experience of Central Asians and Turks during the last five centuries. In modern history the newly-independent Turkic states and Turkey have had very different historical experiences, particularly in regard to nation-building. First, whereas in modern history the Turkic states of Central Asia were colonized by a major external power, Turkey was itself an imperial power annexing alien territories in Asia Minor and Eastern Europe, until the decline and the collapse of the Ottoman empire at the beginning of the century. A central tenet of the contemporary Turkish state is the rejection of Turkey's imperial past. This rejection of the imperial past is an important factor in the legitimizing of the Turkish model of the secular state. Second, the development of the ethnic antecedents of the modern state in Turkey followed a path more akin to the development of the modern nation-state in Europe than that of the decolonized, developing countries of Asia, Africa and the Middle East. Even before the Ottoman takeover of the Seljuk empire, tribal identity was being lost in Anatolia. On the 'marches', or war frontiers between the nascent Turkish empire and Byzantium, special military organizations had emerged on both the Byzantine and the Turkish sides.[15] The Byzantine 'march' warriors were the *Akritoi*. The Turkish host was made up of *Ghazis* (Warriors of the Faith), who came from the most distant parts of the world. These frontier forces were an eclectic mixture of nationalities and languages, forming a distinct population. Prisoners, deserters and intermarriage with local women facilitated cultural exchange and assimilation. In the Muslim 'marches' the Turkish element became dominant, becoming the most important factor in the creation of the Seljuk and particularly the Ottoman empire.[16] In the modern nation-state system, the Turks of Anatolia and those of Central Asia hardly have any shared history.

Until their annexation by Russia, the Turkic peoples of Central Asia were more likely to be engaged in clan or tribal conflict than in integrating political enterprises generated by a common Turkic identity, or by a shared Islamic heritage. Instead, the region has evidenced to our day ethnic diversity and distinct tribal mores.

The modern as much as the ancient history of the predominantly Turkic people of Central Asia suggests the nature of the problem attending the creation of genuine and cohesive nationalities which can provide territorial integrity to the new states. Modern nationalisms remain in great part to be achieved. Centuries of foreign invasions and domination have aborted the process of nation-building. Central Asia's leaders are aware that, although each state carries the name of a local nationality, none is a genuine homeland. Kirghiz, Uzbeks, Tajiks, Turkmen and Kazakhs all have border claims on each other and sizeable irredentist populations to legitimize them.

Equally relevant and important for Central Asian states is the question of the autonomous modern state. When the Russians conquered Central Asia and when the Bolsheviks took it over, no national entities possessing the structure of government properly definable as a modern state existed. The kingdoms of Bukhara, Khiva and Kokund, the most successful indigenous political entities facing the Russian advance, were comparable politically to the European kingdoms of the early Middle Ages.[17] The modern state, when it is not a totalitarian dictatorship directed by a despot, is ultimately legitimized by taming power through the depersonalization of its exercise. In the modern state, the relation between the state and the law is particularly close, and the latter is legislated by genuinely representative bodies.[18] Given the indigenous, Russian and Soviet antecedents to independence in the states of Central Asia, this dimension of the modern state remains to be constructed. The Turkish state model appeals undeniably to the current national leaders. The Turkish model of the secular state was not imposed by a foreign power but created by the Turks themselves as they defined their nation, after the end of the Ottoman empire. However, the historical experience which produced the modern secular state in Turkey is distinctly different from that of the Turkic states of Central Asia.

Ethnic, religious and linguistic loyalties are major hurdles in the way of national develoment and consolidation. To achieve a modern nation requires the integration of groups which are struggling to maintain their identity in the national society. A state as a territorial unit can maintain itself when a central authority has enough coercive power to monopolize governance and maintain public order. A nation, on the other hand, is a subjective belief about the legitimacy of the state. The essential instrument required is the creation and development of institutions that promote a national identity.

After 1924, the Soviet state organized administrative entities with local cadres to run the Central Asian republics according to the dictates of Moscow. These dictates focused on political, economic and military control from the centre, in Moscow, and this situation prevailed until the recent collapse of the Soviet Union. It has changed dramatically in the political sphere, only partially in the economic one, and remains confused and relatively least changed in the military realm. The Russian military presence in Central Asia, notwithstanding the ambiguous status of Russian forces, remains preponderant. The juridical basis for the CIS in regard to Russian troop deployments in Central Asia, and particularly Russian involvement in Central Asian conflicts, is the 1992 CIS Treaty of Collective Security.[19]

Both in the formulation of foreign policy and its diplomatic implementation, the Turkic states of Central Asia lack foreign policy experience and have a severe shortage of diplomats. Moreover, these states continue to be dependent on Moscow-based communications and transportation networks, thus creating a diplomatic isolation that will take time to surmount and can be rectified only by reaching out to foreign sources.

The leaders of the Central Asian states were not nationalist leaders seeking independence before they took over the stewardship of the state. Most of them are members of the traditional ruling élite drawn from the former Soviet apparatus. Because the form the polity will take is yet to be established, their political legitimacy is contingent. The legitimacy of their tenure is based ultimately on their ethnic credentials and the effectiveness with which they handle the extraordinary challenges facing the new states. Their expertise in governing is nevertheless almost exclusively based on their Soviet experience. Their tenure was made and unmade in Moscow, according to the power plays of the contending Communist party élite. The legacy of that experience in shaping policy is best illustrated by Nursultan Nazarbaev, President of Kazakhstan, who, after the failed 1991 *coup*, forcefully spoke in favour of a revitalized Soviet Union, organized as a confederation.[20]

Because of their inexperience in foreign affairs, the leaders of the Central Asian states are currently finding it difficult to define their respective national interests and to pursue them, especially in regard to Russia. They represent incipient modern nations and weak polities. Neither in terms of the nation nor the state are the countries of Central Asia likely to reach maturity in this century. Theirs is a quest which has only just begun.

Turkey's Strategy for Central Asia

Turkish policy toward Central Asia and the former Soviet republics is tentative and part of a broader revision of Turkey's basic foreign policy strategy that is being forged in the light of the end of the Cold War. For the first time since the foundation of the Turkish Republic, in 1924, the basic tenets of the Kemalist foreign policy tradition, set up by Kemal Ataturk (Mustafa Kemal) are being challenged by the unprecedented changes in international relations that have been taking place since 1991. The strategy that Turkey forged after the Second World War was consistent with the foreign policy objectives set up by Ataturk. It basically adjusted Turkish policy to the changes that the Second World War wrought.

The most basic component, and legacy, of the Ataturk strategy was to establish territorial boundaries that legitimized the Turkish national homeland – hence the central importance of security as an organizing principle of the new state. These boundaries were achieved by the national war of liberation and were made legitimate in the international system that followed the First World War by the 1923 Treaty of Lausanne. A pivotal consideration of the negotiations that led to the signing of the treaty was the status of the Straits and of the Dardanelles. The Straits had been historically the linchpin of the strategic assets of Ottoman Turkey and remain to this day the focal point for the defence of Turkey. Lausanne confirmed Turkish sovereignty over the Straits and regulated their international use for commerce.

The preservation of the territorial integrity of Anatolia assured the continued existence of the homeland for the Turks established by their ancestors after leaving Central Asia about nine centuries ago. This was the first objective that governed Ataturk's strategy, and continues to be an irreducible tenet of Turkey's strategy. The policies that have flowed from this core have all been subsidiary and designed to serve this objective in the light of changing historical circumstances. Until recently the subsidiary goals of the Kemalist foreign policy strategy have been relatively constant and without contradictions *inter se*. They can be succinctly labelled modernization, or (put another way) Westernization; and correct (that is, non-provocative) relations with the Soviet Union.[21]

Westernization came to mean not only following the secular state model of internal governance and economic activity, but also a definition of Turkey as a member of the European interstate system and the West. This outlook among the Turkish élite was reinforced by Turkey's participation in the North Atlantic Alliance. Most Turks believe that their aspirations concerning their well-being can be satisfied in the framework of a democratic and secular political system. Kemalism as a national philosophy continues to be accepted by most Turks of all social classes. In spite of the dominant and respected role of the military in public life, Turks show no signs of being interested in territorial expansion elsewhere.[22] Relevant for a Turkish policy towards Central Asia is the fact that the average Turk is awakening to an interest in the life and welfare of their Turkic kinsmen in Central Asia and the Balkans.

The second component of the Kemalist foreign policy tradition is the nature of the relations with the Soviet Union, a state that began almost at the same time as modern Turkey. Until the radical changes brought by its collapse raised fundamental questions about Turkish policy towards Russia and Central Asia, Turkish policies had consistently avoided any involvement in the intra-Soviet politics of the region. The Soviet Union had been the first country to sign a treaty of friendship and aid with the emergent Turkish republic. To assure tranquility at its borders with the Soviet state, Kemalist Turkey disengaged from the politics of the neighbouring peoples in the Soviet Union and maintained a basically friendly posture towards Moscow. At the same time, it remained an unflinching ideological opponent of Communism at home.[23]

However, as the Ottoman state had done, republican Turkey continued, after the First World War, to give asylum to all refugees of Turkic blood from the Caucasus and Central Asia. This policy was continued when Turkey abandoned its neutrality after the Second World War.

After the end of the Cold War, Turkish caution remained and it was not until the actual disintegration of the Soviet Union, following the failed *coup* in 1991, that Turkey focused on Central Asia. The focus was engendered as much by the interests of the leaders of Uzbekistan, Tajikistan, Turkmenistan Kyrgyzstan, Kazakhstan – and in the Caucasus Azerbaijan – as by a preconceived Turkish foreign policy design. Once the decision was made to engage with the region in 1991, however, Turkish policy became actively involved in a process of exploration. In September 1991, the Turkish foreign ministry sent diplomatic teams to all Central Asian republics to assess political developments and to set up formal Turkish recognition and establish Turkish diplomatic posts.[24]

Turkish policy remains pragmatic and tentative. Nevertheless, by the end of 1993, some policy goals had begun to emerge. Taken together, they can be said to outline the beginnings of a Turkish policy.

Except for considerations having to do with Turkey's territorial integrity or security, the core tenet of Kemalist strategy, Turkish diplomacy must invent a Central Asian policy from a relative vacuum. The only concrete antecedent of this century regarding the Turkic peoples of the Caucasus and Central Asia is the negative experience of pan-Turanism which still haunts Turkish foreign policy.

In their policy declarations concerning relations with the Turkic republics, Turkish political leaders have all been sensitive about interpretations of Turkish policies that suggest a reawakened Turanism. President Turgut Ozal, before his death and in connection with official visits to Central Asia, stressed that 'fantasies of pan-Turkism are totally out of the question, especially in today's world'.[25] Both Suleyman Demirel, as prime minister and as president, and Erdal Inonu, when acting prime minister, have made similar statements. Official declarations underscore that Turkey will not play the role of 'big brother'.

Emerging Turkish Policy Objectives

The policies that Turkey is tentatively pursuing towards Central Asia and the Caucasus do not amount to a grand foreign policy design, but they do begin to develop approaches that could become the components of a Turkish strategy for the region. Succinctly stated, the following are emerging as foreign policy goals:

- to develop trade and expand markets for Turkey;
- to abort Muslim fundamentalism in the region;
- to promote the secular model of the state;
- to help create geopolitical stability in the region;
- to establish for Turkey a hegemonic role in the region.

These objectives are interrelated and some feed into each other. For example, the successful promotion of the secular state is the most effective tool for combating Muslim fundamentalism. It also facilitates Turkey's road towards hegemony in that it severely undermines Iran's competition for leadership in the region. Such an outcome is reinforced by the achievement of the economic goals of Turkish policy. Achieving economic goals would help the Turkish economy and also help to improve economic conditions in the newly-independent states of Central Asia and the Caucasus. Moreover, the less economically dependent on Russia these states are, the more independence in foreign policy they would have. Such an outcome would create opportunities for Turkey's inchoate aspirations for regional hegemony.

Regional geopolitical stability would remove many obstacles to the achievement of the other goals. These incipient goals do not have dedicated paths or priorities in the current enunciations of Turkish diplomacy. They may be deduced from the positions and actions of Turkish diplomacy towards the Caucasus and Central Asia.

Turkish Foreign Policy Instruments

'Turkishness', the most psychological diplomatic tool available to Turkey in its relations with Central Asia, has been indicated. An examination of the references to a common Turkic heritage with Turkey by the leaders of the new states makes clear that they are aware of and appreciate the culture they share with the people of Turkey.

This is a subtle and unique asset for Turkish diplomacy in its policies toward Central Asia. Iran's diplomacy does not possesses it in its ideological competition with Turkey. Turkey is on record as being ready to extend help to the new states in the training of statesmen and military personnel. Turkey is already hosting over 7000 students from these republics.[26]

To Turkic leaders confronted with attempting to set up national entities which aspire to being democratic and to operate as market economies, modern Turkey can be an inspiration and a model for development. On the political side, the secular state Ataturk set up over 70 years ago should be a more congenial model for Turkic élites. They, who for several generations have been the product of an atheist Soviet education, would find it quite difficult to run, or even understand, a theocracy patterned on fundamentalist Iran. Although rivalry with Iran about the model of the polity the new states should adopt is already quite intense, Turkish politics and economics have a demonstrably better record.

The present leaders in Central Asia unambiguously prefer the Turkish model. In the words of President Irlam Karimov of Uzbekistan:

> Uzbekistan, as an independent state, is faced with the dilemma of which course of development to choose and one that accords with our own interests. I can definitely say that the Turkish path of development is more acceptable for us first and foremost because it leads to the development of a secular, civilized society. Of course, we must work out our own path of development, using Turkey as a model. The Iranian model will not work for us.[27]

Turkey obviously cannot compete economically in Central Asia with major industrial nations. Nevertheless, on balance the potential of the Turkish economy provides Turkish diplomacy towards Central Asia and the Caucasus with an additional instrument of foreign policy. Turkish traders and industrialists have been exploring opportunities in the Turkic republics for contracts, investments and trade, officially aided and sponsored by the Turkish government.

The following are illustrative of the increasing Turkish economic presence in Central Asia. Turkish investors have invested US$1,358,650,000 (nearly 13,315 billion Turkish lira) in the Turkic republics during the past few years. In Azerbaijan, the NETAS telecommunications company has invested $10 million. The Koc automobile company is investing $30 million for the production of Land Rovers and minibuses, and the Simtel holding company $20 million for the manufacture of washing machines, vacuum cleaners, television sets and stereo systems.[28]

In Kazakhstan, the Pet holding company has allocated $2.5 million for facilities to be used for oil prospecting and drilling. The Turkish division of Mercedes Benz has concluded an agreement to start production in one of that republic's large factories. The StarMod company has allocated $35 million for the construction of a factory to process leather and leather clothes. In Kyrgyzstan, the Borusan corporation will invest $50 million for a factory to produce metal and plastic pipes. The Teletas company is investing $10 million for the Kyrgyzstan broadcast relay stations, while the Tefken company will invest $5.5 million in the electronics industry, $2 million to set up a fur processing factory, $25 million for the construction of a hotel, and $60 million for the construction of shoe factories.[29]

In Turkmenistan, there is concentrated Turkish investment from the opening of banks and the construction of an airport to supermarkets, refrigeration facilities, a cultural centre, hotels, and textile, brick, cement and clothing factories. Total investment is around $883 million. In addition, the Simko company will invest $100 million to produce wire and cables. In Uzbekistan, the Yazeks company plans to invest $100 million in textile factories.

The Turkish government believes that the most important help to be extended to the Central Asian republics is in the sectors of banking and commerce, and sees active and closer co-operation in economic relations as contributing to political stability in the region.[30] Some movement in that direction is under way. Uzbekistan and Kazakhstan are aiming to form a common market by the year 2000, and will soon begin to co-ordinate economic policies. All tariffs between them are to be eliminated, and border customs as well, allowing free movement of goods, services, capital and labour. The Turkish government sees Turkey acting as a bridge in the economic development within the Islamic Conference Organization and to provide assistance to the economic development of the Turkic states.[31]

It is clear that the collapse of the Soviet Union has opened a geopolitical space for Turkey's foreign policy in Central Asia and the Caucasus that had been hermetically sealed against it since the Bolshevik Revolution. It is also becoming apparent that Turkey possesses foreign policy assets and instrumentalities that can advance Turkish national interests in the region. It remains to be seen whether the dynamic situation in the region has created opportunities for Turkey that outweigh the possible costs.

Turkey and Russia in Central Asia

For Turkey, Central Asia offers an irresistible opportunity to enhance its international standing. For Russia, it represents a loss in its international status. Nevertheless, this situation does not represent, in and of itself, a formula for competition and conflict between the two nations in the region, though it creates both divergent and shared interests. It is too early to assess which of these might prevail in the long run. For the present, it seems that mutually shared interests prevail, and foremost among these is the attainment of regional stability.

The potentially unstable character of Central Asia is due to the present borders which cut across regional, ethnic and tribal disputes over land and resources. Turkey's ancestral kinship with the peoples of the area, recognized by them, may make it an effective mediator of unresolved conflicts. Turkish success here would help Russian relations with the former Soviet republics.

By the end of 1992, Russia had become acutely aware of the possibly emergent threat of Muslim fundamentalism and focused on establishing new relations with the former Soviet Central Asian republics. Here, there is a coincidence of Turkish and Russian interests in the promotion of the Turkish model of the secular state. The situation nevertheless carries the seeds for potential rivalry between Russia and Turkey in Central Asia, particularly in regard to Kazakhstan – largely because of the Russian desire to nurture a more intimate security, political and economic relationship with that state.

In the area of regional military security, there is a mix of shared and possibly divergent interests between Turkey and Russia. The Russian Federation has deployed military forces in the region on several occasions, occasionally in the dual role of peace-keepers and protectors of Russian minorities. This has sometimes led to accusations that Russia is supporting one of the parties against the other. One case has been the role of Russian forces in the Azerbaijani–Armenian conflict. In that situation, Turkey protested at the increase of Russian armour not far from its borders, though Russia justified its military deployments in terms of the July 1992 CIS Tashkent agreement. The CIS foreign and defence ministers agreed to create CIS peace-keeping forces to be used in regional ethnic conflicts, and the agreement requires an invitation by all the involved parties prior to the deployment of such forces. Based on statements by CIS Commander Marshal Yevgeny Shaposhnikov, peace-keeping activities will be added to the centralized control of nuclear weapons and co-ordination of military doctrines and reforms in member states as the main function of the CIS military command.

Turkey, not a member of CIS, cannot directly challenge the influence of the Russian military in the Central Asian republics, and its own ability to influence the political outcomes, by the capacities and impact of its own military forces in regard to such conflictual situations in the region, remains at the discretion of Russian policy.

In this connection, and germane to Turkish anxieties, is the agreement of September 1993, which allows the return to Azerbaijan of the Russian forces that had been withdrawn and the return to Russian control of the Baku Caspian naval base.[32] Turkish officials have revealed that they are concerned that Russia considers the republics of the Former Soviet Union as being within its 'zone of influence'. Yeltsin's demands that the Conventional Forces in Europe Agreement be modified to allow an increase in Russian forces deployed in the Caucasus was viewed with apprehension in Ankara. This area of relations suggests the potential for friction between Russia and Turkey.

The other area of potential co-operation or friction between Turkey and Russia is in economic and trade activities with the states of Central Asia and the Caucasus. It is less fraught with conflict because Turkish investments and trade there are modest. Excluding barter deals, Turkey's exports to the region during 1992 amounted to less than 2 per cent of total Turkish exports.

Nevertheless, Turkey is endeavouring to exercise selective control over the raw materials and commodity markets in Central Asia and the Caucasus. It consists primarily of energy resources and their transportation systems. The importance and the impact on Russian plans and economic requirements cannot be assessed simply in percentages of trade. The issue becomes more cogent when viewed from the perspective of the greater economic independence from Russia that some of the Turkic republics are striving to achieve in the energy sector. They have rejected an integrationist approach within the CIS.

Even if Turkey does not have the financial resources, it can act as a bridge with wealthy and politically moderate Arab countries and Europe in joint ventures and commercial deals without raising any fears of economic hegemony.

Notes

1   Ciro E. Zoppo, 'The Geopolitics of Nuclear Deterrence', in C. Zoppo and C. Zorgbibe (eds), *Geopolitics: Classical and Nuclear* (Boston, 1985), p. 161.
2   Michael Rywkin, *Russia in Central Asia* (London, 1963), pp. 15–31.
3   Geoffrey Wheeler, *The Modern History of Soviet Central Asia* (New York, 1964), pp. 57–63.
4   C. Lamouche, *Histoire de la Turquie* (Paris, 1953), p. 140; and Stanford Shaw, *History*

of the Ottoman Empire and Modern Turkey (Cambridge, 1976), pp. 254–5.This is the most comprehensive recent scholarly work.

5 Wheeler, *The Modern History of Soviet Central Asia*, p. 29.

6 Martha Brill Olcott, 'Central Asia: The Reformers Challenge a Traditional Society', in Lubomyr Hajda and Mark Beissinger (eds), *The Nationalities Factor in Soviet Politics and Society* (Boulder, Colorado, 1990), p. 262.

7 Gerard Chaliand and Jean-Pierre Rogeau, *Atlas Stratégique* (Paris, 1983), pp. 8, 92.

8 Rajan Menon and Henri J. Barkey, 'The Transformation of Central Asia: Implications for Regional and International Stability', *Survival*, vol. 34, no. 4, 1992–3, p. 81.

9 This issue is treated in detail in Hajda and Beissinger (eds), *The Nationalities Factor in Soviet Politics and Society*, pp. 1–87.

10 A Russian explanation of the meaning of CIS by the Russian Ambassador to the United States, Vladimir Lukin, is 'Russia in Far and Near Circles', *Segodnya*, Moscow, 2 September 1993 (FBIS-SOV-93-172).

11 'Investments in Turkic Republics', *Sabah*, Istanbul, 2 May 1993 (FBIS-WEU-93-088, 10 May 1993).

12 Ettore Rossi, *Il Kitab-i Dede Qorqut* (Vatican City, 2nd edn, 1981), pp. 14–48.

13 A comprehensive treatment of Ziya Gokalp's ideology is in Anar Suat, 'Social and Philosophical Foundations of Modern Turkish Education: The Impact of Ziya Gokalp', University of Michigan Dissertation, 1986, pp. 66–126.

14 Alan R. Taylor, *The Islamic Question in Middle East Politics* (London, 1988), pp. 29–30.

15 Paul Wittek, *The Rise of the Ottoman Empire* (London, 1938), pp. 33–4.

16 Ibid., pp. 29–30, 40–1.

17 Heinrich Mitteis, *The State in the Middle Ages* (New York, 1975), pp. 11ff.

18 Gianfranco Poggi, *The Development of the Modern State* (Stanford, California, 1978), pp. 101–2; Charles Tilly (ed.), *The Formation of National States in Western Europe* (Princeton, New Jersey, 1975), pp. 3–83.

19 General V. Samsonov, Chief of Staff of CIS Joint Armed Forces General Staff, *Krasnaia Zvezda*, 3 July 1992 (FBIS-SOV, 9 July 1992).

20 Martha Brill Olcott, 'Central Asia's Catapult to Independence', *Foreign Affairs*, vol. 71, no. 3, Summer 1992, pp. 111–12.

21 A very informative analysis of Turkey's strategy in a historical perspective is Duygu Bazoglu Sezer, 'Turkey's Grand Strategy Facing a Dilemma', *The International Spectator* (Rome), vol. 27, no. 1 (1992).

22 Paul H. Henze, 'Turkey: Toward the Twenty-First Century', RAND Note N-3558-AF/A, RAND Corporation, Santa Monica, California, 1992, pp. 4ff.

23 Sezer, 'Turkey's Grand Strategy'.

24 Graham E. Fuller, 'Turkey Faces East', RAND Report 4232-AF/A, 1992, pp. 36–40.

25 Turgut Ozal on Turkish National Television, 2 April 1993 (FBIS-WEU-93-096, 5 April 1993).

26 Erdal Inonu on TRT Television Network, Ankara, 18 May 1993 (FBIS-WEU-93-096, 20 May 1993).

27 FBIS-NES-91-021, 31 January 1993.

28 *Sabah*, Istanbul, 2 May 1993, p. 7 (FBIS-WEU-93-088, 10 May 1993, p. 56).

29 Ibid., pp. 56–7.

30 *Anatolia*, Ankara, 5 May 1993 (FBIS-WEU-93-088, 10 May 1993).

31 RTT Television Network, Ankara, 6 May 1993 (FBIS-WEU-93-088, 10 May 1993, p. 57).

32   'Tajik Conflict, Lack of Russian "Unified" Policy in Region', *Nezavisimaya Gazeta*, Moscow, 29 July 1993, pp .1–3 (FBIS-USR-93-113, 30 August 1993).

The author wishes to thank Alexei Vasilyev of the Russian Academy of Sciences, Moscow, for a useful critique of this study; and Lili Dzirkals, Robin Hardy and Anita Drever for helpful research assistance.

12   Security in the Balkans: A Greek Perspective

George Mourtos

The Balkans is an area with a loose geographical definition. We know roughly the area it covers but its borders are ill defined. Conventional wisdom defines the Balkan peninsula as the former Yugoslavia, Romania, Bulgaria, Albania, Greece and Eastern Thrace. This would mean that all those states emerging from the ruins of the former Yugoslavia belong to the Balkans. However, Slovenia and Croatia deny any connection with the area and rather see themselves as within another geographical region, Central Europe. The Romanian foreign minister, Theodoru Melescanu, describes Romania as a Central European country close to the Balkans.[1] This chapter will focus upon Serbia, Kosovo, Bosnia, the former Yugoslav Republic of Macedonia (FYROM) and Albania.

There are some general initial remarks worth making. First, the crux of the security problem that faces the Balkan states lies in the disorderly and sudden disintegration of Yugoslavia. Second, the losers of the Second World War now seem to want a new share of the 'pie'. Third, it was Serbia that was on the winning side in both world wars, annexing territories which were previously under Italian and Austro-Hungarian occupation. Fourth, one-third of the Serb population lives outside present-day Serbia. Fifth, the Balkans are the meeting-place of three divergent cultures: Western which is mainly Catholic, Islam and Byzantium-Orthodox Christianity. Sixth, almost all the states in the area foster irredentist ideas with an implied territorial expansion, the only exception being Greece; by failing to realize the 'Megali Idea' (Greater Greece) in the disastrous armed campaign in Asia Minor in 1922, Greece became a *status quo* country.

It is often said in the Western press that the causes of the break-up of Yugoslavia are purely internal: the people there could not live together. But then the question arises, why in Yugoslavia and not in other 'mosaic' states? After all, less than 10 per cent of states world-wide are ethnically homogeneous. Only half have one ethnic group that accounts for as much as 75 per cent of their population. Africa, for instance, is a continent of 1000 ethnic and linguistic peoples squeezed within and across some 40 states.

The world community, particularly the European Union, was persuaded by the Germans to recognize Slovenia and Croatia as early as possible, in order to stop the bloodshed between the contestants. But if that was Bonn's real motivation then why does it not recognize Northern Ireland or Kurdistan where fighting has continued for decades? Why did the West so promptly recognize the secession of the constituent administrative parts of former Yugoslavia without applying the same norms and constraints in other parts of the world, and particularly in their own cases? A declaration of independence by any state in the United States, for example, must be approved by something like a two-thirds majority in favour in the Congress.

There are endless questions that can be levelled at the motivations of the international community in the Yugoslav crisis, but one thing seems certain: the external factor still plays an important role in the whole area, where a big Yugoslavia did not fit after the Cold War. Belgrade was considered independent, brave and tough, pro-Russian, Orthodox and self-sufficient (especially in armaments). Big Yugoslavia was a desirable ally during the Cold War, but in the post-Cold War era a big Serbia, it was thought, would be hegemonic. For this reason the international community denied the Serbs outside Serbia the right to self-determination while at the same time accepting that right as a legitimate cause for the independence of the Slovenians, Croats, Muslims and 'Macedonians'. Furthermore, the imposition of a total embargo upon Serbia for aiding the Bosnian Serbs, without imposing a similar embargo upon Croatia for helping the Bosnian Croats, indicates, to say the least, double standards.

The anti-Serbian attitude of the international community puts Greece in an awkward position because a weak Serbia may induce third countries, perhaps hostile to Greece, to move in and fill the power gap. We have already seen Turkey move in eagerly. It is for this reason that Greece is inclined to favour a big and strong Serbia. A strong Serbia will be, from the Greek point of view, a stabilizing factor in the Balkans and a security guarantee for states like Greece and Bulgaria.

The secession of Kosovo, the south-western part of the former Yugoslavia, will render Serbia a much weaker state and invite endless bloodshed. In any case, an uprising in Kosovo will adversely affect the security not only of Greece but also of the wider area. The Albanian government has often emphasized the 'unity' of all Albanians, implying their absorption of part of Serbia (Kosovo). If a conflict starts in Kosovo they hope to resettle the southern part of Albania, called Northern Epires, with Albanians from Kosovo, and expel the ethnic Greeks who live there at present. Such a move by

Tirana could compel intervention from Greece to protect the Greek population in Northern Epires. In response, the Turks may rush to the support of their fellow Muslims in Albania, leading to a major explosion of conflict in the Balkans. Nobody can dismiss the plausibility of this scenario.

It is obvious that any alteration of borders in the Balkans creates havoc throughout the region. What would work better is a form of autonomy for Kosovo and Northern Epires that will give both minorities the power to develop their own cultural, educational and religious institutions as they wish, but keep them within existing borders.

In Bosnia-Hercegovina Greece would ideally favour the strong presence of Serbs with a sizeable presence of Croats, leaving the Muslims with an unimportant political role to play. This has nothing to do with religious prejudice but rather with hard geostrategic and security considerations. First, Bosnia has never been a nation and there is no specifically Bosnian cultural identity. Historically the area has always been inhabited mostly by Serbs and partly by Croats. Those Slav Muslims now in the region have only been in the majority since the 1950s. Despite this majority, the Serbs have retained the dominant place in the territorial make-up of Bosnia-Hercegovina. According to the 1981 census, Serbs were an absolute majority in 2439 out of a total of 5857 inhabited places. This means that the population centres with Serb majorities take up 27,255 square kilometres (53.3 per cent) of the total territory of Bosnia-Hercegovina (51,129 square kilometres).[2]

Second, Alija Izetbegovic, the president of Bosnia-Hercegovina, is a typical hard-core Islamist-nationalist leader. He spent three years in gaol from 1946 to 1949 for promoting social hatred and in 1983 was sentenced to 14 years' imprisonment for propagating his 'Islamic Declaration', first written in 1970.[3] Even his own men, such as his former deputy, Adil Zeulfikarpasic, consider him an extremist. Greece has never felt threatened by Islam, and for centuries has maintained good relations with almost all Islamic countries. Greece does not even feel threatened by Islamic fundamentalism, portrayed by the West as the new threat. The real threat comes from the politicians and 'laymen' who use Islam to advance their political–nationalist aims. The late president of Turkey, Turgut Ozal, the president of Albania, Sali Berisha, and Izetbegovic, by invoking the Islamic faith, hide their nationalistic–expansionist aims. Western countries turn a blind eye as they are not directly affected. The West seems concerned with those fundamentalists who propose a new societal, political and economic model which is in sharp contrast with that of their own. That is why those religious fanatics who do not question the Western model, such as the Saudis and Pakistanis, are not considered fundamentalists by Western governments.[4]

Third, there is the demographic factor. The Muslim presence in the whole peninsula, including Bosnia-Hercegovina, has upset the social and political balance in the area. The numbers are revealing. In the 1950s, the Serbs constituted the majority of the population in Bosnia-Hercegovina and almost half of the population in Kosovo. Before the eruption of the civil war in Yugoslavia, the Serbs constituted about 37 per cent in Bosnia-Hercegovina and 10 per cent in Kosovo. In both areas the fertility rate among the Muslim population is the highest in Europe, almost 4 per cent, while the average European rate, including that in Serbia, Bulgaria and Greece, is around 1.4 per cent. The apprehension in Greece is that the Yugoslav precedent might reappear in the future in the Greek part of Thrace where there is a Muslim minority. Bulgaria also faces a similar problem with their Muslim minority, the numbers of which jumped to 10 per cent of the whole population from 5 per cent in the 1950s.[5] The fear is that if the standards of sovereign rights become determined by numbers rather than factors such as history and culture, that will open up a Pandora's box. It would encourage other Muslim compact communities to assert similar rights, and result in their calling for outright secession or autonomy. In that way the map of the Balkans would change from within.

Lastly, the present crisis in the Balkans, to some degree, has to do with the idea of pan-Turkism; that is to say, with the dream of a great number of Muslims in that area to rebuild the old connections with the Ottoman metropolis, Turkey. The paradox is that almost all those Muslims who live in the former Yugoslavia are not ethnic Turks. Despite that, the vast majority of Muslims in the area are strongly pro-Turkish with pan-Turkish sentiments. During the days of the Ottoman empire all Muslims were considered ethnic Turks and could reach the highest positions within the political hierarchy. It is not surprising therefore that there is no single political party representing Muslims in the Balkans that can be considered anti-Turkish. It could be said, then, that the Muslim élites in the peninsula are more Turkish than the Turks themselves. For instance, the leader of the moderate party Muslimansko Bosngaska Organizacija in Bosnia-Hercegovina, Zeulfikarpasic, declared: 'until the Balkan war there was one state, our own state, the Ottoman.'[6] It becomes evident that a strong Islamic presence in Bosnia-Hercegovina will add a new ring to the so-called 'Turkish arch' comprising Bosnia-Hercegovina, Novi Bazar (Sandzah is its Turkish name), Albania, FYROM, South Bulgaria and Turkey. This squeezes Greece from all sides.

Greek security concerns stem mostly from the fact that outside powers with little knowledge of the peculiarities of the area step in at will as if readjusting the pawns on a political chessboard. Henry Kissinger expressed it well in a newspaper article:

The most irresponsible mistake of the current tragedy was international recognition of a Bosnian state governed by Muslims, blindly following Germany's hasty recognition of Slovenia and Croatia. But whereas Croatia and Slovenia had their own identity, Bosnia was a Yugoslavia in microcosm. It is a mystery why anyone could think that Croats and Serbs, unwilling to stay together in the larger Yugoslavia, could be induced to create a joint state in Bosnia – together with the Muslims they hated for centuries.[7]

Further, the most irresponsible mistake might yet prove to be not the recognition of Bosnia but that of FYROM, for the simple reason that while the former case has turned into a cruel interethnic civil war, the latter could turn into an interstate war engulfing the whole region.[8]

With regard to FYROM, its population is ethnically disparate with a predominant Slav component (of just a little over half), an important ethnic Albanian minority (35–40 per cent) and a sprinkling of other nationalities which include Serbs, Turks, Gypsies, Vlachs and Greeks. The Albanians have a strong feeling of their distinct national identity, claiming descent from the ancient Illyrians. Politically they support autonomy, decided upon by a referendum held in January 1992. As for the Slav majority, it was originally of Bulgarian ethnic affiliation, but intensive Communist propaganda over half a century has to a degree succeeded in creating among some a sense of a 'Macedonian' national consciousness. But ties with Bulgaria remain, as evidenced by the fact that the leading political party in the republic, the Internal Macedonian Revolutionary Organization (IMRO, first in popular votes and parliamentary seats, and well ahead of Kiro Gligorov's 'Democratic Reform' in the elections of 1990) is linked with Bulgarian nationalist circles. Gligorov himself, FYROM's president, is of Bulgarian descent, while Bulgaria considers the inhabitants to be Bulgarians and not Macedonians.

The signs are that this rootless state has all the potential of becoming a troublemaker for the area. First, the preamble and Articles 3 and 49 of its constitution imply territorial claims. Second, the new flag of FYROM appropriated the emblem of the ancient Macedonian dynasty, found a few years ago in the royal tombs in Vergina, northern Greece, and dating back to the fourth century BC (although the Slavs have inhabited the area only since the seventh century AD). Third, IMRO conducted their political campaign on the slogan of the 'unification' of all the Macedonian regions. Fourth, throughout the republic irredentist literature is fanning the flames of nationalism, encouraged by the government. In addition, numerous calendars, maps, tourist mementoes, car stickers and other paraphernalia have appeared everywhere in the republic depicting a larger Macedonia. This points, unequivocally, to the existence of a 'Greater Macedonia' movement, and general recognition of this state with the name of 'Macedonia' would give the green light to further claims.

A state with the name of 'Macedonia' would be a serious security concern, if not a defence problem, at least for Greece. The 'Macedonians' may presently be small and weak in military terms, but then so has been the Irish Republican Army in the United Kingdom and Euskadi Ta Askatasuna (ETA) in Spain. Once recognized on its own terms, this new state could be ruled by anybody who might interpret 'Macedonia' in the most mystical, ethnic sense of the term. This would create problems not just for Greece but for Albanians too, who will feel trapped within a state in the hands of another ethnic group.[9]

The Western press and governments alike tend to treat the Macedonian issue lightly, often making a mockery of the sensitivities of the Greek nation. The German government, for instance, tends to forget that until the early 1970s its sensitivity over the German Democratic Republic's name was so great that, as a rule, diplomatic relations were broken with any state recognizing it. Even after recognition, the Bonn government refered to the East Berlin regime as 'GDR'. How would the German government react if Austria used the name of Bavaria and made irredentist claims upon Germany or appropriated the symbols of Bavaria? Suppose that Slovenia or Croatia decided at the time of their breaking away from Yugoslavia to take the name of the 'Republic of Venice' under the pretext of being partly under Venetian rule at some point of their history. It is anybody's guess as to how Italy would have reacted.

International politics is not, however, about ethics, but simply about power and national interest. Only under this consideration can the issue of 'Macedonia' be explained. Today the Balkan countries are experiencing the harsh reality of being fought over by the great powers. The northern part of the peninsula seems to be heavily under German influence and the southern part (Albania, FYROM and Bulgaria) under US influence. Washington already has an infantry task force of 320 men in FYROM and has dramatically increased contacts and visits to that republic. In military terms this force is totally insignificant but symbolically is important because it stands as an indication to other extra-regional contesters of a US interest in that part of Europe.

It seems certain that the smaller Serbia becomes the greater the influence of outside powers in the Balkans. Russia, at the moment, is playing a passive role in the area, being more interested in the Caucasus and Central Asia, and in consolidating its strategic alliance with the United States. It seems certain, however, that Moscow would not prevent the inevitable stream of Russian volunteer fighters to Serbia if and when the West intervenes militarily.

Another important factor in the security equation of the Balkans, which is of great concern to Greece, is Albania. Despite its small size, with 3.2

million inhabitants, Albania is a divided nation by ethnicity, culture, ideology, religion and economic situation. The antidote to all its mishaps offered by its government is 'Islamic nationalism', which increasingly is becoming the dominant ideology of the state. Although the leading exponent of Islamic nationalism is the party of Berisha, fanatics cross all the party lines. For Greece, the prevailing Islamic 'north' of Sali Berisha has added problems to its northern borders; under its present nationalistic leadership, the governing party is fiercely anti-Greek. The present Albanian government is heavily influenced by Washington. The latter has signed with Tirana a memorandum of understanding over military co-operation; this is the first of its kind with a former Communist country, where, in essence, the Americans will organize the Albanian armed forces. This agreement cements an American zone of influence in the Balkans which comprises Albania, FYROM, Bulgaria, Turkey and Greece, and there are indications of the United States courting Belgrade.

There are two obvious issues of contention and friction between Athens and Tirana. First, there is the issue over the maltreatment of the Greek minority living in Albania which, according to objective estimates, accounts for 12.5 per cent of the total population. Secondly, there is a flow of illegal immigrants from Albania whose numbers are estimated to be between 200,000 and 400,000. Perhaps one-fifth of Albanian men are now in Greece, and it is these people who many Greeks hold responsible for an increase in crime and a growing sense of insecurity within the country.

In conclusion, though it faces few immediate military dangers, it seems certain that there will be an extended and intensified perception of insecurity within the Balkan region towards the end of the twentieth century. The ultimate reason lies in the prevailing climate of mistrust and suspicion existing among all its people.

Notes

1   See T. Melescanu, 'Security in Central Europe: A Positive-sum Game', *NATO Review*, no. 5, October 1993, p. 14.
2   See 'Area and History of Bosnia and Hercegovina', Sofia Centre for Analysis and Strategic Research, p. 6.
3   Ibid., pp. 16–18.
4   See G. Mourtos, 'Islamism: The New Threat?', *New Frontier*, 1 February 1993 (in Greek).
5   See the very interesting articles in *Kathimerini*, 10 January 1993 and 28 February 1993.
6   Lecture delivered by Professor Geltic in Athens, 20 May 1993.
7   See *Daily Telegraph*, 20 May 1993.
8   For an excellent account of the Macedonian problem see 'Borders, Symbols, Stability: Issues Relating to the Recognition of FYROM', The Citizens' Movement, Athens, January 1993.

9   See the article by the spokesman for the Greek government, V. Maghinas, *The European*, 10–15 December 1992.

13 A Romanian Perspective on Security

Ioan Mircea Pascu

The end of the Cold War has brought about a paradoxical situation: on one hand, it has marked the end of the post-war confrontation between the two main political and military alliances, especially in Europe, and, on the other, it has plunged us into an era of great uncertainty and even open conflict, mainly in the eastern part of the continent. Consequently, we are now in search of a new balance of power with both European and worldwide connotations.

Europe, therefore, is now at a crossroads, and its future path depends entirely on the interaction between East and West, which, in turn, depends on the maturity of its decision-makers in both parts of the continent. The West could 'export' its *stability* towards the East, giving Europe the chance to become a truly integrated area, or the East could 'export' its *instability* towards the West, and the whole continent could plunge back into a type of politics characteristic of the nineteenth century. Although the necessity for recognizing such a choice seems to have been grasped by the current politicians in both East and West, the process of establishing a new balance based on the redistribution of power after the collapse of Communism appears to dominate practical approaches. As a result, in spite of any possible desire to move away from a nineteenth-century type of politics, it seems that the attraction of the old ways is much stronger than anticipated and than it should actually be. Spheres of influence, shows of force, covert actions, internal and external conflict (which we all thought to be things of the past) are with us again, and we find ourselves shaping our future with the instruments of the past. If we continue to do so, there should be no surprise if that future actually looks similar to our past, in spite of any initial intentions to the contrary.

Concretely, we are witnessing all sorts of 'movements', from tectonic (see the current struggle between the North Atlantic Treaty Organization

(NATO) and Russia for control over East-Central Europe), through lesser ones (such as the attempts to recreate the old empires which dominated the Balkans in the last century) to indeed small, individual 'games' of picking up the leftovers from the great powers' table (as in some of the border areas of the former Yugoslavia).

Considering the large security framework of the continent, one should note a drastic change in the nature of the threats which have occurred since the end of the Cold War. Until then, recognized threats were quite visible and mainly external – meaning war was likely to arise either as the result of an error or of a local conflict escalating into a global nuclear war, given the unitary, integrated character of the world balance of power between the two superpowers and their respective allies. Since the end of the Cold War, with the relative independence achieved by the 'local' balances of power and with the transition process engulfing the former members of the Warsaw Treaty Organization (WTO) the threats have tended to become less visible and more internal. In other words, internal subversion rather than external aggression seems to be the main threat confronting particularly the East-Central European states at present. This threat takes two main forms. First, there is inherent internal weakness in some states arising from the inevitable process of transition. Second, some states see the obvious opportunity to achieve their offensive objectives in another country by appearing to work for the fulfilment of an 'international mandate'. The scenario is simple: foment discontent, bring it to the point of conflict, internationalize it and then call for the international community to work for its resolution.

Until the end of the Cold War, the European security system was based on the balance of power between the two political and military alliances. Reflecting the *détente* of the early 1970s and the need to bring in the neutral and non-aligned European countries, the Conference on Security and Co-operation in Europe (CSCE) process was initiated in those years. The aim was to create an all-European system based on the two political and military alliances, capitalizing on their need for co-operation. The restructuring of the entire system effected by the collapse of the WTO and the former Soviet Union seriously damaged the chances of the CSCE assuming the role of a truly continental system of security. On the one hand, the Conventional Forces in Europe (CFE) Treaty – negotiated and concluded under totally different circumstances from those prevailing today – is like an extinguished star from which we continue to receive light, and, on the other hand, the CSCE is a security structure only in name, because it totally lacks teeth.

Consequently, the task of forming the basis for a future continental security system has to be assumed by the existing Western multilateral institutions. Of them, most certainly, the best equipped is NATO. The main difficulty for NATO is that it remains an alliance designed to protect the security of its current 16 members. However, by initiating the 'Partnership for Peace' programme and by taking a tough stand on Yugoslavia, it has indicated its desire to assume, in addition to its initial mission, those pertaining to a wider security system. In its turn, the Western European Union (WEU) is still an organization in search of a role, whose future will depend on the kind of relationship to be finally established between the United States and the Western European powers, after the collapse of Communism and the 'opening' of East-Central Europe. Last but not least, the European Union (EU) itself could assume a larger role in security matters either directly – by succeeding in converting the WEU into its armed component – or indirectly by slowly and surely building security through projecting stability and economic progress towards the East of the continent.

We are driven, however, to only one major conclusion: namely, that none of these institutions can assume the functions of a continental security system acting alone because each as presently constituted forms only a fraction of the necessary 'total'. Rather, we need their co-operation in a general framework built upon an intelligent and co-ordinated distribution of roles among them.

How does all this strike a Romanian? What are the implications for Romania's security? After the revolution of December 1989, the dissolution of the WTO, and the violent break-up of the former Yugoslavia and the former Soviet Union, Romania's security can be said to derive from a combination of the following three parameters: a lack of formal alliance structure; a diminished internal capacity to cover its security requirements; and its location in a turbulent international environment with open conflicts on both its north-eastern and south-western borders. But because of its power potential (second only to Poland in the area between Germany and the Former Soviet Union) and its strategic location, it is clearly a country which can hardly be ignored in any calculations concerning this part of the continent and even beyond.

Of the potential threats to Romania's security the most dangerous might arise from a marked deterioration in the situation in the north-east of its territory – for example, if there is a conflict between Ukraine and Russia or civil war in Russia or Moldova. This is why Romania supports the democratic development of these three countries and wishes to maintain good relations with them.

In the south, Romania cannot completely ignore the intermittent accusations that it intends to regain the lost territory of the 'Cadrilater' (now belonging to Bulgaria). But Bucharest and Sofia are convinced that they both have much more to gain from co-operating, especially now that the Yugoslav conflict is physically limiting their links to the West.

The Yugoslav conflict may possibly create problems for Romania by spreading either to the south, into Kossovo, Macedonia and the Sanjak, thereby threatening a general Balkan war, or to the north, into Vojvodina, and encouraging ethnic violence.

Last but not least, Romania's relations with Hungary are far from friendly. Both countries have, however, demonstrated that they can manage such relations without allowing them to degenerate into open conflict. Moreover, bilateral military relations between Bucharest and Budapest are good, thus exercising a positive restraining role on the entire bilateral relationship.

Romania's foreign policy is based upon both independence, realizing that it can only count on itself, and an approach to security that is rather more subtle than is usual. Thus, to be secure it is not sufficient either to protect oneself or be protected by others; it requires also enough political maturity and responsibility to avoid trouble. It is a bit like the insurance business: higher risks require higher premiums. Consequently, a boxer will have to pay more for a life insurance than a normal citizen and all the more so if he is a street brawler as well.

In accordance with both its own situation and that of its immediate international environment, Romania has four principal security guidelines. First, priority has to be given to relations with the West, motivated on the one hand by the recognition that it is the primary source of capital, technology, information and security, and on the other by the fact that Romania has always considered itself an extension of the West towards the East, taking into account its Latin origins. Second, it needs to keep balanced and friendly ties with the East, particularly with Russia and Ukraine. Third, it must practice good neighbourliness in its relations with all its neighbours. Fourth, it needs to be actively involved in conflict resolution around its borders. It should be noted that, if the first point is meant to take care of the first layer of the concept of security – namely, protection – the other three are meant to answer the requirements of the second layer – namely, avoiding trouble.

Lastly, it is necessary to mention Romania's response to the 'Partnership for Peace' programme. The idea of extending NATO's co-operation towards the East receives a positive reaction, representing material evidence of the West's resolve to promote stability and security in this area. The difficulty is, however, that, given the indivisible nature of security in the entire area east of the German border, partial solutions – like an early and hasty admission of a 'select' group of former WTO countries into NATO – would almost certainly complicate rather than simplify matters. Therefore, the idea of an equal start for all these countries, without discrimination, is considered in Bucharest to be more realistic and fair. That is exactly why Romania saluted the 'Partnership for Peace' initiative and signed the framework document, seeing in it both a contribution to the gradual transformation of NATO into the pivot of an all-European security system and an instrument through which the performance of its armed forces in accomplishing their mission could be improved.

14 Hungary and the Problems of National Minorities

György Réti

The problem of national minorities is a key question for both Hungarian foreign and internal policy. First, about 5,000,000 Hungarians – one-third of the nation – live beyond the borders of our country. Second, about 900,000 people belonging to national minorities live in Hungary. As a consequence of the territorial changes following the First World War (and confirmed after the Second World War) Hungary lost about two-thirds of its territory and about one-third of its population. Among all the national minorities living in Europe (except the newly created Russian one) the Hungarian ranks the highest: nearly 3,500,000 Hungarian people live in minority status in the states surrounding Hungary. This figure does not include the nearly 1,500,000 Hungarians living in Western Europe and North America and elsewhere. There are nearly 2,000,000 people of Hungarian origin in Romania, about 600,000 in Slovakia, in the former Yugoslavia about 500,000, in the Ukraine nearly 200,000 and in Austria 5000.

After the election held in May 1994 a new government based upon a socialist-liberal coalition was formed in Hungary. As the 1994 Programme of the Hungarian Government declares:

> From the viewpoint of internal security, stability and co-operation the Government attaches special importance to vouchsafing and effectively protecting the rights of national and ethnic minorities. True to its political and moral obligations, as spelled out in the [Hungarian] Constitution, the Government intends to pay careful attention to the situation of ethnic Hungarians beyond Hungary's border. It considers the assertion of their rights as a special area of Hungary's foreign policy relations, an important domestic task, and a question of national solidarity.
>
> The Government considers the Hungarians beyond the borders as a part of the Hungarian nation in a cultural sense. Using the means at its disposal – and

165

acting in harmony with the relevant international norms – the Government will strive to bring about for the Hungarian minorities beyond Hungary's borders economic, political and legal conditions and a social atmosphere in which they live a meaningful life in the country of which they are citizens. The Government will use its influence to bring about a situation in which in every country the right of ethnic affiliation may be fully asserted. True to the relevant document of the UN, the Council of Europe and the Conference on Security and Co-operation in Europe, the Government considers as a precondition of the effective protection of minorities, preferential treatment and the assurance of special rights so that the disadvantages of minority existence can be compensated. It is the conviction of the Government that the attitudes of states towards minorities are an important component of the assertion of human rights, and an inseparable part of proper international relations.

The Government believes that the situation of ethnic Hungarians beyond Hungary's border is a key component of Hungary's relationship with its neighbouring countries. It holds that if the rights of Hungarian minorities beyond Hungary's borders are to be vouchsafed, there is a need for dialogue with the political leaders of neighbouring countries and a search for mutually advantageous and wide-ranging co-operation. The Government will resolutely and consistently use its influence to bring about that the Hungarian minorities beyond Hungary's borders, and their organizations, should enjoy genuine equality in the exercise of their rights. It intends to settle present and future problems chiefly within the framework of bilateral relations, though it will also resort to international forums and organizations if need be. It deems it necessary to win broad international support for its cause. The Government plans actively to seek the formation of an effective bilateral and multilateral international system for the protection of minorities.

In line with this programme the new Hungarian government submitted to the Hungarian parliament the European Charter on Regional or Minority Language and the European Convention on Arbitration and Courts of Arbitration for ratification.

In order to ensure that ethnic Hungarians beyond the borders can live a meaningful life in the countries where they are citizens it is essential that they should be able to create a secure livelihood and have the opportunity to improve their welfare, to become members of the middle class, to participate in local and state-level government and the voluntary organizations of local society. The Hungarian government and people are determined – in accordance with the practice of European institutions – to help ethnic Hungarians beyond the Hungarian borders to avail themselves of the opportunities offered by local municipalities and the business community in specific trades. They accord special importance to the integration of the entrepreneurial activities of Hungarian minorities in Hungary's economic co-operation with neighbouring countries. Hungary regards the autonomy of the minorities as a framework suitable and desirable for the assertion of human, minority, economic and social rights within the borders of the country in which they are citizens, in harmony with the relevant principles of international law and with international practice.

The Hungarian governmental official and social organizations support the voluntary organizations of the Hungarian minorities beyond the Hungarian borders in the fields of culture; scholarship and adult education; the teaching of the mother language, religion and various trades; and the co-operation of the organizations of the Hungarian minorities with their counterparts inside Hungary and with related international organizations and institutions. They help the young ethnic Hungarians beyond their borders to study in the colleges and universities of Hungary with a view to their returning to the country of which they are citizens upon graduation. The new Hungarian government intends to establish relations with each and every legitimate and democratic organization and party and with the leaders of ethnic Hungarians beyond the borders. It is an axiom for the new government that the official Hungarian standpoint on minority issues should be elaborated after consideration of the views of minority organizations and their representatives.

In its policy towards the Hungarian minorities the government seeks continuous dialogue and co-operation with the opposition parties and the various organizations of society. The Hungarian government considers it right to support financially the educational, cultural and religious organizations of the Hungarian minorities, as well as their mass media and their business and enterprise development. The nature of this support must be transparent. For Hungary it is also important to have the co-operation of Hungarians living in the developed Western countries in rendering more effective the international efforts for the protection of minorities.

The Office for Hungarian Minorities Abroad co-ordinates the entire scope of governmental activities concerning the Hungarian minorities. It works out its minority policy, fosters relations with the organizations of the Hungarian minority as well as similar organizations in other countries, and participates in the representation of minority affairs in various international organizations.

Hungarians, living as a minority, are usually strongly devoted to their language, customs and national identity. This is well illustrated by the fact that during more then 70 years of minority life their numbers have not decreased significantly. In the last four years, as a consequence of the great political changes in Central and Eastern Europe, more advantageous possibilities have emerged for the political and economic activities of the minorities. At the same time, however, in certain countries, formerly more or less muted nationalistic tendencies have also arisen on the part of the majority. In many cases signs of a phobia over cultural and economic performance and even over the very existence of the minorities can be detected.

The organizations of the Hungarian minorities created for the safeguarding of their interests have more or less the same basic aims. They have nowhere demanded a change of borders, but have urged the creation of provisions for self-government or local autonomy which would guarantee equal opportunities for and the survival of the identity, language and culture of the minorities.

We may now turn to the situation of the Hungarian minorities in the various neighbouring countries. In Slovenia and Croatia the status of the small Hungarian communities was formerly good, and they had all the political and cultural rights that a minority deserves. But the civil war in the former Yugoslavia has caused great problems, many Hungarians being forced to escape to Hungary. Now their situation is again improving. It is important that Hungary has signed agreements on minority rights with both countries. In the Vojvodina, the formerly autonomous province of Serbia, conditions for the approximately 400,000 Hungarians were gradually normalized after the Second World War, but in recent years the civil war and the revival of Serbian nationalism have put an end to their relatively favourable position. Provincial and local autonomy have been abolished and their institutions have been curtailed. Their proportion among the casualties in the army was relatively high. We can only hope that with the end of the civil war the former favourable situation of the Hungarian minorities will be restored.

The situation of the Hungarians living in the Sub-Carpathian region bordering Hungary has improved substantially since Ukraine achieved independence. The 1991 Hungarian–Ukrainian Declaration on the Rights of National Minorities has set a positive example of recognizing national minorities as organic components of the statehood of the country in which they live. A joint committee has been established for supervising the fulfilment of the declaration.

In Slovakia, which gained independence in 1993, the constitution defines the country as a national state with one national language. At the same time the constitution states that the implementation of minorities' rights may not infringe the territorial integrity and the sovereignty of the Republic of Slovakia. The constitution does not guarantee the right of minorities to their ethnic identity, and offers no protection against their forced assimilation. Their political parties may be dissolved at any time. All this shows a certain distrust and fear of the nearly 600,000-strong Hungarian national minority community. Several dozen amendments submitted by the representatives of the Hungarian coalition were all rejected, and hence the constitution represents a retrograde step from the legal situation of minorities previously in force. The representatives of the Hungarian minority thus walked out of the

Slovak Chamber in protest. In the 1994 parliamentary election, however, the coalition of the three Hungarian parties obtained 10.2 per cent of the vote and became the third force in the highest Slovak political forum. The Hungarians in Slovakia have many elementary schools where the education is in the Hungarian language, but there are 130 villages with Hungarian majorities where none exist. There is no Hungarian university in Slovakia and the only Hungarian high school is in a very difficult situation. Slovak radio broadcasts 36 hours of Hungarian language programmes weekly, and television 25 minutes a week. There are two professional and many amateur Hungarian theatres. One daily newspaper and some quarterlies are published in the Hungarian language. There has been something of a 'political battle' around the use of Hungarian names in Slovak towns and villages, for according to a law of 1990 this was prohibited and many names in the Hungarian language were removed. However, a law adopted in July 1994 makes the use of Hungarian names possible again. The newly elected Hungarian prime minister, Gyula Horn, made his first visit abroad to Slovakia in August 1994. This visit contributed to the reduction of tension in Hungarian–Slovak relations. We can only hope that the forthcoming visit of the Slovak prime minister, Vladimir Meciar, will reinforce this positive process.

In Romania, according to the last census conducted under the Nicolae Ceausescu regime the number of Hungarians, living mainly in the region of Transylvania was 1,651,000, but responsible sources put the figure at about 2,000,000. This is one of the largest national minorities in Europe. In the euphoria caused by the events of 1989, the Government of National Salvation declared equality before the law of national minorities with the Romanian majority, underlining the right to use a mother tongue freely and to instruct in mother languages at all levels. The reopening of the Hungarian University was also mentioned. However, according to a memorandum written by the Democratic Alliance of Hungarians in Romania (DAHR) on Romania's admission to the Council of Europe in August 1993:

> the rights enumerated in this declaration have not been guaranteed by any law and have not been put in practice yet ... . Deprivation of these basic human rights creates a disadvantageous situation for minority citizens in each field of social life: education, the law and administration.

This memorandum formulated in 15 points the DAHR's objections concerning Romania's legal system, and made 13 proposals for change.

The Romanian constitution of 1991 underlines that Romania is a national state, and the only official language is Romanian. Hungarians in Romania say that they are particularly worried about discrimination in economic life (such as ethnic discrimination in lay-offs, in issuing entrepreneurial licences, and in opportunities to participate in privatization) as well as about the refusal to build a full-scale educational system in the Hungarian language. The Hungarian University and the Hungarian Consulate-General in Cluj-Napoca (or Kolozsvár in Hungarian) were closed under the Ceausescu regime and have not reopened.

In Romania, according to many observers, some political forces still cling to the ideology of state nationalism. Stephen Griffiths writes in his excellent book with the significant title *Nationalism and Ethnic Conflict: Threats to European Security*:

> However, there is a great deal of evidence that over the past two years inter-ethnic relations in the region [Transylvania] have polarized dramatically and that much of the trouble has been caused by Romanian extremists working with the 'approval' of seemingly compliant officials. Following the violence in Tigru Mures in 1990, which claimed the lives of some 30 people, the extreme right-wing organization Vatra Romaneasca has been involved in more reported incidents designed to raise the level of nationalist hatred in Transylvania.[1]

There are many state and church elementary and secondary schools teaching in the Hungarian language, but, according to the DAHR, 'an independent educational system (from nursery school to university) adequate for the needs of approximately 2,000,000 Hungarians is absent in Romania'. In 1994 about 1000 Transylvanian students were studying in Hungary, but their diplomas are not fully recognized in Romania. There is one opera house and five Hungarian theatres in Romania, but all are in a deplorable financial situation.

The Democratic Alliance of Hungarians in Romania has grown into a significant political factor in society. In the last election, held in 1992, it gained over 881,000 votes, and with its 27 deputies and 12 senators it has become the second largest group in the Romanian parliament. The leaders of the Hungarian minorities never fail to underline that their efforts to protect the interests of Hungarians is intended to promote the internal consolidation of Romania. They have nevertheless often been subjected to attacks violating their human rights and reputations, and occasionally even to physical atrocities.

The situation of Hungarians living in Romania was one of the major questions raised during the visit to Hungary of the Romanian foreign minister, Theodoru Melescanu, in September 1994. After this visit the meetings of the experts of the two countries were renewed. As in the case of Slovakia, we can only hope that these positive signs will lead to an improvement in the relations between the two countries, including the problems relating to national minorities.

Demanding rights for the Hungarian minorities living beyond its borders, the Hungarian government tries to ensure these same rights for the minorities living within the country. According to the 1990 census and the estimates offered by minority organizations there are about 200,000 ethnic Germans, 110,000 Slovaks, 80,000 Croats, 25,000 Romanians, 25,000 Serbs, 5000 Slovenes and about 500,000 Gypsies in Hungary, which has a total population of 10,300,000. The minorities are scattered all over the country's 18 counties. Urbanization processes, as well as those of auto-assimilation, have taken place during the past decades and have led to the disruption of many traditional minority communities.

The basic principles concerning national and ethnic minorities are codified by the Hungarian constitution. It says that they 'are constituent elements of the State' and 'have their share in the power of the people'. The constitution provides for the collective participation of minorities in public life, the care of their own particular culture, and the wide-ranging use of their mother tongue, including education and the right to use names in their original ethnic forms.

After a two-year-long discussion, on 7 July 1993 the Hungarian parliament adopted the Act on the Rights of National and Ethnic Minorities by an overwhelming majority vote. The Act was prepared and elaborated jointly by the best Hungarian experts on this question and by the Minority Roundtable which consists of the representatives of all minority groups. Before adoption the draft Act was sent to the Council of Europe which formed a positive opinion on it, remarking that the specific form of self-government contained in it was a rare occurrence even in Europe. The Council found that the normative definition of a national or ethnic minority, the principle of the free choice of national identity, the regulation of collective rights of minorities, and cultural autonomy based on the personal principle were highly progressive achievements.

The Act consists of an introduction and nine chapters devoted to the following items: fundamental provisions, individual minority rights, collective rights of minorities, self-government of minorities, the local spokesman (ombudsman) of minorities, the cultural and educational autonomy of minorities, use of minority languages, financial support, economic management and assets of minority self-government and closing provisions. The object of the Act is to identify and create conditions under which the 'auto-assimilation process' of national and ethnic minorities can be halted and made reversible. This assimilation process is due to the fact that minorities, except the Gypsy communities, in Hungary live in a scattered pattern, in practically all regions of the country and in most cases mixed with the overwhelming majority of Hungarians. In these circumstances, the minorities' strong intellectual strata could not develop. Therefore the fundamental principle of the Act is related to the active protection of minorities, helping to preserve their identity.

Concerning the protection of the minorities the programme of the new Hungarian government declares:

> The social status of minorities and the protection and assertion of their rights are regarded as key criteria of democracy by the Government. In accordance with general European norms, it will fully ensure the rights for all minorities in Hungary. It will seek to evolve a social climate in which no minority has cause to be afraid and nobody suffers discrimination.
>
> The Government takes the view that it is an essential human right to maintain a national and language-related identity and to have the right to openly declare affiliation to an ethnic group.
>
> The survival and progress of national and ethnic minorities, the reduction of inequalities between the majority group and the minorities, and the lessening of other disadvantages besetting the minorities, all require preferential treatment and special rights to which communities, just as much as individuals, are entitled. The rights are enshrined in Law LXXVII of 1993 on the Rights of National and Ethnic Minorities, the implementation of which the Government considers a priority task.

That means that the Hungarian government underlines the necessity of positive discrimination towards national minorities, as each member of an ethnic minority has the right to special treatment and their status should not be dependent on the manner in which the rights of ethnic Hungarians living outside Hungary are honoured. The Hungarian government rejects the principle of reciprocity on this question. It supports the spontaneous self-organization of minorities in Hungary – which in recent years has shown a welcome upsurge – as well as efforts to strengthen their legal and cultural autonomy. It attaches importance to, and encourages, the formation of self-governing bodies of minorities at both local and national levels. It helps their regional organizations which are built from the bottom up, based on local initiatives. It intends to create institutional forms for the integration of the legitimate representatives of minorities in the work of the Hungarian parliament, and it treats as a partner each legitimate and democratic minority organization and regularly consults them.

A principal condition of the strengthening of the minority identity is genuine progress in minority education. Hungary tries to ensure adequate conditions for the operation of minority nursery schools, teaching in minority languages in elementary and secondary schools, tuition in institutes of higher education, the operation of libraries and other cultural institutions, the training of minority teachers and the supply of textbooks and teaching aids needed for minority education. Central budget subsidies for these purposes, based on the principle of preferential treatment, are guaranteed. There are now in Hungary 295 minority kindergartens with about 14,000 children receiving education in their mother language. There are also about 320 primary schools offering education not only in Hungarian but also in the language of the various minorities. In addition, there are seven specialized minority secondary schools, three being German and Slovak, two being Croatian, and one each being Serbian and Romanian.

In the field of the mass media every minority group has at least one weekly newspaper (their number has multiplied since the change of regime in 1989). Hungarian radio broadcasts a 20-minute programme in all minority languages every day, while television broadcasts two 30-minute programmes each month for every minority plus a 5-minute news magazine each week. Hungary also promotes the exchange of teachers, students and cultural assets, as well as mutual recognition of certificates and diplomas with the mother countries of the national minorities in Hungary, and the government also supports church activities in the mother tongues of Hungary's national minorities.

The hardest national minority question for Hungary concerns the situation of about 500,000 Hungarian Gypsies, who have been particularly seriously affected by the economic crisis and recession of the past 15 years and by increasing unemployment. The Hungarian government considers the task of relieving their difficulties as complex and special, one that requires interdepartmental co-ordination. From the standpoint of domestic policy, because of the problems that Gypsies have in adjusting to conventional society, the Gypsies are not considered as just another minority. They are a social group requiring particular attention. The government considers it a priority to halt the deterioration of the situation of Gypsies of Hungary, and gives support to Gypsies to compensate for their disadvantaged social and labour market position. The government is focusing its attention on upgrading the educational standards of Gypsies and consolidating and broadening the stratum of professional people among them. It is also elaborating a crisis management programme which takes into account all aspects of this issue. After the end of the Communist system over 100 Gypsy organizations emerged, and there are several summit organizations such as the Association of Interests of Gypsy Organizations. The problem is that they are divided among themselves. In the field of culture there has been a further increase in the number of different Gypsy folk ensembles and clubs. They have two regular television and radio programmes and three newspapers financed by the state. No political party in Hungary follows an anti-Gypsy ideology or practice. Skinhead groups, however, do exist and occasionally clash with Gypsies.

In order to improve the efficiency of the use of the funds related to the minorities, the Hungarian government has rendered transparent the public financing of minority programmes. This support is now activity-centred rather than organization-centred, as had hitherto been the case. Public support must be free of any partisan, ideological and personal bias. The Hungarian government helps national minorities to exercise the right to maintain free relations with their mother countries (that is, with the nation of common language) and/or other ethnic groups and organizations outside Hungary, and encourages national minorities in Hungary to participate in bilateral, multilateral and other forums that aim at the international protection of minorities. The Hungarian government and people consider it natural that people who belong to a minority regard themselves as both Hungarian citizens and, in cultural and sentimental terms, part of their mother nation.

The Hungarian government has decided to act firmly and consistently against all forms of prejudice, national or ethnic hatred and discrimination, against xenophobia, chauvinism, racism, anti-Semitism and hostility toward Gypsies. The Hungarian legal system provides a sufficient basis for countering discrimination against minorities, but if the legal practice is unsatisfactory the government considers it to be its duty to promote laws and other activities that consistently combat discrimination against minorities. That is why a parliamentary commissioner for minority affairs was chosen. The task of implementing the principles outlined above and co-ordinating the relevant government efforts belongs to an independent government agency, the Office for National and Ethnic Minorities.

Research on minority questions is co-ordinated by the László Teleki Foundation. At the same time, the Hungarian government supports the relevant activities of the minority groups themselves.

On 13 December 1994 the first elections of self-governing minorities bodies – along with the elections for local municipalities – were held. There were elected 639 local minority self-governing bodies (including 423 Gypsies, 103 Germans, 41 Croatians, 29 Slovaks, 17 Serbs and 11 Romanians). Now the task is to bring about co-operation between the self-governing bodies of minorities and the local organs of power.

The Hungarian government attaches great importance to the achievement of cultural and political autonomy by the national minorities in Hungary, but it also seeks autonomy for the Hungarian minorities beyond its borders. In this region of Europe there is a fear of autonomy for the minorities, but without it there can be no solution of the minority question. Autonomy is for a minority like water for a fish. Such autonomy has been possible in the cases of South Tyrol and Catalonia, and the Swedish minority in Finland and the Germans in Denmark have been given different forms of autonomy without endangering the territorial integrity of the state. Such autonomy should also be possible in Central and Eastern Europe.

Some progress has been made concerning the question of minority protection in Europe, but it appears to be very little considering the complexity and danger of certain conflicts. At the same time the Hungarian government greatly appreciates both the activity of the Chief Commissioner for Minorities of the Organization for Security and Co-operation in Europe (OSCE), Hans van der Stoel, and the monitoring system of the Council of Europe, since these could form the main pillars of an emerging European minority protection system. The Copenhagen document contains the most precisely defined system of minority norms in the OSCE, as well as internationally.

Csaba Tabajdi, Hungarian Political Secretary of State on Minority Questions, has written:

> As an instrument of the internal integration of the Central and East European societies, the national question has, or can have, two opposite effects. In the first case it is a force mobilizing the national sense of responsibility, awareness, patriotism and national integration for overcoming the crisis of the countries concerned, raising them out of their peripheral situation and promoting their integration into Europe.
>
> In the other case, the nationalist integration makes use of the appeals for national co-operation to postpone the organic introduction of modernization and Western experiences, to reinforce the power positions of the ruling élites. In the name of a false and distorted national integration or nationalism – creating phantom internal and external enemy images – it strives to curb political articulation and pluralism, to suppress the opposition, to curtail human rights and suppress the minorities. A very thin line separates these two types of internal integration.[2]

There is a Hungarian saying: 'The more languages you know, the more you are worth.' The members of minority groups usually know two languages and two cultures, which is why they are an enriching factor in the life of a country and should not be a dividing one. Languages are, or should be, bridges between two countries and between two nations. The overwhelming majority of Hungarians think that in the Europe of today the borders should not be changed but 'spiritualized'. The present writer is convinced that a country and its leadership can join the family of a democratic and united Europe only with the implementation of a policy of 'positive discrimination' towards its minorities. That is one of the most important touchstones of democracy, humanism and internationalism.

Notes

1 S.I. Griffiths, *Nationalism and Ethnic Conflict: Threats to European Security* (Oxford, 1993), p. 21.

2   Csaba Tabajdi, *Functions and Dysfunctions of the National Factor in Central and Eastern Europe* (Budapest, 1994), p. 12.

15 Italy and the Central European Initiative

Stephen P. Koff

Introduction

The Central European Initiative (CEI) has had a short history, but one strongly marked by the enormous changes which have occurred in Eastern Europe. Born in 1989 as an association of Italy, Austria, Hungary and Yugoslavia, it is dedicated to economic development more than to anything else.

It must be examined in terms of two major developments. The first, the fall of the Communist alliance system in Eastern Europe with all its ramifications, including the huge power void it left, made the initiative possible. The second, the fall of Communism itself, permitted Italy to develop a new sense of the possibilities of independent action in the foreign policy sphere. The leadership of Italy in the creation of the initiative is a prime example of the new foreign policy focus. Obviously, there were other related factors which impacted on the CEI and its development, such as the reunification of Germany and the resultant power configuration in the new Europe, the need for the European Union to develop ties to East European nations, the importance of aiding the development of democracy in the former Communist nations, and the break-up of Yugoslavia, to mention a few.

The CEI is, first and foremost, a regional organization which transcends borders which were recently hostile; as a regional grouping it is consistent with other major developments of this kind in recent years. In the case of the Balkans–Danube–Adriatic region, the basis of the beginning of the initiative, it had special geographic and historic importance for Italy. Within the regional concept the original emphasis was to be a national and sub-national co-operative programme.

When it was created in 1989 with four members it was called the Quadrangle. Czechoslovakia joined the group on 20 May 1990 and the name was changed to the Pentagonal. A year later, on 27 July 1991, Poland became a member and the name had to be changed again, to the Hexagonal.

When Czechoslovakia divided into the Czech Republic and the Slovak Republic both countries joined the group. With the break-up of Yugoslavia, Slovenia, Croatia and Bosnia-Hercegovina also became members. The organization then became known as the Central European Initiative.

With the fall of Communism the former satellite countries faced the enormous problems of economic and political reforms simultaneously. Ties to Western Europe appeared essential to these nations. As these fledgling democracies made strides to stabilize political systems while moving to market economies, they saw considerable advantage in joining programmes of co-operation with Western countries which emphasized development at a basic level. In this period of massive adjustment, it was recognized that there would be some economic decline and that it was essential to improve the infrastructure of these countries to provide the foundation for long-term economic development. With this kind of development the CEI was seen as helpful in paving the way for former Communist countries to obtain membership of or special relations with the European Union.

The CEI was an illustration of a new-found maturity in Italian foreign affairs. After 1945 Italian foreign policy rapidly evolved from a flirtation with neutralism to a total commitment to the West, and more specifically to the United States, to the North Atlantic Treaty Organization (NATO) and to the European Union (EU). Italy soon became known as one of the most faithful partners of the United States, though as a result there were many critics both at home and abroad who saw Italy as subservient to the Americans on many occasions. It was also an accommodating and faithful ally in NATO and the EU.

Following its economic miracle, Italy's status in the world improved considerably. Of symbolic importance was its surpassing Great Britain in terms of gross national product and its invitation to join the Group of Seven. Culturally, it also maintained its substantial international reputation. Unfortunately, political instability at home along with terrorism and other factors negatively affected its international standing and curtailed its independent activity in foreign affairs. Obviously, the division between the East and West further limited its potential initiatives.

With the end of the Cold War, however, Italy began to look for ways to assert itself on the international scene. There was no intention of breaking with the United States, but rather loosening its ties and pursuing its own special interests. It also wanted to become a more important international actor in the eyes of its European allies. The three areas viewed as central to Italian foreign policy were the North Atlantic–European, the Mediterranean and the Balkans–Adriatic. The Italians saw them as closely related. Italy saw itself not only as a force in the Mediterranean and South-Central Europe, but also as an agent of NATO and especially of the EU in these arenas. If one of the goals of the CEI was to ease the way for member states to join the EU, Italy was to be the facilitator.

Geopolitics

In recent years there has been a general renaissance of interest in geopolitics, in Italy and elsewhere. This has resulted in numerous new books and several new journals devoted to the subject. A great deal has been written about the architecture of the new Europe since the fall of the Iron Curtain, which utilizes old and new arguments about geopolitical factors. One new journal in Italy called *Limes: Rivista italiana di geopolitica* has dedicated considerable space to geopolitical analyses of Italy's relations with the changing Eastern Europe, especially the countries of the former Yugoslavia, and has published several articles which discuss the CEI.[1]

Unfortunately, the concept of geopolitics is often used in a vague fashion as different authors have diverse approaches. This chapter will interpret geopolitics as concerning territory, resources (including human), geographic position, nature of terrain and historical experience within and across certain borders. The CEI as a regional organization has qualities which lend themselves to geopolitical analyses. Central Europe, the Balkans and the Adriatic countries (with some overlap) all have specific related historical experiences and common geographic influences, even if the exact territorial configurations are not agreed upon. Italy's position next to what until recently were described as East European nations clearly meant that it had important linkages with these countries, some of which went back to Ancient Roman times. It should not be forgotten that during the Cold War period Italy was a front-line nation. Much has been written about Germany's geographic position during this period, but Italy was also very vulnerable to attack from the East. Italians were reminded of this when NATO planes from bases in Italy attacked Bosnian Serb positions around Gorazde in April 1994, and there was considerable apprehension that retaliation attacks across the Adriatic might take place. Italy shares common frontiers and the Adriatic Sea with countries of the former Yugoslavia.

As a result of its geographic position it seems logical for Italy to look eastwards for a sphere of influence. Undoubtedly, that has been one of its goals in the CEI. Given its economic strength, especially in the 1980s, and its democratic experience, it seemed appropriate that it should become the leader in a co-operative regional effort. Furthermore, while a Mediterranean outlook in the EU was strengthened with the addition of Spain, Portugal and

Greece, the recent addition of Scandinavian countries has caused Italy to be concerned about the organization's southern interests. As a result, the CEI seems to have become more important and, with international trade becoming steadily more competitive, trade potential to the east has more value for Italy.

Historical Experience

In its modern development Italy was very much caught between East and West. Parts of it were occupied by Spain and France, while at the same time the Austro-Hungarian Empire controlled important areas. It should not be forgotten that when Italy was created in 1860 Venice and the area around it remained in the hands of the Austro-Hungarians. This was a thorn in the side of the new nation until the situation was settled in 1866.[2] As a fledgling nation it had little room to manoeuvre, but saw its eastern neighbours as important, as was demonstrated on the occasion of the request for aid by newly-born Romania. All Italy could offer was counsel, and it advised the Romanian government to improve its treatment of Jews in order to gain the respect of the Western nations.[3] In this period, if there was a major thrust to Italy's foreign affairs attitudes it was irredentism, the desire to retrieve unredeemed lands. In pursuing this goal it played off Germany, France and Austria to retrieve its northern and eastern territories.

A fateful decision was taken in 1882 when Italy became a partner with Germany and Austria in the Triple Alliance. While being a minor actor among the three nations Italy's goals were to enhance its international reputation and to increase its influence to its east, though in the early years of the Alliance Italy's Balkan aspirations were frustrated by its allies. True, Italy did win a compact with Austria which guaranteed that there would be no change in the *status quo* without the agreement of the two nations, with the further proviso that compensation would be in order for any changes agreed.[4] However, the lands to the north continued to be a source of serious disagreement between the two nations as Italy kept up its claim to Trentino and Trieste. The status of Trieste was to cause friction between Italy and its neighbours for many years. By the turn of the century Italy felt strong enough to work towards parity with Austria and Russia as the latter became increasingly interested in the Balkan area. The Italians worked to block the dominance of both big powers.

The years 1908 and 1909 saw Italian–Austrian relations become still more antagonistic when Austria annexed Bosnia-Hercegovina. A joint Russian–Italian effort to block the Austrian action came to naught and brought humiliation to both. Austria did make some concessions to Italy, but Austria was still seen as the barrier to Italian goals. Italian public opinion, with some support from its political class, clamoured for Trentino and Trieste to become part of Italy.

With the coming of the First World War Italy at first remained neutral. It had made a strong effort to forestall the war by invoking the element of the Triple Alliance treaty which called upon Austria to consult and reach an agreement with Italy before it disturbed the *status quo* in the Balkans.[5] Italy continued to pressure Austria for concessions and compensation, but, unsuccessful in this, it opened secret negotiations with the British which culminated in the Treaty of London. Great Britain would support Italy in its claims for extensive territory beyond its north-eastern boundaries and provide naval help against the Austrian Adriatic fleet. Italy then entered the war on the side of the Allies. The war was longer and more costly than the Italians anticipated and the peace settlement was a great disappointment to them. The Treaty of London was disregarded by President Woodrow Wilson who felt that, not being a signatory to it, he was not bound by it. Italy's rewards in the peace settlement were not only meagre but left ambiguity, such as that concerning Fiume, an area which Yugoslavia claimed.

Gabriele D'Annunzio, a renowned writer and poet, led what may be described as a tragi-comic invasion of Fiume. It was supposed to be the first step in a plan to give Italy all of the East Adriatic. D'Annunzio's action had the support of the Italian people and the covert appreciation of the government. A banana republic situation developed, which has since been seen as a dress rehearsal for Italian Fascism.[6] The occupation lasted over a year and ended only when the Italian government became embarrassed by the lingering situation. In 1920, in what is considered a considerable diplomatic achievement, Italian foreign minister Count Carlo Sforza reached an agreement with Yugoslavia and signed the Treaty of Rapallo.

The break-up of the Austro-Hungarian Empire was seen by the Italians as an opportunity to expand their influence in Central Europe. Their hopes were first blocked by Wilson's ideal of self-determination and afterwards by France which developed ties with several East European nations.[7] When Benito Mussolini came to power it soon became clear that the Danube–Balkans and related areas were important to Fascist foreign policy. A treaty of friendship with Yugoslavia was signed in 1924, but Mussolini did not feel limited by it. He made overtures to other countries in the area, often involving contradictory interests. Yet the influence of France in the Balkans remained strong and the Italian dictator made little headway.

In March 1934 protocols were signed with Austria and Hungary which bound those countries closer to Italy. At the same time Rome reduced tensions with France over the Balkans–Danube region, but Paris still would not recognize the area as one of Italian influence. It was not long before

Adolf Hitler replaced France as the major barrier to Italy's aspirations in South-Central Europe. The test came with the German *Anschluss* with Austria. The world and Hitler wondered how Mussolini would react since Italy had considered itself the protector of Austrian independence. When Mussolini did nothing he clearly became the junior member in the dictators' partnership. It should also be noted that before the Second World War the Italian foreign minister Galeazzo Ciano dreamed of forming an alliance of small neutral countries in the Danube–Balkan area, but nothing was to come of it.[8]

With the rapid approach of the Second World War the Italians became increasingly concerned about German power in the nations located to Italy's east. Following the German occupation of Prague in March 1939 Italy took complete control of Albania. This country had been firmly under Italian influence but Mussolini wanted to show Hitler and the rest of the world that Italy was also ready for imperial adventures in nations near its borders. During the Second World War, after brief successes, things went badly for Italy. Its major thrust to the east was an invasion of Greece which was unsuccessful and necessitated German military help.

In the peace settlement after the Second World War Italy lost its imperial possessions. In addition to these, its major losses were in its north-east areas where a large number of Slavs lived. Once again the city of Trieste, which was to become important in the CEI, became a major point of contention between Italy and Yugoslavia.[9] It should be recalled that Yugoslavia, now led by Josip Broz Tito, emerged from the war as a victor, while Italy approached the peace table as a loser.

The issue of Trieste quickly became caught up in the Cold War. As East–West tension became increasingly intense, Italy went to the polls in a crucial election in 1948. It is agreed that the election turned on whether Italy would become neutral or pro-Western. On the eve of the elections the United States, France and Great Britain issued a three-power declaration in which they pledged to support the return of Trieste to Italy. This inflamed the situation and Tito reacted angrily. Further complications occurred when Tito split with Moscow and the Western powers became hesitant to upset him. So they began to back-pedal on their pledge to Italy on Trieste.[10] When they decided to support the Italian administration of a part of the area Tito explicitly stated that if Italy occupied any of the disputed territory he would consider it an act of aggression. Tension between the two disputant nations rose rapidly and war appeared to be a real possibility as both sides amassed troops. Cooler heads and advice from the allies prevailed and the issue was settled by the Treaty of Osimino in 1954.

With the onset of the Cold War, after some doubts, Italy soon became firmly ensconced in the Western camp, while its neighbours to the east became just as solid in their positions in the Soviet circle. The one exception was Yugoslavia which went its own way on an independent road to Communism. The East–West division effectively blocked major interactions between Italy and the Balkans–Danube countries. There was some trade but not much. Finally, in the 1980s, it picked up as numerous commercial contracts became more important. In addition, a few sub-national transborder projects were initiated. All of this helped pave the way for the CEI.

Precursors of the CEI

There were co-operative groups in the same general area which became the foundation of the CEI. These were the Working Community of the Western Alps (Arge Alp) and the Community of the Western Alps (Cotrao) which transcended the East–West political divide. The most important precursor was the Working Community of the Alpe-Adrea.[11] It was begun in 1978 when the Cold War was still in full force. It was founded as an organization based on sub-national co-operation among regions in Yugoslavia, Hungary, Austria and West Germany. It aimed at the co-operation of its members in fields such as trade, tourism, and the environment (fields which also became the concern of the CEI). The total population in the regions involved was close to 40 million and covered over 275,000 square kilometres.

It is probably too strong to claim, as some of its proponents did, that Alpe-Adrea played an important part in melting Cold War barriers. At the grass roots level, however, it did encourage dialogue and real co-operation. It also had the recognition of other international organizations. It started out with eight fields of operation: the economy; agriculture; regional planning; environmental protection; culture; traffic and transportation; health and hygiene; and forestry. Each sector had a commission which established working committees to research problems and organize conferences, exhibitions and the like. No overall organizational structure was established and no single headquarters or secretariat was created. This was done to encourage more flexibility and forestall the development of a bureaucratic power centre. As will be seen, a similar strategy was pursued by the CEI. The goals of Alpe-Adrea were not political, but the operation of the organization did have political significance. It definitely provided a bridge between East and West and very important markets for the regions in Yugoslavia, especially Slovenia.

The fall of Communism and the move away from statist economies to liberal ones has facilitated the activities of the Alpe-Adrea, though, while some projects have been completed, few of these have been of major importance. There is also little evidence that life has been markedly improved for the people of the participating regions. This has led one author to state that this resulted in 'limited "productivity" of cross-frontier initiatives and a wasted round of studies and conferences with few concrete results'. He continued: 'to this can be added a tactical error of the participating regions which, faced with the real difficulty of co-operation, found the only remedy in continuously widening both the number of participants and the fields of co-operation'.[12]

In addition, it is clearly the great disparities in strength among the participating regions which have caused problems. In spite of this, there is a considerable sense of satisfaction among the participants that the activities of the Alpe-Adrea have put the regions on a course of development that otherwise would not have come about. Also, it offers a thrust which is consistent with new approaches to co-operation among the new democracies.

Almost concurrently with the creation of the CEI, Italy increased its contacts with Yugoslavia which was already facing critical internal problems. These contacts were at the highest level, including prime and foreign ministers. On 17 September 1989, less than two months prior to the founding meeting of the CEI, a letter of intent was signed between the two nations creating an Adriatic Initiative. It was to deal with the protection of the environment of the Adriatic region and economic help for Yugoslavia, at a time when inflation was running rampant and the continuation of the Yugoslav federation was threatened. The Adriatic Initiative was not to be a closed operation but was to be open for collaboration with other states, such as Albania. Events in Yugoslavia soon took over. When it became evident that an organization at the national level was needed to further develop co-operation in the whole Italy–Austria and Balkans–Danube area, the CEI was created.

The Aims of the CEI

At its birth in 1989 the CEI was described as ambitious and somewhat nebulous.[13] Furthermore, according to the author of the most complete study of the initiative in Italy to date, it and similar activities were an expression of an Italian policy vision which looks towards a Europe free of blocs and the Paris–Bonn axis, with a focus upon East–West development and a dissipated power equilibrium.[14] The organization can indeed be described as an Italian initiative. As noted earlier, that in itself had importance. After years of being a follower nation in international affairs, Italy now considered itself a front-line player, not only developing an independent thrust in foreign affairs but also acting as a regional leader and a broker towards the East on behalf of the EU.

Much of the credit for the creation of the CEI has been given to Gianni De Michelis when he served as foreign secretary. Diplomat and author Sergio Romano has written: 'After Sforza, De Michelis certainly was the most exuberant and dynamic of all Italian foreign ministers.'[15] Although he came to the position with little experience in foreign relations, he was certainly an activist who believed that Italy should command more respect in world affairs. Unfortunately, his reputation has been tarnished as he has been caught up in the political scandals which have rocked Italy in recent years. Not only was De Michelis the 'father' of the CEI, he articulated more than anyone else the goals of the group. These were first stated in an article in *Corriere della Sera* on 9 November 1989.

He began with the premiss that it was necessary to stabilize the countries of Central Europe and to help in their integration with Western Europe, of which they were historically considered part. He further emphasized that the initiative had clear limits and was not meant to interfere with Italy's other international obligations to the EU, NATO and the Conference on Security and Co-operation in Europe (CSCE, now the OSCE). In fact, he believed that the new organization should not touch on formal security arrangements, though this aim was to change later. He believed that it should be recognized that the Final Act of Helsinki specifically mentions regional associations as part of the push for the reconstruction of Europe, and it was in this context that he suggested that regional co-operation would offer a flexible and pragmatic way to approach specific grass-roots projects. He conceived the Quadrangle as an interim operation with the partners moving towards membership of the EU in the near future.

De Michelis openly admitted that one of the Italian aims of the initiative was to block German penetration into South-Central Europe. As it had historically, Italy continued to believe that the region east of Venice and Trieste was its natural area of influence, and that Germany with its considerable wealth and strength should be kept out if at all possible. According to Romano, 'The non-declared scope was that of impeding these countries from falling wholly in the German orbit and becoming economic satellites of a new Germanic Commonwealth from Reno to Brest Litovsk.'[16]

When considering the aims and objectives of the CEI it must be repeated that the operation was above all a pragmatic one in which infrastructure was to be constructed for the most part at the sub-national level. Clearly a modern infrastructure is a requirement for economic growth and integration into the European complex. Highways, railways, energy projects and the like have been the central thrusts of the CEI.

There has been some criticism that the CEI expanded too quickly and too widely. However, the expansion appears logical. There is little question that Czechoslovakia belonged as it represented the heart of Central Europe, and for Italy and Austria it was a natural development to the east. On the other hand, the admission of Poland represented to some a departure from the original concept of the CEI. It gave the organization a true north–south axis. It meant that there was a bridge from the Adriatic to the Balkan Sea. For Poland, it meant southern economic relations and an alternative to a united Germany as its only major trading partner. In addition, there was a certain logic in including Poland when Hungary and Czechoslovakia were members and the three nations were so interrelated historically and geographically. The close relations of the three countries were underscored by the creation of their own regional organization in February 1991, known as the Visegrad Group. These three former Soviet satellites saw the CEI as enhancing their desires to join the EU.

It is to the credit of the organizers of the CEI, especially De Michelis, that they saw considerable flexibility in the organization as necessary. This flexibility included membership expansion. Italy recognized the need for growth and encouraged Polish membership; when the Yugoslav federation dissolved the CEI was quick to admit Slovenia and Croatia and prepare the way for collaboration of other states of the former Yugoslavia and other nations in the region, such as Romania.

From the very creation of the CEI, the rapidity of changes both in the region and beyond made planning and operations difficult. The dissolution of Yugoslavia was the most serious development. Among other things, the potential flow of refugees from the former Yugoslavia threatened general destabilization and severe economic problems in the CEI member nations and beyond.

Meetings

The first meeting of the CEI in November 1989 in Hungary identified the diverse areas in which the new organization would become involved. Working groups were established in the fields of transportation, telecommunications, the environment, small and medium businesses, and culture and tourism. The organization began with both considerable hope and commitment. All was not, however, total consensus. There was Hungarian pressure to enlarge the scope of the Quadrangle into the military–security area. This came as a considerable surprise to the Italians. The idea was rejected, but it is clear that the Hungarians were looking beyond the end of the Warsaw Treaty Organization (WTO) and were concerned about potential German unification. Later, other former Communist countries wanted security matters considered.

The first meeting of the Pentagonal, with the inclusion of Czechoslovakia, also saw the development of a common position on the problems of minorities. This was prepared for presentation to the conference of the human rights group of the CSCE which was planned for 5 June 1990. Although the common position was accepted, it was done so begrudgingly by some of the partners. Italy had to push hard to obtain agreement. Other areas emphasized at the meeting were environmental problems (particularly the pollution of the Danube), telecommunications and transportation. The last was of special interest to Italy.

At the May and June meetings of 1990 four new working groups were created, concerned with scientific and technological research, information, energy and migration. At the August meeting of prime ministers in Venice (Italy was represented by its deputy prime minister, Claudio Martelli) observers from the Council of Europe, the Economic Commission for Europe of the United Nations (UNECE), the World Bank, the EU and the European Bank for Investment were present.

The 1991 meetings were in part devoted to the Polish request to join the group. The Italians proposed that Poland first be invited to join working groups which were of special interest to it. Subsequently, Poland was permitted to join all working groups and to send observers to other CEI meetings. Poland became a full member of what became known as the Hexagonal the following year.

The Hexagonal met in a crisis situation on 26–7 July 1991 in Dubrovnik. Events in Yugoslavia had deteriorated significantly and were seen as a threat to peace in Europe. Things were so tense that the Hungarian delegation was accompanied by heavily armed guards.[17] Observers present from Albania, Switzerland, the Alpe-Adria and European and international funding bodies looked for solutions. The discussions underscored the need to pacify the entire Balkans and help develop an organic plan for economic reconstruction.[18] However, in spite of Yugoslavia's membership of the organization, its efforts had little impact on the situation there. A spokesman for the Ministry of Information in Yugoslavia stated: 'The Hexagonal will fundamentally be useful. But because an action is so complicated, it must operate without time limits.'[19]

An extraordinary meeting of national co-ordinators, high-level functionaries of the member nations, took place on 6 September. Events in Yugoslavia continued to threaten peace in the region, and developments in the Soviet Union were unsettling, particularly for Poland. Much discussion took place, especially about possible future developments in the Balkan republics, the Ukraine and Belarus. The possibility of these nations collaborating with the Hexagonal was examined, as well as aid to Russia.

The 1992 meetings of the CEI continued to be dominated by the situation in Yugoslavia. An agreement was reached at the summit meeting in Vienna on 18 July 1992 to open channels for the millions of refugees trapped in

Bosnia to leave. A few days after the Venice meeting children from the war-torn area began to arrive in Milan. The number of children involved at first was small but symbolically very significant to the people of Sarajevo. The flow soon became larger in spite of many difficulties.[20] In addition, the CEI, seeing this as the worst refugee crisis in Europe since the end of the Second World War, appealed to the UN to do something quickly for the refugees. A decision was taken to plan a huge refugee camp in Austria. It must be noted that while Italy took refugees for humanitarian reasons, its fundamental policy was to discourage a diaspora and to urge that as soon as conditions permitted these people were to be returned to their homes.

On 22–23 March 1993 the foreign ministers of the CEI met in Budapest. The ministers of Italy, Austria, Croatia, the Czech Republic, Hungary, Poland, the Slovak Republic and Slovenia attended. The membership of the group had changed greatly in less than four years. The foreign minister of Bosnia-Hercegovina was unable to attend but offered his full support to the conference. The Czech Republic and the Slovak Republic were accepted as members from 1 January 1993. The ministers expressly declared:

> a commitment to strengthening the role of the CEI as a specific form of regional co-operation in promoting the process of stabilization and integration of Europe through:
> 1) a pragmatic approach to strengthening economic relations, with special emphasis on assisting in developing market economies in the countries in transition and bringing about closer collaboration among themselves and their future integration in the European Community;
> 2) intensifying political consultation in accordance with the responsibility of the member states for the future of our region and Europe as a whole.[21]

These two points have been central to all CEI meetings.

General developments in Central and Eastern Europe continued to trouble the CEI. The foreign ministers' statement speaks of anxiety over developments in Russia, dismay at the war in Bosnia-Hercegovina, and disappointment over the lack of progress in the implementation of the UN peace plan. Emphasis was given to the need to preserve ethnic diversity in the countries of Central and Eastern Europe as well as the importance of full respect for and effective protection of minority rights.

General approval was given for Belarus, Bulgaria, Romania and the Ukraine to participate in some CEI activities, and Bavaria's involvement in some of the working groups was welcomed. At this point no one seemed concerned about any threat from Germany. The response to an application for admission from the government of the Former Yugoslav Republic of Macedonia was non-committal, promising further consideration later.

By this time the CEI had developed relations with a wide range of regional groups and organizations, including UNECE, Black Sea Economic Co-operation, the Baltic Sea States, Balkan Co-operation, Barents–Euoartic Region and the Working Communities of the Danubian Countries. It was also agreed to extend relations with the Alpe-Adrea Working Community through regular exchanges at the working group level.

There were two other major meetings of the CEI in 1993. The heads of governments met in Budapest on 16–17 July and the foreign affairs ministers convened in Debrecan on 19–20 November. At the former meeting much of the same ground was covered as at the foreign ministers' session earlier in the year, especially concerning Yugoslavia, and the Former Yugoslav Republic of Macedonia was welcomed as a member. The heads of government also emphasized the need for increased economic co-operation among CEI members and a renewed push for EU membership by the CEI countries desiring it. They also discussed co-operation with other major international bodies, particularly the European Bank for Reconstruction and Development (EBRD). In addition, a working group on natural disaster relief was singled out for commendation.

As was to be expected, the November 1993 meeting of the ministers for foreign affairs was again dominated by the Yugoslav issue. After follow-up discussions of issues raised at earlier meetings the ministers 'noted with satisfaction that the co-operation within the CEI, as an element of the new European architecture, is a substantial contribution to the strengthening of the political and economic stability at an all-European level'.[22] Bearing this in mind, the ministers agreed to continue to strengthen the role of the CEI as important for:

- identifying the most urgent needs of its member states, particularly in the fields of economic and infrastructural development, science, technology and culture, with a view to finding appropriate solutions;
- organizing political dialogue on selected issues among the member states;
- formulating, whenever possible, joint positions to be presented at international fora, and elaborating common documents in special cases;
- exchanging information on experiences concerning the implementation of internationally accepted norms and principles of democracy, human and minority rights as well as of market economies in the CEI region.[23]

The next meeting of foreign ministers, on 5–6 March 1994, was once again overshadowed by external events. The issue of Italian troops being sent to Bosnia-Hercegovina under the peace-keeping aegis of the United Nations was publicly raised as the foreign ministers gathered. The Italian foreign minister, Beniamino Andreatta, indicated the willingness of Italy to place troops at the disposal of the UN. However, Croatia quickly vetoed the idea on the basis that countries near the conflict should not participate in the peace-keeping forces. Andreatta spoke to journalists at the conclusion of the CEI foreign ministers' meeting. The troops issue totally overshadowed the CEI deliberations.[24]

With the Yugoslav situation continuing to dominate the discussion, a new development involved ministerial support for an Italian proposal urgently to convene a meeting in Florence of donor states and international agencies to develop a specific programme of action for humanitarian assistance in Bosnia-Hercegovina. The ministers also indicated their concern over the Greek government's imposition of trade restrictions on the Former Yugoslav Republic of Macedonia. The Working Group on Minorities was asked to finish their elaboration of the instrument for the protection of minority rights in the CEI region. The ministers noted that such an effort could be a significant contribution to the work of the Council of Europe on the same subject.

Organization

From its birth the CEI was never intended to develop into a highly organized group. The very name Central European Initiative is not felicitous, since it has little meaning outside its membership group and interested international bodies. The use of English as the language of reports appears strange since it is not the language of any member state. Avoiding a formal structure was thought to give the organization more flexibility. It saw itself as a temporary entity which would disappear when all its members joined the EU. Not only does it have no fixed structure but it does not have an international juridical personality.[25] From its beginning emphasis was to be placed on problem-solving and collaboration at the political and technical level.

The group works through a six-month rotating presidency, responsible for general co-ordination. However, after the internal conflict in Yugoslavia began members thought it unwise for that nation to occupy the presidency, and Yugoslavia's turn was bypassed, creating some friction. Three regular and occasional extra summits are held annually. The prime ministers meet once a year, while the foreign ministers convene twice annually. Interested parties representing other potential member states and representatives of international or regional organizations and institutions generally attend these meetings as observers.

No secretariat has been established, though the issue has been considered. Austria offered to act as host to such an administration, if it were created; however, when fellow member states did not wish to provide funds for such an apparatus the offer was withdrawn. There is a national co-ordinators' group which consists of high-level bureaucrats who perform some of the work of an on-going secretariat.

The major efforts of the CEI are conducted through working groups. These groups are dedicated to specific subjects and it is in their activities that the pragmatic grass-roots operation is conducted. In discussing the projects of the working groups, one author states:

> The main value of these projects is in providing the means and instruments for a greater degree of integration between the countries of the area (the integral potential of the projects), the creation of common standards, creation of infrastructures to facilitate communication, the reopening of cultural channels and the promotion of good relations between populations and minorities.[26]

In 1990, working groups on energy, information, scientific and technological research and migrations were added to the five original working groups (dealing with telecommunications, the environment, transportation, small and medium-size enterprises and culture). In 1991 three additional working groups were created in the fields of tourism, statistics and disaster relief. Membership of the various groups is voluntary and not all the CEI members are involved in all the groups, while non-member nations participate in some of the working groups. The term 'variable geography' has been borrowed from the EU to indicate participation by non-member nations.

Over 125 projects have been initiated by the working groups, those dedicated to infrastructural improvement being considered the most important. As one writer puts it, 'One of the Hexagonal's fundamental objectives is the comprehensive development of physical (and partly also human) infrastructure in Central Europe.'[27] Primary projects are new highways, such as the Trieste–Ljubljana–Budapest road, and railway connections, such as the Trieste–Venice–Treveso–Vienna corridor. The railway system was aimed, in part, at improving the routes to the Adriatic ports and making better use of container trains. A very promising project in telecommunications has involved a fibre-optics network that connects the Czech Republic, the Slovak Republic, Italy and Hungary, and originally included Yugoslavia. Further expansion of this network is being considered. Proposals for new gas pipelines from east to west and access to North African natural gas through Italy have developed beyond the feasibility study stage. Infrastructure projects are of the greatest assistance to former Soviet satellite countries as they endeavour to reform their economies. As privatization progresses, improved infrastructure makes foreign investment more attractive and aids trade among the CEI partners as well as with the rest of Europe.

As might be expected, financial resources are a major problem for the CEI. The financial shortfall increased rapidly as the organization developed, and the world recession has had a severe impact. Italy, under the influence of De Michelis, who thought in grandiose terms, was prepared to underwrite a considerable part of the costs of the operation. Unambiguous support for the CEI early on by most representatives in the Italian parliament was evident. Two hundred million lire were voted initially, and used for environmental concerns. The money went to the International Institute for Applied Systems Analysis which studied pollution emissions in East-Central Europe. The following year, in 1991, 1400 billion lire was specifically designated for 'frontier areas', and some of this money was used for CEI projects.[28]

Other member states were not in a financial position to make major contributions. When Italy's economy weakened with the world recession, funds for the CEI were no longer available. Furthermore, when the Italian government changed in 1992 the enthusiastic supporter of the CEI, De Michelis, was replaced as foreign secretary by Andreatta, an economist who was sceptical of the organization and its costs. Given Italy's huge public deficit, Andreatta favoured a cut-back in large-scale CEI projects. He clearly favoured smaller sub-national efforts aimed at local economic development. Specifically, Andreatta believed that the CEI could be most useful in organizing chambers of commerce and similar groups to enhance trade.

De Michelis and others counted on funds from international organizations but, while some help was forthcoming, it was not sufficient to cover major projects. However, the EBRD has proposed that it become a technical secretariat for the CEI projects, and this has the support of Italy.

Two other organizational sectors deserve a mention. The first are the meetings of parliamentary delegations of member states which usually take place concurrently with CEI summit meetings. This has facilitated the exchange of views and has built support among leading politicians in the various nations. Less successful have been the meetings of trade union leaders for enhancing the concern for social problems.

Conclusion

Any evaluation of the CEI would have to recognize mixed results. It did not achieve all that its founders, especially De Michelis, had hoped for it. It has not become the centrepiece of a new, more active Italian foreign policy, and has not enhanced Italy's reputation as a foreign policy leader. This has been a disappointment. Its efforts in the Balkans–Danube–Adriatic region have, nevertheless, encouraged stability and democracy in Eastern Europe.

One of the goals of the CEI has been to enable member organizations to apply for EU membership, and progress has been made towards that goal. At the same time the liberalization of trade and extension of credit by the

EU to the East European members of the CEI has made the organization less important among these members.[29] In addition, Austria's membership of the EU has changed the CEI situation somewhat.

The lack of a formal organization has adversely affected the CEI. The benefits of avoiding bureaucratization have been outweighed by a general lack of coordination, overlap, inefficiency and very slow development of activities. With over 150 projects, the meagre resources of the CEI have been overstretched, and it is generally agreed that the number must be cut back. Summit meetings have considered consolidation and elimination of repetitious activity. Curiously, for an organization aimed at improving infrastructure at the sub-national level, the summit meetings seem to be more successful than the working groups.

There are also those who believe that membership has expanded too rapidly. The debate about the issue is similar to the issues over the EU expansion. Some would have preferred it to deepen its relationships and make further achievements before broadening its membership. In addition, the organization may have grown beyond its natural geographic configuration. However, it would have been politically difficult to exclude those new members, given the volatile situation in Eastern Europe.

At the same time, as originally conceived, the organization was not to have political and security matters as a major thrust. However, events such as the unification of Germany, the break-up of the Soviet Union and, above all, the dissolution of Yugoslavia, caused some shift in emphasis. The Yugoslav situation quickly threatened the peace and security of the area. While much time in summit meetings was devoted to the problem, and communiqués were issued concerning it, the CEI had little success in bringing pressure to bear for a peaceful solution. The Yugoslav situation also complicated several of the infrastructure projects, and a few had to be dropped or substantially modified as the war intensified. Work in the fields of the environment, tourism and, above all, transportation was affected. Furthermore, the issue of refugees and the protection of minority rights had to be addressed, detracting attention from basic economic developmental goals.

In spite of its shortcomings, however, the CEI cannot be described as a failure. Although not well known among the general public, it has been well received by the political class in Italy. There is a feeling that, as a regional development, the CEI is consistent with the way the world is evolving. It is in tune with larger international organizations, such as the UN, the OSCE, the EU and other groups which support regional development. It succeeded in establishing important channels of communication within the region, the importance of which cannot be overestimated. In an area of the world where a power vacuum exists following the fall of Communism, the incorporation of evolving democracies into international patterns of friendship, co-operation and consultation is vital.

Although many of the projects have had their problems, their overall importance should not be disregarded. First, the feasibility studies done on infrastructural problems have provided necessary needs assessments, particularly in the transportation and energy sectors, and work on road and rail connections has progressed. Many of the projects offer experimentation on a small scale; when successful the approach can be transferred to a more general level.

For those who believe that contacts with the former Soviet satellite countries are helpful, the CEI has been positive. There is hope that these contacts will reduce the overlap of work and a more rational approach to development will evolve. Broad east–west and north–south corridors have produced infrastructural improvements which hasten economic improvement across all of East-Central Europe.

If expectations for the CEI are kept in proper perspective, the organization's utility cannot be questioned, and, while not a major development in world affairs in itself, it does demonstrate Italy's ability to undertake independent activity on the world stage.

Notes

1   See Luigi Vittorio Ferraris, 'Dal Tevere al Danubio: L'Italia scopre la geopolitica da tavolino', *Limes: Rivista italiana di geopolitica*, nos. 1–2 (1993).
2   Denis Mack Smith, *Italy: A Modern History*, rev. edn (Ann Arbor, 1969), pp. 76–82.
3   William Oldson, 'Italy and the Question of Romanian Independence', *Il politico*, vol. 150, no. 2 (1989), pp. 197–217.
4   William C. Askew, 'Italy and the Great Powers before the First World War', in Edward R. Tannenbaum and Emiliana P. Noether (eds), *Modern Italy: A Topical History since 1861* (New York, 1974), p. 315.
5   Ibid., p. 325.
6   Smith, *Italy*, p. 335.
7   René Albrecht-Carrié, 'Foreign Policy Since The First World War', in Tannenbaum and Noether (eds), *Modern Italy*, p. 341.
8   Sergio Romano, *Guida alla politica estera italiana* (Milano, 1993), p. 204.
9   Gastone Guidotti, 'Trieste', *Rivista di studi politici internazionale*, vol. 44, no. 2 (1982), pp. 207–16.
10 Giuseppe Mammarella, *Italy after Fascism: A Political History* (Notre Dame, Indiana, 1966), pp. 162–5.
11 Riccardo Cappellin, 'Alpe-Adria: Opportunità e prospettive', *Relazioni internazionali*, vol. 53, no. 2 (1989), pp. 60–7.
12 Gianni Bonvicini, 'The Political Aspects of the Relationship between the "Esagonale" and Regional Co-operation Across Borders' in 'Inter-Relations between the "Esagonale" and the "Alps-Adria" Initiatives in a Changing Europe', First Workshop of the Institutes of International Affairs of the Central-European Initiative (Trento, 1992) p. 144.

13   Ferraris, 'Dal Tevere al Danubio', p. 213.
14   Calogero Di Gesù, 'La nuova proiezione italiana nell'area adriatico danubiana: L'iniziativa pentagonale e l'iniziativa adriatica'. Typed text, Rome, 1991, p. 114.
15   Romano, *Guida alla politica*, p. 204.
16   Ibid., p. 205.
17   *La stampa*, 26 July 1991, p. 7.
18   Ibid.
19   *Corriere della sera*, 27 July 1991.
20   *La stampa*, 19 July 1992, p. 8.
21   Ministers of Foreign Affairs of Member States of the CEI, 'Declaration', Budapest, 22–23 March 1993, pp. 1–2.
22   Minister of Foreign Affairs of Member States of the CEI, 'Document', Debrean, 19–20 November 1993, p. 3.
23   Ibid.
24   Il sole-24 ore, 6 March 1994, p. 3.
25   Di Gesù, 'La nuova proiezione', p. 128.
26   Bonvicini, 'The Political Aspects ...', p. 149.
27   Andras Inotai, 'Economic Aspects of Cooperation in Central Europe', in 'Inter-Relations Between "Esagonale" and the "Alps-Adria" Initiatives in a Changing Europe', p. 170.
28   Maurizio Cremasco, 'From the Quadrangolare to the Central European Initiative: An Attempt at Regional Cooperation', Istituto Affari Internazionali Document (Rome, 1993) p. 6.
29   Tito Favaretto, 'Per una visione coerente degli interessi italiani nell'Europa dell'Est', *Limes*, no. 1–2, 1993, p. 199.

Index

N.B. Page references to footnotes are suffixed by the letter 'n'.